D1714822

ST. JEROME

Commentary on Ecclesiastes

Ancient Christian Writers

THE WORKS OF THE FATHERS IN TRANSLATION

No. 66

ST. JEROME: COMMENTARY ON ECCLESIASTES

TRANSLATED, AND
EDITED WITH A COMMENTARY,

BY

RICHARD J. GOODRICH AND DAVID J. D. MILLER

THE NEWMAN PRESS
New York/Mahwah, NJ

Caseside design by Lynn Else
Book design by Lynn Else

Copyright © 2012
by
Richard J. Goodrich and David J. D. Miller

Library of Congress Cataloging-in-Publication Data

Jerome, Saint, d. 419 or 20.
   [Commentarius in Ecclesiasten. English]
   St. Jerome : commentary on Ecclesiastes / translated and edited with a commentary by Richard J. Goodrich And David J. D. Miller.
      p. cm. – (Ancient Christian writers ; no. 66)
   Includes bibliographical references and index.
   ISBN 978-0-8091-0601-1 (alk. paper)—ISBN 978-1-61643-090-0
1. Bible. O.T. Ecclesiastes–Commentaries–Early works to 1800. 2. Jerome, Saint, d. 419 or 20. Commentarius in Ecclesiasten. I. Goodrich, Richard J., 1962- II. Miller, David, 1935 Nov. 11- III. Title. IV. Title: Saint Jerome. V. Title: Commentary on Ecclesiastes.
   BS1475.53.J4713 2012
   223'.8077–dc23

                                              2011035415

Published by The Newman Press
an imprint of Paulist Press
997 Macarthur Boulevard
Mahwah, New Jersey 07430

www.paulistpress.com

CONTENTS

ACKNOWLEDGMENTS

In creating this work we have received a great deal of help from a number of people. In particular we would like to thank the following: Gillian Clark, Sam Giere, Dennis McManus, Eva Schulz-Flügel, and David Sedley. We would also like to thank those at Paulist Press who have worked with us to bring this work to press: the late Lawrence Boadt, Nancy de Flon and Paul McMahon; and Maurya Horgan and Paul Kobelski of the HK Scriptorium. Finally, we must acknowledge our debt to those who have suffered the most during our long hours spent among dusty tomes and at the keyboards. Richard would like to thank his wife, Mary, and his daughters, Ann and Grace, for tolerating his frequent mental absences and unfortunate obsession with Jerome. David would like to say the same of his wife, Ida.

INTRODUCTION

LIFE

Eusebius Sophronius Hieronymus,[1] St. Jerome, was born around the year AD 345, somewhere along the western coast of the Balkan peninsula (the Roman province of Dalmatia, modern Croatia). He lists his hometown as Stridon,[2] a village that was located on the border between Dalmatia and Pannonia. Beyond these details, we actually know very little about Jerome's early life. His father owned land and was apparently well off. Jerome had at least one younger brother (Paulinian), a sister,[3] and a maternal aunt from whom he was estranged.[4]

Like many Roman children of good family, Jerome began his education in a local village school.[5] After he had mastered the fundamentals of reading, writing, and arithmetic, probably around the time he turned twelve,[6] his parents sent him off for advanced education. Anxious to place their son on the high road to an imperial career, Jerome's parents arranged to send the boy to Rome, where he took lessons from Aelius Donatus, who was one of the most famous grammarians of his day, having written textbooks on composition as well as commentaries on Vergil and Terence. In later life Jerome would point to his education under Donatus with pride; indeed, even in his *Commentary on Ecclesiastes* he cannot resist quoting his old master.[7] When his studies with Donatus were complete, Jerome went on to a Roman school of rhetoric, where he polished his skills as an orator in preparation for a political career.

Details about Jerome's movements immediately after finishing his education in Rome are fairly thin. It would appear that he and his friend Bonosus traveled to Trier, hoping to secure a post in the imperial civil service.[8] The emperor Valentinian had made Trier a base for his defense of the northern imperial border; Jerome and Bonosus must have believed that proximity to the imperial court might yield positions for two well-trained young men.

This lofty ambition appears to have been frustrated, and Jerome quickly realized that his interests lay elsewhere. We know nothing about the events that turned his attention toward the church; Jerome is frustratingly vague about the end of his aspirations for a bureaucratic career. In a later letter he recounts his change of heart at Trier, but fails to mention the catalyst for abandoning his secular ambitions.[9] While in Trier he transcribed two books written by the Latin theologian Hilary of Poitiers, *On the Synods* and *Tractates on the Psalms*.[10] The *Tractates on the Psalms* drew heavily on the allegorical exegesis of Origen, and this may have been Jerome's first contact with the work of the great Alexandrian.

Jerome abandoned the imperial capital, first making his way to Stridon and then spending an indeterminate amount of time in northern Italy. Here, in the company of his school friends Bonosus and Rufinus, he appears to have experimented with ascetic Christianity, possibly in a community at Aquileia. This interlude was shattered by a break with his family and unspecified charges against Jerome that caused him to flee to the East.[11] His nominal destination was the Holy Land; his route took him through Athens and Anatolia. Unfortunately illness dogged his steps and by the time he reached Syria, he was a very sick man.

Jerome found a haven in Antioch with an old friend, the presbyter Evagrius. Jerome spent nearly a year as a guest in Evagrius's home, recovering from the diseases that had interrupted his pilgrimage. As he healed, the urge to resume an ascetic life returned. Antioch was well placed for experimentation, surrounded by Syrian monks who inhabited the lonely places outside the city walls. With his health restored, Jerome moved into a cell on Evagrius's estate at Maronia and plunged into the eremitic life. Jerome's monastic life was as idiosyncratic as he was. As Stefan Rebenich has pointed out, his experiment was a far cry from the strict asceticism of the Egyptian Desert Fathers, cut off from the outside world.[12] While in his "cell," Jerome busied himself with intellectual pursuits: learning Hebrew and Syriac, supervising the team of copyists who were adding new books to his library,[13] and maintaining an extensive correspondence with a network of friends. Jerome clearly had no intention of withdrawing from the world or of allowing the world to forget him.

Jerome claimed that doctrinal differences between himself and the Syrian monks ultimately compelled him to abandon the desert.[14] While this may have been a factor, Jerome's letters written during this period hint at a fundamental unhappiness with his isolation. Jerome longed to be at the center of the political life of the church, and it is unlikely that the radical disengagement from the world that characterized many of the monks of this period would ever have proven congenial to him. As his satisfaction with his ascetic experiment waned, Jerome began writing letters to Damasus, bishop of Rome, in an apparent attempt to bring himself to the attention of the pontiff.[15] This effort appears to have been successful; while Jerome's earliest letters to Damasus sought advice, a letter written from Constantinople[16] redefines their relationship, with Jerome now solving an exegetical difficulty for the pope (an explanation of the vision recorded in Isaiah 6). After spending time in Constantinople with his patron Evagrius, Gregory of Nazianzus, and Gregory of Nyssa, Jerome returned to Rome (ca. 382), where he joined Damasus's staff, possibly in the ecclesiastical archive.[17] He appears to have served as an expert on the affairs of the Eastern church, helping Damasus to understand the theological controversies that raged in the East as well as answering correspondence for the pope.[18]

In 382, at the request of Pope Damasus, Jerome turned his attention to revising the old Latin versions of the Gospels. An astounding number of Latin translations were available at the time. Each manuscript he examined seemed to offer a different translation. This was a well-known problem, and we find St. Augustine registering a similar complaint: "Those who translated the scriptures from Hebrew into Greek can be counted, but the Latin translators cannot be counted at all. For when the Greek [New Testament] came into everyone's hands in the early days of the faith, every man who thought he had a little skill in Greek dared to make a translation [into Latin]."[19] Damasus was determined to bring order to this chaos. The pope commissioned Jerome to collate the extant Latin texts and create a standard version that could be used by the Roman church. The project was completed in 384, when Jerome offered the pope a completed translation of the four Gospels. Jerome's edition brought together the best of the Latin manuscripts, checked against the Greek and altered to match the Greek when necessary.[20] Although Jerome's *On Illustrious Men* would lead his readers to believe that he had revised the entire New Testament,[21] modern scholars believe that Jerome abandoned this project once the four Gospels were completed.[22]

Under Damasus's patronage, Jerome began to build his reputation as a biblical scholar. The pope also brought him into contact with an extraordinary group of women, Roman aristocrats who lived on the Aventine hill. The putative leader of these women was a wealthy widow named Marcella. A member of an ancient senatorial family, Marcella had embarked on a life devoted to asceticism, chastity, and Bible study after her husband died. Jerome, fresh from the Syrian desert, promoted himself as a proficient monk and a teacher of Scripture. His number of contacts among these women soon began to expand, ultimately including Paula and her daughters, Blesilla and Eustochium. These women would play a major role in the rest of his life, wealthy patrons who could support both his work and his fragile ego.[23]

Unfortunately, Jerome's influence over these women was noticed in Rome, and not with approval. Those who held power and shaped public opinion began to mutter about the ascendancy that men like Jerome exercised over these wealthy women. When Paula's daughter Blesilla starved herself to death following a rigorous plan of mortification of the flesh, voices were heard to ask how much longer these detestable monks would be allowed to remain in Rome. Should they not be stoned and driven from the city?[24] Jerome continued to live under Damasus's powerful protection, but clearly the promoters of asceticism were beginning to wear out their welcome in the Eternal City.

This protection vanished in December of 384, when Damasus passed away and Jerome found himself standing alone before his enemies. Although details are scanty and Jerome writes little about the events that led to his exile, it appears that Jerome was tried before a council of Roman clerics. Rather than elect him the next pope (as Jerome seems to have hoped would happen), the council charged Jerome with unspecified crimes and hauled him before an ecclesiastical court.[25] This "Council of Pharisees," as he later would label them, forced a promise from him to leave the city, which he did as soon as possible, taking ship for the Holy Land. Jerome would never again lay eyes on Rome, and it must have seemed that, at age forty-one, driven out of the city, his life and work had been destroyed.

In fact, the most productive part of his career, the work that would earn him the lasting reputation he so craved, lay before him. Upon reaching the East, he was reunited with Paula. The two made a brief tour of Egypt, home of the celebrated Desert Fathers, and then settled in Bethlehem. Here, in the city where Christ had been born, Paula funded the construction of a double monastery and Jerome began the scholarly work that catapulted him into the front rank of Christian scholars.

JEROME'S *ECCLESIASTES*

It is rather astonishing that Jerome chose to launch his exegetical career with a commentary on Ecclesiastes. This book has always been one of the more challenging books in the biblical canon, with its nihilistic appraisal of life under the sun and its gloomy conclusion that the best that humans can hope for is to enjoy what they have been given until death takes them away.[26] Although it is difficult to establish the exact order of Jerome's works, the *Commentary on Ecclesiastes* is one of the earliest, if not the earliest, of his commentaries on the Hebrew Bible.[27] Jerome does not tell us why he chose to begin with Ecclesiastes rather than a more obvious starting point (like Genesis). In the preface to this work he notes that he had begun the project in Rome at the urging of Blesilla, who, however, died before he could complete it. Its appearance among his earliest exegetical writings may have been nothing more than wrapping up unfinished work.

At its heart, Ecclesiastes is a meditation on the apparent arbitrariness of life in this world. One person is born into great wealth and affluence, while another starves to death on the street. Moreover, there appears to be no correlation between virtue and reward. It would be eminently sensible if those who set their hearts on the pursuit of the good, those who sought the face of God, were richly blessed in this life, while those who did evil were punished. If life worked along these predictable lines, then our paths would be clear. We would be able to see the consequences of our actions and choose blessing or condemnation.

Even a reverse correlation between cause and effect would be preferable to what we observe in this world. St. Augustine developed this line in the *City of God*, noting that even if the opposite was true—if the wicked invariably prospered while the righteous were poor and suffering—it would be much easier to explain: the wicked would be receiving their reward here on earth, leaving the righteous to receive an eternal, heavenly reward.[28] But even this reverse correlation does not occur, and that makes a belief in divine providence and God's judgments difficult. The events, chances, and disasters that give shape to our lives and compel our responses appear fairly random. It is difficult to discern a divine hand orchestrating events.

The Preacher took up the task of trying to reconcile this tension between divine providence and the apparent randomness of life beneath the sun. After considering the matter in depth, he concluded that every pursuit humankind attempts is a vanity (read "futile, worthless, pointless"). Nothing that an individual does or accomplishes has any bearing on that person's fate: all people, the great and the poor, the wise and the fools, go down to the grave and are quickly forgotten as the earth spins on. "For there will not be memory of the wise together with the fool in eternity, because look, in the days that will come suddenly, oblivion will overwhelm all things; and how will the wise man die together with the fool?" (Eccl 2:16).

The looming shadow of death darkens the Preacher's vision. From his investigation he concludes that death consumes all, irrespective of what we do or what potentialities we develop in our lives. A void yawns beneath our feet, one that ultimately will swallow fool and wise man alike. Consequently, the only strategy that makes sense in the face of the mind's inability to see beyond the veil of the end is to embrace pleasure and joy whenever possible.[29] This view, which is the logical outworking of the Preacher's premises, has always sat uncomfortably in its Judeo-Christian context.[30] An obvious sign of this discomfort can be found in the epilogue tacked on to the end of the work by an anonymous editor: "Fear God and keep his commandments. That is the whole man, because God will bring every action to judgment on everything hidden, whether it be good or bad" (Eccl 12:13–14). This was not, needless to say, the obvious conclusion to be drawn from the Preacher's sermon.

The reconciliation of the Preacher's fundamentally nihilistic worldview with the good news of the Christian message is the major task facing any Christian commentator on this text. In many ways Jerome brings no new solutions to the problem, but draws on the strategies mapped out by the exegetes (both Christian and Jewish) who had preceded him. Jerome careens between allegorical and literal readings of the text, misunderstands and misreads his text (possibly deliberately), cites a wide range of Jewish and Christian opinions, and generally manages to force the Preacher into a Christian straitjacket, with varying degrees of success. When it comes to the question at the heart of Ecclesiastes, Jerome chooses to place this inquiry outside the boundaries of legitimate Christian discourse.

Inquiry into the secret purposes of God, the question of "why things happen," is a doomed venture. Jerome's position is neatly summed up and reinforced by his repeated citation of 1 Cor 13:12: "for now we see in a mirror dimly, but then face-to-face. Now I know in part; then I shall understand fully, even as I have been fully understood." Jerome cites or alludes to this text repeatedly in his commentary. In his discussion of Eccl 1:8 ("the eye will not be satiated with seeing, and the ear will not be filled up with hearing"), he advances 1 Cor 13:12 as an interpretive key to Ecclesiastes. A knowledge of the natural sciences is difficult to acquire, Jerome writes. Speech cannot unfold the causes and natures of things, the eye does not see where it is blind, nor is the ear able to be filled. Our search for knowledge is doomed to failure because we see in a mirror, dimly.

At Eccl 2:12 ("And I looked, that I might see wisdom and errors and foolishness, because who is there among men, who could go after the king, before his maker?"), Jerome returns to his argument that humans lack the wisdom to grasp the fundamental truths underlying creation. This verse demonstrates that humans, possessing only limited understanding, cannot fathom the wisdom of the Creator. Even in those things that we feel certain we know, we actually only speculate rather than comprehend. We suppose, rather than know, what the truth is. Again, the reason for this is that we now see in a mirror, dimly.

Therefore, no matter how we might struggle to acquire knowledge, it always eludes us. Commenting on Eccl 7:24 ("I have tried all these things in wisdom, and have said: 'I shall be made wise'; and it has become further from me, more than it was"), Jerome noted that Solomon tried to acquire wisdom to know all things, but the more he obtained, he realized, the farther he was from true wisdom. This is comparable to the experience of someone who studies the Scriptures: the more they understand, the greater the obscurity that confronts them. Jerome presumably speaks from his own experience here. But again this is because we see in a mirror, dimly. In the life to come we will be amazed at how far we were from true knowledge and understanding.[31]

In the present life, the fullness of God's knowledge and the mysteries of ultimate reality are things that can only confuse us. At Eccl 7:17 ("Be not just greatly, and do not ask more, lest you become bewildered"), Jerome claims that the Preacher realizes that our minds cannot grasp perfect wisdom and that we also should recognize our own limitations. Jerome supports his interpretation with a precedent from Paul. When a rhetorical interlocutor had questioned the apostle about the purposes of God, Paul replied, "Who are you, O man, to answer back to God?" (Rom 9:20). Paul's answer was a kindness to his readers, wrote Jerome, as there is a certain class of knowledge too great to be grasped by the human mind. This knowledge would only lead to our bewilderment, as the Preacher had stated in this passage.

But even worse than the fact that this knowledge had the potential to bewilder those who might obtain it was the fact that the very pursuit of this knowledge, the desire to probe into these secret mysteries of God in search of answers to the big questions, was a punishment that God has levied on certain people. This view emerges fairly early on in the commentary; in his discussion of Eccl 1:13 ("And I gave my heart to investigating and considering in wisdom about all things that happen under the sun. God gave this evil occupation to the sons of men, so they would be occupied by it"), Jerome argued that the Preacher had gone beyond what was permissible in his search for knowledge. He wanted answers to the great questions that trouble humans, but this was forbidden knowledge, restricted to God alone.

In levying the punishment of this desire on certain people, God makes them hungry for what they may not have, desperate for answers they will never learn. Jerome supports his argument with an odd biblical text, Paul's treatment of God's judgment upon sin in Rom 1:26–32. In this passage Paul wrote about the punishment that had come upon those who refused to honor and follow God, whose nature was known from the goodness of creation. God handed these people over to the lusts of their hearts, and they plunged into and wallowed in disgraceful conduct. Jerome read Eccl 1:13 through the lens of Paul's verses. Humans in general and the Preacher in particular wanted to know more than what was permissible for them to know, so God had handed them over to their wicked desire. He allowed this yearning for forbidden knowledge to have full rein in them, a burning hunger that gave them no rest as they struggled to penetrate mysteries that were off-limits.

Jerome voices a similar sentiment in his comment on Eccl 8:16–17:

> He who seeks the causes and explanations of events, why this or that has happened, and how the world is directed with various outcomes—why one baby is born blind and crippled, while another sees and has a sound body; why this man has poverty, that man has riches; this one noble, that one inconspicuous—this man achieves nothing except to be tormented by his own investigation, and to have discussion acting as torture, and still not find what he seeks; and when he claims to have learned, he is then at the starting point of his ignorance and is in deep error.

Throughout his *Commentary on Ecclesiastes,* Jerome questioned the validity of the inquiry that had occupied the Preacher. Unlike Origen, who believed that it was permissible to speculate on the deeper mysteries of God as long as one did not contradict the teachings of the Bible and the rule of faith,[32] Jerome here evinces little patience for an investigation into questions he deems beyond human comprehension. In other words, Jerome's exegesis undermines the entire purpose of Ecclesiastes. Rather than waste our time trying to understand things that lie beyond our limited comprehension, we should be content with what has been clearly taught in the Scriptures. Knowledge of the higher mysteries should be left to a future life where we will be able to understand them. An obsession with these questions is a punishment given by God, a curse levied upon those who had the temerity to question the unfathomable wisdom of the creator.

The effects of this curse are amply evident among the heretics. For Jerome, the desire to probe—as well as the claim to have penetrated—God's hidden mysteries is the hallmark of the heretic. And lurking closely behind every heretic is Satan the deceiver, the fallen angel who prowls the earth looking for humans to lead astray. Christians need to be ever-vigilant, guarding their minds and conduct to prevent Satan from gaining a foothold in their soul. For once he does, he will begin to introduce heretical ideas, and even the best of Christians will slowly slip away from orthodox doctrine into heresy (8.2–4). No one is immune; even the wisest person can tumble into error should his guard falter (10.9). And once that person begins to slide away, Satan will reinforce his thoughts, leading him further astray. With Satan operating behind the scenes, the church of the heretics draws the unwise and careless to it, beguiling the fools to partake of the false sacraments and polluted baptism. The heretics actively work to pour the oil of their ideas over the heads of those who have been deceived (9.7–8). Through their false doctrines and affable, persuasive speech, they catch the unwary like fish in nets (9.12).

The heretics are able to seduce many through futile verbosity (10.13–14). Although the scholars and wise thinkers of the church fight them mightily, their efforts in this life go largely unrewarded. The masses, preferring glib speech to wisdom, are led astray by Satan (10.5–7). The voices of the wise are ignored; popular acclaim goes to the heretics. This injustice will not be redressed until the next life, when wisdom will be revealed and the heretics will earn their well-deserved punishment (11.2). They promise themselves joys and prosperity, but their minds are clouded and unable to see what truly lies in store for them: they and their doctrines will perish, bringing no value either to themselves or to those who have been led to embrace them (2.2; 5.12–16). Jerome seemed to believe that once a person becomes a heretic, there is no road back to orthodoxy. The heretic has a nature that has been twisted and irredeemably corrupted (1.15). There is no path into the city of God that any heretic can find; if Plato, Aristotle, and all the rest of the philosophers—the wisest men in worldly terms who have ever lived—were unable to find the path to God, how will a Satan-deceived heretic ever find a way (10.15)?

Many heretics line the path that a true Christian must walk, preaching eloquently in the churches about God's hidden mysteries. The only sure and certain course for those who wish to arrive in God's kingdom is to stopper their ears and meditate upon what has been revealed. Questions about providence, the ways in which God does and does not act in this life, are out of bounds for the Christian. Jerome's exegesis never really engages with the heart of the Preacher's project, save to deem it a question off-limits to Christian speculation.

JEROME'S SOURCES

The Biblical Text

In writing his *Commentary on Ecclesiastes,* Jerome drew heavily on the Hexapla, the critical edition of the Hebrew Bible created by Origen. This parallel version of the Hebrew Bible featured six columns of text. The first column contained the Hebrew text written in Hebrew characters. Column 2 was a transliteration of the Hebrew characters into Greek letters. Columns 3 and 4 contained Greek translations of the text made by Aquila and Symmachus; column 5 contained the Greek text of the Septuagint, and the final column featured the Greek translation of Theodotion. This massive work of erudition was housed in a library at Caesarea, and Jerome demonstrates both in this commentary and elsewhere that he had consulted the text.[33]

By the time Jerome embarked on the *Commentary on Ecclesiastes,* he was aware of the shortcomings of the Septuagint.[34] Other Christians in late antiquity did not share this dissatisfaction. Since the beginning of the Christian movement, the Septuagint had served as the standard version of the Old Testament. It had, after all, been produced under the direct inspiration of God's Holy Spirit. According to the *Letter of Aristeas,*[35] the Septuagint translation had been commissioned by King Ptolemy II Philadelphus in the third century BC. Desiring a translation that he could read, the king had assembled seventy-two translators and set them to work making independent translations of the text.[36] When the seventy-two manuscripts were compared, it was found that they all agreed, a certain miracle and validation of the divine inspiration that had led the translators to their amazing concord.

Setting legend aside, it is clear that the Septuagint had been created for Hellenistic Jews who had been scattered in the Diaspora. These Jews were losing their ability to read Hebrew, so the Septuagint was produced to facilitate their study and worship. After the death of Jesus, the Septuagint was adopted by the Christians, and for nearly four hundred years it served as the "Authorized" version of the Christian movement. As a consequence of this attachment, Jerome's contemporaries grew alarmed when, sensitive to the flaws of the Septuagint, he began to move away from that text and return to the Hebrew manuscripts.[37] For many Christians, Jerome's work seemed to undermine the authority of the Bible. Changes to this text, even to correct its deficiencies, were bound to excite controversy. Augustine reported one case in which an African church service was reduced to a riot after the presiding bishop read Jerome's new translation of the Book of Jonah aloud in a church service. The congregation was accustomed to hearing the word *cucurbita* ("gourd"), while Jerome's new translation offered the word *hedera* ("ivy"). Hearing that the plant had been altered in Jerome's revision, the congregation broke into a tumult. The bishop was forced to take Jerome's version to a local group of Jews to seek their opinion on the emendation. Most unfortunately, the Jews supported the Septuagint reading, leading Augustine to conclude that perhaps Jerome would be better off simply collating and refining the Septuagint rather than trying to create a novel translation based on the Hebrew text.[38] After all, Jerome was simply one man, prone, like any other man, to making mistakes. Was he, Augustine seemed to imply, so above error that he could serve as judge and arbiter over the holy texts?[39] Rufinus offered another objection to Jerome's translation: it gave the pagans and Jews grounds for unbelief when they saw that Jerome was changing the sacred law of the Christians.[40] If a change was required, then it must be self-evident that the earlier version was incorrect. Things that underwent changes at human hands could not be considered divine. Jerome's project jeopardized the foundation on which the faith was constructed.

Jerome was not deterred by his critics, however, and, beginning in 390, he set out to make a fresh Latin translation of the Old Testament. For the next fifteen years Jerome devoted his attention to making (and defending) a new translation *iuxta Hebraeos* ("according to the Hebrew"), ultimately creating his greatest contribution to Christianity, the Vulgate.[41]

Jerome's use of the Septuagint in his preparation of the *Commentary on Ecclesiastes* is more complicated than it might appear at first sight. There are clear indications in the *Commentary* that he was dissatisfied with the work of the seventy-two, but he was not yet prepared to jettison the Septuagint and begin with a fresh translation from the Hebrew.[42] In the preface to this work, he noted that the Latin translation he offered was based on the Septuagint where it did not deviate too far from the Hebrew original. Implicit in this statement is the need to compare and, if required, correct the Septuagint text in accordance with the Hebrew. This seems like a straightforward position for Jerome to adopt: the Hebrew was the authentic version, the final authority. The Septuagint was useful only insofar as it conformed to the correct Hebrew text.[43]

Yet, whether Jerome realized it or not, this clear position is muddied by at least two issues. The first is his own expertise in Hebrew. There are a number of places in which Jerome, appearing to misunderstand the Hebrew text, follows the Septuagint in its mistaken interpretation.[44] Jerome's recognition of these mistakes and his growth as a Hebrew scholar are attested by the corrections found in his later Vulgate translation of Ecclesiastes, in which the Septuagint readings he had incorporated in the *Commentary* are abandoned for a translation that corresponds more closely to the Hebrew text.[45] The intermediate position occupied by the *Commentary* in Jerome's literary corpus provides some insight into the course of his developing expertise in Hebrew.

The second issue complicating Jerome's position on the Septuagint is more fascinating. At a number of points in the *Commentary* he clearly recognizes that the Septuagint had deviated from the Hebrew text, yet he still admits the Septuagint translation as a basis for exegesis and interpretation. For instance, at 2.15, 16, the Hebrew text clearly states that, at the end of his quest, the Preacher had concluded that there was no point in acquiring wisdom; the end of the fool and the wise man is the same. Both die. The Preacher does not admit the possibility of an afterlife in which the inequities of this life might be redressed, so he suggests that the hard work of study is fruitless. Jerome, who did believe in an afterlife and wanted to believe that an unrewarded life of wisdom in this world might receive recompense in the next, had to find some way to put a Christian spin on the verse. The Hebrew text offered no help, although, in his first translation, Jerome rendered it accurately. The Septuagint, on the other hand, had modified the verse by adding a phrase that was not present in the Hebrew. At the end of v. 15, the Greek translators had appended the phrase διότι ὁ ἄφρων ἐκ περισσεύματος λαλεῖ (*dioti ho aphrōn ek perisseumatos lalei*, "because the fool speaks from excess").

This emendation threw doubt on the Preacher's judgment. Did the Preacher really intend to condemn wisdom, or was this a sentiment he had voiced in error? Jerome noted that the Septuagint, although not keeping close to the Hebrew wording, had rendered the sense of the verse better than the Hebrew had![46] In other words, the mistranslation, the pious defanging of the Hebrew text, had given Jerome a handle to alter the Preacher's meaning completely, substituting an explanation more palatable to a Christian readership. At several other points we find Jerome clearly indicating that the Septuagint translators had mistranslated the Hebrew but then offering the Septuagint version and making exegetical points based on what he knows is a mistake.[47]

Jerome was, of course, writing for an audience that was accustomed to reading the Septuagint version of this text. But if he inserted these readings simply as a palliative to those readers, how can we explain the great number of places in which he does not make this concession? Augustine would later develop an eccentric explanation for the clear mistakes and mistranslations found in the Septuagint: God had directly inspired both versions, the Hebrew and the Septuagint, and the differences between the two versions exist because God chose to say the same things in different ways, adding, subtracting, or changing texts to show that translation was no act of servile labor but was the fruit of divine action.[48] While it is unlikely that Jerome would have endorsed this explanation (as his later Vulgate translations from the Hebrew attest), at the time he wrote the *Commentary* it is clear that he had no reservations about using the Septuagint if he felt that a text he knew to be wrong would allow him to make a point that could not be drawn from the Hebrew.

The Recentiores

The Septuagint (at least the version found in the Hexapla) was an important source for Jerome's work on Ecclesiastes, but, as discussed above, he offers clear signals throughout that he had significant doubts about the quality of the text. Jerome also makes use of the three other Greek translations arrayed in the Hexapla, the work of the *recentiores*, Theodotion, Aquila, and Symmachus.

Theodotion

There is some controversy over the biography of Theodotion. Jerome labeled him an Ebionite,[49] while Irenaeus claimed that he was a Jewish scholar from Ephesus.[50] In patristic sources the works of the *recentiores* are usually given in the order Aquila, Theodotion, and Symmachus, which, until recently, scholars thought reflected a chronological arrangement of these three translations. This arrangement has been cast into doubt in recent years, however, with some scholars arguing that Theodotion might have predated Aquila and that material traditionally attributed to Theodotion in the Hexapla might have been written by an earlier translator or translators.[51] Theodotion has long been regarded as a translator whose style adopts a middle course between the wooden literalness of Aquila and the freer rendition of Symmachus. This characterization of his work is being reconsidered as Septuagint scholars reassess the materials traditionally attributed to Theodotion. There was no such hesitation in the early Christian church; quotations attributed to Theodotion appear in early works such as the *Shepherd of Hermas* and Justin Martyr's *Dialogue with Trypho*.

Aquila

The first reference to Aquila in patristic literature comes in Irenaeus, who wrote that Aquila of Pontus, a Jewish convert, had made a translation of the Hebrew Bible into Greek that denied the divinity of Christ.[52] Modern scholars suspect that Aquila was a Gentile who converted to Judaism during the time of the emperor Hadrian (ca. 117–138).[53] His translation was a very literal, word-for-word translation of the Hebrew[54] that ignored the basic rules of Greek syntax in order to follow the word order of the Hebrew text. The resulting text was very clumsy, a translation whose fidelity to the Hebrew led to obscure Greek.

Symmachus

Symmachus was the final Greek translator incorporated into the Hexapla. In most respects, the translation of Symmachus was the best of the three. He wrote an idiomatic Greek that captured the flavor and meaning of the Hebrew more accurately than the other two *recentiores*. The fragments that survive of his translations veer toward the paraphrase—replacing idiomatic Hebrew words and phrases with matching Greek idioms and avoiding the literalism found in Aquila.[55] The early fathers of the church attest that Symmachus was an Ebionite.[56] Eusebius claimed that, in addition to his translation of the Hebrew Bible, Symmachus had written a commentary on the Gospel of Matthew in which he attacked the idea of the divine birth. Jerome's regard for Symmachus is evident throughout the *Commentary*, and Symmachus's version of the text is often cited with approval.[57]

Old Latin Versions

It is difficult to evaluate the possible influence of earlier Latin translations on the translation that Jerome offers in this commentary. As a general rule he is rather disdainful of these earlier Latin translations, and, as discussed above, he had dedicated a good part of his earlier literary career to revising and supplanting these versions. Nevertheless, the *Commentary on Ecclesiastes* does reveal that Jerome consulted one or more Latin versions in preparing his own work. At 1.13, for instance, Jerome offers the translations for the Hebrew word *ʿinyān* found in the Greek texts as well as that given by a "Latin interpreter." Jerome also noted an error found in "the Latin manuscripts" at 2.5. These references lead us to suspect that although Jerome claims to have made his translation from the Hebrew, with reference to the Septuagint and *recentiores*, in fact he also had one or more Latin versions of the text at hand.

THE COMMENTARY

Before examining the sources that Jerome employed in creating his commentary, it might be prudent first to ask, What was a commentary in the ancient world? In modern theological studies commentaries are such an accepted part of the scholarly landscape that we may give very little thought to their role and place in Christian literature. Although Jerome was not the first Christian author to employ the commentary form, he was an important contributor to the genre.

The commentary, in antiquity as now, is a multifaceted work. On one level it operates as a piece of persuasive rhetoric: the commentator must convince readers that he has correctly understood the text under discussion, and, as a result, his interpretation is to be regarded as authoritative, normative for Christian belief. A failure to do so, whether through mistakes or a general weakness of scholarship, undermines the argument of the commentary. A persuasive reading and exegesis, on the other hand, allow the writer to advance an agenda. The writer's reading of the text is advanced as normative or correct; this interpretation is to be given preference over the interpretations of other writers. Over a period of time, as a commentator crafts a body of work (as Jerome did), his reputation expands and his views begin to determine orthodoxy: the correct interpretation of a text.

The commentary was also a place to demonstrate expertise. For Jerome, the act of writing commentary could serve as an advertisement for his unique talents. In the pages of the *Commentary on Ecclesiastes* he demonstrates his considerable philological skills, handling Hebrew, Greek, and Latin with apparent ease. He also evinces a mastery of the books that make up the biblical canon, as well as classical and philosophical literature. Moreover, he shows that he has studied a broad range of Christian writings, especially, as will be discussed below, the writings of Origen. His formidable erudition shines through every page of his commentaries. Based on the evidence of these works alone, an ancient audience would have been compelled to acknowledge his expertise.

Why would Jerome seek to build his reputation through the writing of commentaries? The obvious answer would be one of emulation. The great Origen had written a number of biblical commentaries, and, in recasting himself as the Latin Origen,[58] Jerome may have seen commentaries as one way to compete with Origen's legacy. It is also the case that Origen's literary work would have served as an advertisement for the catechetical school he oversaw in Alexandria. The writing of commentaries also figured in the promotional effort of Jerome's teacher, Aelius Donatus. Donatus had gained much fame (and undoubtedly increased the number of students in his school) through writing commentaries on Vergil and Terence. If Jerome ever considered opening a Christian school in Bethlehem, then self-promotion through the writing of commentaries would have been one way to attract students.[59]

Jerome's exegetical works also allowed him to demonstrate his expertise to a wide Christian audience. Having been driven out of Rome by his jealous contemporaries, Jerome set to work with a passionate urgency, producing a vast quantity of Christian scholarship in a relatively short time. It is almost as if, denied the praise and position he felt he deserved in Rome, he resolved to show his detractors the quality of the man they had lost. The *Commentary on Ecclesiastes* was simply one of the opening salvos in the battle to distinguish himself among the Christian literati. Jerome would gain the renown of an Origen or bury the world in papyri trying.

Having sketched out a few of the reasons why Jerome might want to write a commentary, we would do well also to ask how Jerome conceived his task as the writer of a commentary. In the mid-twentieth century, a number of scholars began to question Jerome's competence and ability as both translator and exegete. Jerome's frequent and often unattributed borrowings of material from Greek scholars such as Eusebius of Caesarea and Origen led many to doubt the originality and contribution of Jerome. Was he a celebrated *vir trilinguis* as he claimed, or an industrious plagiarist, stitching together the work of earlier Christian writers? The noted French patristics scholar Pierre Nautin did the most to disparage Jerome's reputation. Writing about Origen, Nautin claimed that Jerome's frequent references to Jewish exegesis were in fact drawn from the works of Origen. In fact, asserted Nautin, Jerome himself did not know how to read Hebrew and any references he drew from that language had been lifted from the Greek masters.[60] Although this position has been largely debunked,[61] there is little doubt that Jerome is indebted to more sources than he explicitly names.

This is by no means a discovery of modern scholarship. Jerome's contemporaries, especially Rufinus of Aquileia, were more than aware of the extent of Jerome's appropriation of the work of other writers. When the relationship between Rufinus and Jerome soured, the former did not hesitate to charge Jerome with borrowing from Origen and other writers and employing them in his own works. Jerome was forced to respond to Rufinus's charges, explaining his own conception of a commentary:

> What do commentaries have to do?
>
> They explain what someone else has said; they make clear, in straightforward language, what was obscurely written; and they reproduce many people's opinions, saying: "Some explain this passage like this, some like that; such-and-such people, with such-and-such pieces of evidence and such-and-such reasoning, endeavor to confirm their view of its sense, and their understanding of it." This is so that the careful reader, after reading varying interpretations and learning many people's views, whether acceptable or not, may judge which is the truer and, like a sound banker, reject payment in counterfeit coin. Surely a person who gives several people's expositions, in the single work that he is explaining, will not be held guilty of a conflicting interpretation, and of mutually contradictory views?[62]

In a subsequent book of the *Apology*, directed at Rufinus, he wrote:

> In these commentaries, and in others as well, what I have done is to expound both my own and others' opinions, making an open avowal of which are heretical and which

orthodox. It is a normal principle of commentaries and expounders that during their exposition they go into differing opinions, and explain people's views, whether their own or others'. It is not just the interpreters of the holy scriptures who do this; those who comment on secular literature, Latin and Greek alike, also do the same.[63]

These explanations of Jerome's methodology in writing commentary are repeated in a letter written to Augustine:

It is not for me, in my minute little cell along with my monks—that is, with my fellow-sinners—to venture to lay down the law on great issues; but I do venture to admit, frankly, that I read the works of greater men, and that in my commentaries I follow the universal practice of including differing interpretations, so that everyone may follow the one he wishes, out of a large number. This, I believe, is what you have found in your reading, both in secular literature and in the divine books, and have approved.[64]

These reflections on the task of a commentary writer were drawn out of Jerome by the heat of controversy; they are a hurried defense of his methodology, possibly the first time he was forced to articulate it. Nevertheless a couple of important points emerge: (1) It is clear that Jerome would not have valued originality in a commentator. The job of a Christian exegete was not to make up new or novel interpretations of the sacred text, but to indicate the lines of thought explored by earlier writers. In this Jerome manifests the deep conservatism of Roman writers: novelty and innovation were not prized in antiquity as they are now. Indeed, as noted above, one of the main attacks on Jerome's Vulgate translations from the Hebrew was that the project was a novelty, something new and suspicious. (2) It was the task of the commentator, having marshaled a diverse range of views, to pronounce judgment on them. The commentator served the reader by indicating which views were orthodox, which heretical. This was a later development in Jerome's thought, one that does not appear in the first defense of his methodology (Hier. *Ruf.* 1.16). In this task Jerome saw himself standing in a long line of commentators, both Christian and secular, spelling out for the masses orthodox interpretations of literary works. Jerome sought to present himself as a gatekeeper over orthodoxy, a trusted and wise scholar who would sift the chaff to help his readers find the kernels of truth.

Jerome's statements about the nature of commentary all postdate the *Commentary on Ecclesiastes*. In this work Jerome borrowed freely from other writers, largely (as Rufinus hinted) failed to identify his sources, and made little attempt to delineate catholic from heretical thought. We suspect that this borrowing was extensive; by the time he composed the *Commentary on Ecclesiastes* a number of other Christian authors had tried their hands at explaining the text. Some of these works are lost, making a direct comparison with Jerome's text difficult or impossible. Nevertheless, in the following paragraphs we shall briefly identify authors who predated Jerome in writing on Ecclesiastes. An extended discussion of their direct influence on Jerome will be found in our notes on the *Commentary*.

Dionysius of Alexandria

Dionysius of Alexandria (died ca. 264) was a student of Origen and became the bishop of Alexandria around the year 248. He did not enjoy a quiet life and was forced to flee his post during two of the third-century persecutions of Christians (under Decius in 250 and Valerian in 257). In *Vir. ill.* 69, Jerome notes that Dionysius had claimed in a letter that he was beginning a commentary on Ecclesiastes. Jerome's entry does not make clear whether Jerome had seen a finished version of this commentary, but, since he did not list it among Dionysius's completed works, it could be argued that he had not.

The commentary on Ecclesiastes attributed to Dionysius survives in an incomplete form going no further than chapter 3 of the text. Although the two commentaries share thematic interests, Jerome omits arguments from Dionysius that would have buttressed his own views. For instance, in commenting on the Preacher's claim that there was a time to speak and a time to remain silent, Dionysius stated that the time to speak is when your hearers will receive what you have to say, while the time to keep silent is when the listeners are heretics who will pervert what you say.[65] In view of Jerome's repeated excoriation of heretics (see above), it is hard to believe that he would not have incorporated this interpretation into his own commentary had he known it. That he did not, coupled with the entry in *On Illustrious Men*, suggests that he had not read this text.

Gregory Thaumaturgos

Gregory Thaumaturgos (ca. 213–270) was also one of Origen's students. A pagan who was converted to Christianity through his association with Origen, he later became bishop of Neocaesarea, in the province of Pontus and Bithynia (located on the southern border of the Black Sea in modern Turkey). His nickname (Thaumaturgos) refers to the wide range of miracles he is reputed to have performed while a bishop. This reputation was enhanced when Gregory of Nyssa wrote an account of his life (*De vita Gregorii Thaumaturgi*); Jerome numbers him among his illustrious men (Hier. *Vir. ill.* 65), and in the same place also attributes the *Metaphrasis on Ecclesiastes,* a "short, but valuable" Greek paraphrase to this author.[66] That Jerome had read the *Metaphrasis* is made evident at 4.13–16, where he cites a passage from Gregory's work. This is the only direct citation of Gregory in the work. Gregory's work is a paraphrase of the text of Ecclesiastes, rather than a commentary on the work. Consequently, Gregory makes his argument about Ecclesiastes indirectly, through the Greek words and phrases he employs in his translation.[67] Although there are similarities of thought between the two works, direct dependence is much harder to establish.

Origen

There can be little doubt that the works of Origen (ca. 185–254) exercised considerable influence on Jerome's *Commentary on Ecclesiastes.*[68] Aside from the Hexapla, which Jerome studied in making his translation (see discussion above), Origen also provided many of the exegetical arguments that Jerome deployed in explaining the text of the book. These range from his schematization of the three books of Solomon—Proverbs is intended to instruct the young; Ecclesiastes is intended for one who has mastered the basic lessons and now needs to learn to despise the world; the Song of Songs is for the perfected (see 1.1; Or. *Cant.* Prol. 3.6–8)—to Origen's doctrine of *apokatastasis,* the view that in the fullness of time all of the souls who have fallen away from God will return to be reunited with him (see 1.15 and Or. *Princ.* 1.6.3; 3.6.5). At this time, in the late 380s, Jerome was still completely enamored of the work of the Alexandrian exegete, and it is almost certain that, had a commentary on Ecclesiastes written by Origen survived, a comparison would reveal even more appropriations than are indicated in the notes of this work.

Victorinus of Poetovio

Victorinus (died ca. 304) was the bishop of Pettau in the Roman province of Pannonia. One of the earliest fathers to write commentaries in Latin, he was probably martyred during the persecution of Diocletian. Jerome notes that among Victorinus's theological works was a commentary on Ecclesiastes. Unfortunately Victorinus was not much of a linguist, and Jerome characterized his works as "inferior in style."[69] The only reference to Victorinus in the *Commentary* occurs at 4.13–16, where Jerome paraphrased (along with others) Victorinus's view on the passage, a view that he stated was quite close to the position adopted by Origen.

Apollinarius of Laodicea

Apollinarius (ca. 310–390) was, during the time Jerome wrote the *Commentary*, the controversial bishop of Laodicea. He had been a faithful supporter of the Nicene cause, a friend and partisan of Athanasius of Alexandria, but after the Council of Constantinople (381), some of his views about the nature of Christ's incarnation cast him into disrepute. His minimization of Christ's human nature earned censure by councils in Rome, and from 381 onward, he was forbidden to preach in the church.

Jerome avoids mentioning Apollinarius's controversial positions in his entry on the man in *On Illustrious Men*,[70] preferring to highlight Apollinarius's formidable language skills and his defense of the faith in a work written against the pagan philosopher Porphyry. Apollinarius was also well known for his biblical commentaries, of which only fragments remain. Although Apollinarius's commentary on Ecclesiastes is no longer extant, Jerome's citation of the work at 4.13–16 and 12.5 establishes the fact that there was such a volume and that Jerome had consulted it. While Jerome avoids outright censure of the work, his comments about it fall well short of praise. At 4.13–16 he offers a quotation from Apollinarius, noting that, as usual, Apollinarius was straining to express great matters in a brief discourse. At 12.5 he suggests that Apollinarius, led astray by following the translation of Symmachus, had produced an interpretation of the verse that pleased neither the Jews nor the Christians. Unfortunately Jerome fails to record Apollinarius's interpretation.

Gregory of Nyssa

A final possible Christian source for Jerome could have been Gregory of Nyssa's *Homilies on Ecclesiastes*. Gregory of Nyssa (ca. 330–395) was one of the three great Cappadocian fathers. Jerome had met Gregory of Nyssa and Gregory of Nazianzus while in Constantinople, and in *On Illustrious Men* he noted that Gregory of Nyssa had read a portion of his tract against the heretic Eunomius to him.[71]

Eight of Gregory's homilies on Ecclesiastes are extant;[72] when these works are compared with Jerome's commentary, it becomes evident that Jerome either had not read them or chose to ignore them. The few points of contact between the two works—for instance, in identifying the Preacher with Christ (see 1.1)—are either theological commonplaces or can be attributed to the influence of Origen on both writers. In fact, a systematic comparison between the work of Gregory and that of Jerome tends to highlight Jerome's deficiencies as a theological writer. His often pedestrian approach to the text lacks the imaginative range and depth of Gregory's analysis. For instance, the two men take radically different approaches to *Eccl* 1:13: *"And I gave my heart to investigating and considering in wisdom about all things that happen under the sun."* In his commentary, Jerome chose to emphasize the literal/historical interpretation of this verse: the Preacher had embarked on a course of inquiry designed to gain an understanding of why the world seems to be vanity. Unfortunately, his investigation was a probe into the hidden things of God, the mysteries that no human fathoms. These topics are off-limits to human investigation. As a punishment for his investigation, the Preacher was made to suffer, his mind subjected to torture. This is the same fate that awaits the heretics.

Jerome's fundamental lack of sympathy for the Preacher's attempt to understand why things happen as they do stands in sharp contrast to the interpretation offered by Gregory of Nyssa. Gregory, identifying the Preacher with Christ (as did Jerome when it suited him), developed the full implication of what it meant to have Christ uttering these words. Clearly Jesus already knew everything that was happening in heaven, so what was he investigating? It must be the events taking place on earth. This is the reason that God chose to become incarnate as Christ. He wanted to come to earth and, like a good physician, probe the maladies that had sickened his creation. Jesus was born to investigate the ills of the world and then offer himself to heal those diseases.[73]

Throughout what remains of his work, Gregory read the words of the Preacher through the lens of the Incarnate Christ. Ultimately his allegorical speculations may prove less congenial to a modern reader than what Jerome offers, but there can be little doubt that it is a great deal more imaginative and holds together in a more integrated and theologically coherent manner than Jerome's ad hoc exegesis. We have made a point in our notes of contrasting the two writers in order to highlight the different approaches open to late antique Christian exegetes of the text.

Jerome's Hebrew

As J. N. D. Kelly noted in his biography of Jerome, one of the distinctives of this work was Jerome's incorporation of rabbinic exegesis in its pages.[74] Throughout the commentary Jerome refers to the beliefs of "the Hebrews," or of "his Hebrew," the teacher who had instructed him in the language. One of these teachers is identified in Hier. *Ep.* 84.3: "then, in turn, I came to Jerusalem and Bethlehem, where, with much work and expense I retained Barania as a night-time tutor. For he feared the Jews and presented himself as a second Nicodemus to me." Barania not only developed Jerome's ability to read the Hebrew language but also seems to have served as a source of contemporary Jewish readings of the text. The assistance of Barania ranged from clarifying the meaning of individual Hebrew words (see, e.g., 1.14, where Jerome states that his Hebrew teacher had explained that, contrary to what the Greek translators had written, the Hebrew word *rĕ'ût* actually meant "affliction" or "badness," rather than "pasture" or "will") to actually offering interpretations of Ecclesiastes that Jerome preferred over the Christian interpretations (see, e.g., his discussion at 3.9–11).

Jerome's use of Hebrew sources was fairly controversial. Rufinus, for instance, attacked Jerome's reliance on Hebrew exegesis, averring that when the time had come to choose a teacher, Rufinus had chosen Christ, while Jerome had followed Barabbas.[75] For Jerome, however, a knowledge of both Hebrew and contemporary rabbinic exegesis was important to his self-presentation as a biblical scholar.[76] The ability to read the Hebrew Bible in its original language conferred unparalleled authority in the late antique world of Christian exegesis. Jerome could discuss the original text at a level that no other Christian could reach. His knowledge of Hebrew in many ways made his judgments unassailable by his contemporaries. Consequently, Jerome emphasized this facet of his learning, parading his linguistic skills whenever possible.

Frequently, Jewish exegesis is employed simply to confirm a point. At 7.9 Jerome cites an explanation of the passage offered by his Hebrew teacher and says nothing more about it. In some cases, however, the Jewish interpretation is offered as superior to Christian views on the text. When discussing *Eccl* 1:7, for instance, Jerome noted that some had understood the verse to mean that the sun evaporated freshwater or the sea swallowed it. The Hebrews, on the other hand,

had seen in this verse a metaphor for humans who soon return to
the earth from which they sprang. This latter interpretation, Jerome
claimed, was preferable to the literal exegesis of "some."

Jewish sources were also employed to provide the literal or
historical interpretation of a passage. For instance, at 1.12, Jerome
explains that the Jews believed that the historical context for the
Book of Ecclesiastes was Solomon's repentance for placing his trust
in wisdom and wealth, while simultaneously offending God with his
foreign women. At 3.2 he notes that the Jews related *Eccl* 3:2 to their
experience of captivity under the Babylonians, and at 7.16 two biblical
episodes, the sons of Aaron (*Lev* 10:1–2) and King Manasseh (*2 Chr*
33:11–13), are employed to explain the text. For Jerome, then, Jewish
exegesis was important to establish the literal or historical context of
the text under examination.

Unfortunately, since the Jews had turned their backs on Christ
and failed to accept him as Messiah, they lived with blinders on,
unable to see the higher, spiritual meaning of these words. They
had failed to rejoice in the coming of Christ and consequently had
received the Antichrist (4.13–16). The Jews and the synagogue had
been supplanted by the Christians and the church (1.4; 3.6, 7; 6.1–6;
9.4b–6). As time passed Jerome would develop and refine his ideas of
how Jewish exegesis fit into his thought. Jewish interpretations were
like a spiral staircase that one ascended to reach the spiritual summit.
They were the literal foundation on which Christian allegory was to
be built, absolutely essential if the Christian interpretation was to be
constructed on rock rather than sand.[77] Consequently, before exegetes
could properly understand the text of the Hebrew Bible, they must
first understand the rich interpretive tradition of the Jews.

In later works Jerome would begin to downplay the importance
of the Jewish traditions and interpretations that he cited.[78] Clearly, as
time went by and Jerome's reputation as an accomplished exegete
became well established, he felt that he could dispense with this prop
to his interpretations. Nevertheless, in this early work his reliance
on Jewish exegesis is clear and incontrovertible, and it served as an
important way to lay claim to authority as a biblical exegete.

PLAN OF THIS VOLUME

Our work is divided into two main sections: the first is a
translation of Jerome's book as a whole, and the second is our own

commentary on his work. Our guiding principles in the translation are given in the next three paragraphs.

Before commenting on a section of the biblical text, Jerome prefaces each new section with a Latin translation of it. This normally amounts to a single verse or two of our Bible, but sometimes to several verses. To distinguish the biblical text from his commentary on it, we print our version of these translations in italics, repeating the italics wherever he again quotes the text on which he is commenting—though he does not always do so in exactly the same words.

The initial translations are as literal as possible, as in the Septuagint translation of this book of the Bible. Thus, the Latin wording of them remains very Hebraic in form, consisting of short sentences strung together almost solely by the single conjunction normally translated "and," often with no obvious connection of thought between them. The Hebrew of Ecclesiastes is generally acknowledged by commentators, whether Jewish or Christian, to be difficult; thus these Latin versions, like those of the Septuagint, are also often very puzzling. However, we have seen it as our task to render them into English with the same sometimes painful fidelity that Jerome has given, so as to show what he thought was the actual text that he had to explain.

As would be expected from a pupil of Donatus, the Latin of Jerome's commentary itself is elegantly expressed, though often in sentences too long and elaborately constructed to be comfortable for most modern readers. Here, we have tried to be both faithful to his meaning and readable, but not necessarily with the fidelity to his sentence structure that we maintained in his initial translations of each section.

In our commentary, we attempt to resolve the philological, textual, historical, and theological questions posed by Jerome's work. When it seems appropriate, relevant, and fruitful, we also compare Jerome's exegetical interpretations to those of earlier Christian and Jewish authors. The presence of commentary notes on a word or phrase in Jerome's text is indicated by a superscript asterisk(*) in the translation. The notes are divided into sections by chapter and verse, and each note is prefaced with an English lemma to separate multiple notes in a section. The reader will also find occasional footnote numbers in the main text. These identify points where we have disagreed with the Latin text found in the CCSL critical edition. The footnote numbers are linked to entries in the Appendix, where the readings we have adopted may be found.

Every Greek and Hebrew word appearing in this volume is given in both the Greek or Hebrew font and a transliteration. Where appropriate the word or term is also defined, for example, λόγος (*logos*, "word").

Jerome makes free use of the Septuagint throughout his work. The numbering of the book of Psalms in the Septuagint (and the Vulgate) is different from what is found in English Bibles that are based on the Hebrew text. Consequently, when citing a Psalm quotation, we have identified the verses as in the following example: LXX *Ps* 118:1 [119:1]. In these citations, the reference embedded in the square brackets directs the reader to where the verse may be found in modern English translations. The same system is used also in cases such as the Four Books of Kingdoms, which correspond to the Books of Kings and Chronicles in English versions. All Septuagint references conform to the edition of Rahlfs, with which those of the New English Translation of the Septuagint (NETS) correspond.

In chapters 5 and 7 the verse numbering of the CCSL edition follows that of the modern Vulgate, which differs by one verse from NRSV and other English versions. As the CCSL text is the starting point of our work, we have retained its numbering of these chapters both in our translation and in references to them in our notes. The earliest manuscripts contained no indication of chapter or verse divisions or numbering.

Notes to Introduction

1. The classic biography of Jerome remains J. N. D. Kelly, *Jerome: His Life, Writings, and Controversies* (London: Duckworth, 1975). This has been supplemented in recent years by Stefan Rebenich, *Hieronymus und sein Kreis: Prosopographische und sozialgeschichtliche Untersuchungen, Historia. Einzelschriften 72* (Stuttgart: Franz Steiner, 1992) and Stefan Rebenich, *Jerome, Early Christian Fathers* (London and New York: Routledge, 2002).

2. Hier. *Vir. ill.* 135: "I, Hieronymus, a son of my father Eusebius, am from the town of Stridon which is on the border between Dalmatia and Pannonia, and was overthrown by the Goths." Jerome is the only ancient writer to mention Stridon. Archaeologists have been unable to locate the town (Kelly, *Jerome*, 3).

3. In a letter written to the Roman senator Pammachius, Jerome stated that he planned to send his brother, Paulinian, back to Stridon to sell what remained of the family estates after they had been ravaged by the Goths (Hier. *Ep.* 66.14).

4. In *Ep.* 13, Jerome writes a conciliatory letter to Castorina, his aunt, seeking reconciliation. The nature of their dispute, as well as whether they ever mended their relationship, is not recorded.

5. In *Ruf.* 1.30, he recalls how he had to be torn from his grandmother's lap to attend the lessons put on by his tutor.

6. Kelly, *Jerome*, 10.

7. See 1.9.

8. Kelly, *Jerome*, 27; Rebenich, *Jerome*, 6.

9. See Hier. *Ep.* 3.5.

10. Kelly, *Jerome*, 28.

11. As with many elements of Jerome's early life, details are in short supply. See Kelly, *Jerome*, 33–35; Rebenich, *Jerome*, 12.

12. Rebenich, *Jerome*, 12–17.

13. See Hier. *Ep.* 5.2, in which Jerome lists the books he would like his friend Florentius to send to him in Syria. See the similar request made in Hier. *Ep.* 10.3.

14. See Hier. *Ep.* 17.

15. See Hier. *Ep.* 15, 16.

16. Hier. *Ep.* 18.

17. Rebenich, *Jerome*, 32.

18. Hier. *Ep.* 123.10.

19. Aug. *Doct. chr.* 2.16.

20. Dennis Brown, "Jerome and the Vulgate," in *A History of Biblical Interpretation*, ed. Alan Hauser and Duane Watson (Grand Rapids: Eerdmans, 2003) 358–59.

21. Hier. *Vir. ill.* 135: "I translated the New Testament from the Greek and the Old Testament from the Hebrew." *On Illustrious Men* was composed

in 391, and it is possible that in this claim Jerome was simply anticipating a project that he hoped to complete at a future date.

22. See Kelly, *Jerome,* 88–89; Brown, "Jerome and the Vulgate," 359–60.

23. The *Commentary on Ecclesiastes,* for instance, is dedicated to Paula and Eustochium; see the Preface. Blesilla is there credited with stimulating Jerome to write the commentary, although she died before it was completed.

24. Hier. *Ep.* 39.6.

25. It is presumed, from the statements that Jerome made in Hier. *Ep.* 45, that he was accused of being engaged in an inappropriate relationship with Paula (Kelly, *Jerome,* 113–14).

26. For a history of reception of Ecclesiastes by later Christian writers, see Eric S. Christianson, *Ecclesiastes through the Centuries,* Blackwell Bible Commentaries (Oxford: Blackwell, 2007).

27. Megan Hale Williams (*The Monk and the Book: Jerome and the Making of Christian Scholarship* [Chicago: University of Chicago Press, 2006], 282) dates the *Commentary on Ecclesiastes* to 388–389, placing it after the *Commentarioli in Psalmos* and the *Tractatus in Psalmos,* which she dates to 387.

28. Aug. *Ciu.* 20.2.

29. See, e.g., *Eccl* 2:24; 3:12; 8:15.

30. See Robin Lane Fox, *Pagans and Christians* (London: Viking, 1986), 522–24, for a harsh censure of the early Jewish and Christian attempts to interpret this book.

31. Augustine makes a similar point in *Ciu.* 21.9, when he states that although we do not understand the decisions God makes now, when our knowledge becomes complete after our death, we shall understand and approve what God has arranged.

32. Or. *Princ.* 1. Pref. 2–3. Origen suggested that the apostles concealed many mysteries so that later thinkers would have something on which to exercise their minds.

33. See, e.g., Hier. *Ep.* 106, a lengthy letter that discusses variations between the Septuagint and the translation of the Psalter that Jerome had made in 384 while in Rome. In this letter, Jerome refers frequently to the Hexapla, using it to substantiate the claim that the version of the Septuagint used in the West was flawed. Jerome's postexilic contact with the Hexapla is suggested also by the fact that shortly after settling in Bethlehem he began a new translation of the Psalter, revising his Roman translation in accordance with the better version of the Septuagint text he found in the Hexapla (Stefan Rebenich, "Jerome: The Vir Trilinguis and the Hebraica Veritas," *Vigiliae Christianae* 47 [1993]: 51). See also Hier. *Vir. ill.* 54, in which Jerome states that he had access to Origen's Hexapla.

34. See Adam Kamesar, *Jerome, Greek Scholarship, and the Hebrew Bible: A Study of the Quaestiones Hebraicae in Genesim,* Oxford Classical Monographs (Oxford: Clarendon Press, 1993), 49–54, for the argument that Jerome began to view the Septuagint as suspect earlier rather than later. For the chronology adopted here, see Kelly, *Jerome,* 153–67; Rebenich, "Vir Trilinguis," 52; Brown, "Jerome and the Vulgate," 361.

35. The *Letter of Aristeas* is an anonymous letter, written probably in the second century BC. It purports to come from the pen of a courtier named Aristeas, who describes the favor Ptolemy showed to the Jews and his initiative in ordering the creation of the Septuagint.

36. The translation by individuals and successful collation are found in Iren. *Haer.* 3.21.2.

37. See, for instance, the remarks of Jerome's contemporary, Rufinus of Aquileia, in Ruf. *Apol.* 2.35; see also the objections to this project raised by Augustine in Aug. *Ep.* 71.2.3–4.

38. Aug. *Ep.* 71.3–4. Rufinus also picks up this story, snidely suggesting that the inscriptions on the tombs of the Roman Christians that referred to the Jonah story would require emendation to reflect Jerome's modification (Ruf. *Apol.* 2.35).

39. Augustine states that despite the fact that the Jews confirmed that Jerome's translation from the Hebrew was more reliable than the Septuagint, the churches had decreed that no one man was likely to be more reliable than the authority of the seventy-two who had translated the Septuagint (Aug. *Ciu.* 18.43). See Williams, *Monk and the Book*, 97–133, for the view that Jerome's translation project was one way in which he sought to buttress his authority and standing within the late antique Christian world.

40. Ruf. *Apol.* 2.35.

41. Jerome finished his translation of the Hebrew Scriptures around the year 405, as noted in the prologue to his translation of Joshua (see Rebenich, *Jerome*, 54).

42. As early as 381 Jerome evinced dissatisfaction with the Septuagint. In the preface to his Latin translation of Eusebius's *Chronicon,* Jerome noted that Aquila, Theodotion, and Symmachus had all been driven to make fresh Greek translations of the Hebrew Bible because the Septuagint had not retained the flavor of the Hebrew original. See Hier. *Chron.* Pref.; discussion in Kamesar, *Greek Scholarship,* 44–45.

43. Clear signs of this are present in Jerome's translation of the verses of Ecclesiastes found at 1.16; 2.12; 2.24–26; 5.5; 5.11; 7.8; 8.1; 8.2–4; 8.6–7; 8.12; 9.18; 10.2, 3; 10.5–7.

44. See, e.g., 1.15 ("be adorned"); 2.1 ("even this was vanity"); 2.2; 2.8 ("wine stewards and stewardesses"); 3.18–21 ("about the utterance").

45. See, e.g., the notes found on Jerome's translations at 2.2; 2.3; 2.6; 7.15; 7.26, 27.

46. See 2.15, 16.

47. See, e.g., Jerome's discussions at 8.1; 8.2-4; 8.12; 8.13; and 10.9.

48. Aug. *Ciu.* 18.43.

49. Hier. *Vir. ill.* 54. The Ebionites were a Christian sect who denied the virgin birth of Christ; they believed that Jesus had been the natural son of Joseph and Mary. Later, at his baptism, he had been infused with the Holy Spirit.

50. Iren. *Haer.* 3.21.1.

51. See Natalio Fernández Marcos, *The Septuagint in Context: An Introduction to the Greek Versions of the Bible* (Leiden and Boston: Brill, 2000), 142–46, for a discussion of the problems associated with Theodotion.

52. Iren. *Haer.* 3.21.1.

53. Fernández Marcos, *Septuagint in Context*, 111.

54. Bruce M. Metzger, "Theories of the Translation Process," *Bibliotheca Sacra* 150 (1993): 142.

55. Ibid.

56. Eus. *Hist. Eccl.* 6.17.

57. See, e.g., 7.8; 9.3–4a.

58. See the discussion in Mark Vessey, "Jerome's Origen: The Making of a Christian Literary *Persona*," *Studia Patristica* 28 (1993): 135–45.

59. The nature of Jerome's foundation in Bethlehem deserves more consideration than is possible here. Although he characterizes it as a monastery, he did expend a considerable amount of time trying to attract students to come study with him (see, e.g., Hier. *Ep.* 53, in which Jerome seems to encourage Paulinus of Nola to visit; however in Hier. *Ep.* 58, he dissuades him from making a trip to the Holy Land). Interestingly, Rufinus would later charge Jerome with running a secular school in Bethlehem where he taught pagan authors to young boys (Ruf. *Apol.* 2.11).

60. For a concise summation of Nautin's position, see Rebenich, "Vir Trilinguis," 56–57.

61. See Kamesar (*Greek Scholarship*, 97–194), who argues that, while Jerome utilized whatever Greek information he could find about the Hebrew text and exegesis, these materials could take him only so far; Jerome needed an understanding of Hebrew to achieve what he did.

62. Hier. *Ruf.* 1.16.

63. Ibid., 3.11.

64. Numbered among the letters of Augustine as Ep. 75.5.

65. Dion. Al. *Fr. Eccl.* 3.7.

66. The standard study of this work is John Jarick, *Gregory Thaumaturgos' Paraphrase of Ecclesiastes*, Septuagint and Cognate Studies 29 (Atlanta: Scholars Press, 1990). For an extended discussion of Gregory's career, see Lane Fox, *Christians and Pagans*, 516–42.

67. Jarick (*Gregory Thaumaturgos*) offers a first-rate examination of the choices Gregory made. It is unlikely that Jerome devoted the same care to this work.

68. A short, but useful discussion may be found in Kelly, *Jerome*, 150–52. Sandro Leanza (*L'Esegesi di Origene al Libro dell'Ecclesiaste* [Reggio Calabria: Parallelo 38, 1975], 31–69) offers a more exhaustive analysis of Jerome's use of Origen in the *Commentary on Ecclesiastes*.

69. Hier. *Vir. ill.* 74.

70. Ibid., 104.

71. Ibid., 128.

72. An English translation, with extensive discussion, may be found in Stuart George Hall, *Gregory of Nyssa: Homilies on Ecclesiastes. An English Version*

with Supporting Studies. Proceedings of the Seventh International Colloquium on Gregory of Nyssa (St. Andrews, 5–10 September 1990) (Berlin and New York: W. de Gruyter, 1993).

73. Gr. Nyss. *Hom. 1–8 in Eccl.* 2.2.

74. Kelly, *Jerome,* 150.

75. Ruf. *Apol.* 2.12–13. In his apology, Rufinus twists the name of Jerome's Hebrew tutor (Baranias), making an allusion to *John* 18:40, where, at the trial of Christ, the crowd called for the release of Barabbas rather than Jesus.

76. This point is explored in some length at Williams, *Monk and the Book,* 221–31.

77. Hier. *Zach.* Prol.; Williams, *Monk and the Book,* 222.

78. See discussion and examples in Williams, *Monk and the Book,* 223–24.

COMMENTARY ON ECCLESIASTES

PREFACE

To Paula* and Eustochium*

I recall that about five years ago now, when I was still in Rome and was reading Ecclesiastes to the holy Blesilla,* with the object of challenging her to disregard this age and to regard everything she saw in the world as worthless, I was asked by her to explain all its obscurities in the form of a brief commentary, so that she could understand what she was reading without me. At the preliminary stage of our work she was taken from us by sudden death, and the three of us proved unworthy to have such a partner in our life; I was shattered by this heavy blow, and for the time being fell dumb.

Now that I am in Bethlehem, a more august* city, I am paying the debt I owe both to her memory and to you, with the brief warning that I have followed no one else's authority; however, in translating from Hebrew, I have adapted myself more to the usage of the Septuagint translators, at least where they were not far from the Hebrew text.* I have occasionally also paid attention to Aquila, Symmachus, and Theodotion,* without deterring the reader's study by excessive novelty and, again, without losing the source of the truth by following side channels of interpretation against my inner certainty.

CHAPTER 1

1.1 The words of the Preacher, the son of David, king of Jerusalem.

The Scriptures most clearly teach that Solomon was called by three names: "the peacemaker," that is, "Solomon";* also "*Ididia*,"* which is "the beloved of the Lord"; and what is said here, "*Coeleth*,"* that is, "the Preacher." Now the name "Ecclesiastes" in the Greek language* means "one who assembles the gathering" (that is, the

33

church).* We can call this person a rouser* of the people, because he speaks to the people,* and his discourse is not directed to one person in particular, but to the world at large.* He was also called the "peacemaker" and the "beloved of the Lord," because there was peace during his reign,* and the Lord loved him. For Psalms 44 and 71* are each prefaced with a title: "Of the Beloved," and "Of the Peacemaker."* Although, relating as they do to the prophecy of Christ and the church, these titles surpass the fortune and powers of Solomon, they were nevertheless, according to history,* written about Solomon.

And so, like the number of his names, he produced three books: Proverbs, Ecclesiastes, and Song of Songs.* In¹ Proverbs, he is teaching a young person and instructing him, as it were, about his duties through maxims*—hence, too, he repeatedly directs the discourse toward his son. On the other hand, in Ecclesiastes he is educating a man of a mature age not to believe that anything among the affairs of the world is perpetual.* To the contrary, he asserts, everything that we see is transitory and brief. Then at last, in the Song of Songs, he joins to the embraces of the bridegroom a man who has been perfected and prepared by treading the present age underfoot.* For unless we first have relinquished our vices, renounced the ostentation of this present age, and prepared ourselves unencumbered for the arrival of Christ,* we cannot say: "Let him kiss me from the kiss of his mouth."* Philosophers, too, educate their followers in a way that is not far from this order of teachings: they teach ethics first, then they interpret natural science, and when they see a student has advanced in these arts, they lead him up to theological study.*

We must pay close attention to the fact that the author's name is different in the three books.* In the book of Proverbs, it is given as: "The Proverbs of Solomon, the son of David, the king of Israel."* In Ecclesiastes: "The words of the Preacher, the son of David, the king of Jerusalem."* Clearly the word "Israel," which is wrongly found in the Greek and Latin manuscripts,* is here unnecessary.* On the other hand, in the Song of Songs neither the "son of David" nor the "king" of either Israel or Jerusalem is written in the heading, but only "The Song of Songs of Solomon."* Just as the Proverbs and the elementary instruction pertain to the twelve tribes and all of Israel, and just as contempt of the world is not fitting except in the case of dwellers in the City (that is, those who dwell in Jerusalem), so the Song of Songs is especially suitable for those who desire only heavenly things.* For those who are beginning and those making progress, both his father's dignity and the authority of his own monarchy are rightly claimed. For the perfect, however, where the disciple is taught not through fear but by love,[*] his personal name suffices, for the teacher is an equal[*] and he does not recognize himself to be a king. So far, this refers to the literal sense.

But, according to the spiritual sense,[*] "the peacemaker," "the beloved of God, the Father," and "our Preacher," is Christ,[*] who pulled down the dividing wall, "and by his incarnation abolished the hostilities" and made both one,[*] saying: "My peace I give to you, my peace I leave with you."[*] Of him the Father said to the disciples: "This is my beloved Son, in whom I am well pleased; listen to him."[*] He is the head of the entire church, and speaks to the multitude of nations,[*] *not* to the synagogue of the Jews. He is king of a Jerusalem built of living stones,[*] not of the Jerusalem about which he said: "Jerusalem, Jerusalem, you who kill the prophets"[*] and: "Behold your house shall be left desolate,"[*] but of the Jerusalem by which he forbids to swear "because it is the city of the great king."[*] He is the son of David,[*] to whom the blind shouted in the Gospel: "Have mercy on us, son of David";[*] and the whole crowd in unison resounded with: "Hosanna to the son of David."[*]

Finally, the Word of God does not come to Solomon, as it did to Jeremiah and the other prophets; instead, he is himself a rich, mighty king, inasmuch as he *is* the Word and Wisdom and the other powers.[*] As such, he speaks words to the men of the church and puts words into the mouths of the apostles, concerning whom, as the Psalm puts it: "Their voice has gone out into all the earth and their words to the ends of the earth."[*] And so certain people are wrong to believe that we are stirred to embrace pleasure and luxury by this book, when, to the contrary, what is being taught is that everything that we perceive in the world is vain, and that we should not strive diligently to obtain things that perish while they are held.

1.2 "Vanity of vanities,"[*] said the Preacher, "all is vanity."

If everything that God made is very good,[*] in what way is all vanity,[*] and not just vanity, but even the *vanity of vanities?* Just as in the Song of Songs what is indicated is "a song above all songs," so too, by the phrase *vanity of vanities*, the magnitude of this vanity[*] is demonstrated. Such an idea was also written in the Psalm: "Nevertheless every person living is entirely vanity."[*] If a living person is vanity, it follows that a dead person is the vanity of vanities.

We read in Exodus of Moses' face having been glorified to such a degree that the sons of Israel were unable to look at him.[*] But the apostle Paul said that this glory was not glory in comparison to the glory of the gospel: "For what was glorified in that case is no longer glorified, on account of the superior[2] glory."[*] Accordingly, we too are similarly able to call the sky, the earth, the seas, and all things contained in this circle good in themselves; but compared to God, these things are as nothing.[*] It is like my seeing the small flame of a lamp and being content with its light, and then, when the sun rose,[*] being unable to tell that the lamp was shining, and even seeing the light of the stars themselves concealed by the splendor of the sun. In the same way, gazing upon the elements and the manifold variety of things, I certainly admire the greatness of the works; but reflecting that all things pass away, the universe declines toward its own end, and only God is what he has always been, I am compelled to say, not once but twice, *vanity of vanities, all is vanity.*

In Hebrew, *vanity of vanities* is written *abal abalim,* which, apart from the Septuagint,[*] everyone has translated similarly as ἀτμὸς ἀτμίδων or ἀτμῶν.[*] We may translate these terms "smoky vapor"[3] and "a faint breeze that quickly dissolves." And so something perishable, something not of the whole, is indicated by this phrase. Those things that are seen are temporal, while those things that are unseen are eternal; or—because the creation has been subjected to vanity and it groans and is in labor and waits for the revelation of the sons of God,[*] and "now we understand in part and we prophesy in part"[*]—all is vanity until what is perfect comes.[*]

1.3 What is left for a man in all his labor, with which he labors under the sun?

After the general proposition that all is vanity, Solomon begins with men, saying that they sweat in vain in the labor of this world, accumulating riches, educating their children, maneuvering for office, constructing buildings[*]—and in the midst of their work they are suddenly snatched away by death, and hear: "Foolish man, tonight your soul will be taken away from you; whose now will be what you have prepared?"[*] Particularly since they carry nothing from all their labor with them, but return naked to the earth from which they were taken.[*]

1.4 A generation goes, and a generation comes; and the earth stands in the age.[*]

One generation dies, and another is born; no longer seeing those you once saw, you begin to see those who formerly did not exist. What is more a vanity of vanities than the fact that the earth endures, although it was made for the benefit of man,[*] while man himself, the master of the earth, suddenly crumbles into dust?[*]

In another sense, the first generation—that of the Jews—departed, and a generation that was gathered from the Gentiles followed.* The earth stands until the synagogue gives way and the whole church comes in. When the gospel has been proclaimed in all the earth, then the end will come.* But when the consummation is at hand, heaven and earth will pass away.* Significantly, he does not say *the earth stands in the ages,* but rather, *in the "age";* yet we praise the Lord, not in one age, but in the ages of ages.*

1.5 The sun rises and the sun sets and draws to its place and it rises there.

The sun itself, which was given as a light to mortals,* points to the transience of the world* daily through its rising and setting. After it dips its burning disc in the ocean, it returns through paths unknown to us to the place from which it had set forth.* When the circuit of night has concluded, it hastily "bursts forth again from its own chamber."*

Now, for what we have written following the common edition,* *it draws to its place,* the Hebrew text has *soeph,* which Aquila* translates εἰσπνεῖ,*⁴ that is, "it breathes." Symmachus* and Theodotion* translate this "it runs back," because clearly the sun returns to its own place and takes a breather in the place from which it had earlier set out. Still, all of this is to teach, through the changes of seasons and the rising and setting of the stars, that the life of mankind declines and dies, while it is unaware.

In another meaning, the sun of justice, in whose wings is healing,* rises with people fearing him* and sets for the false prophets at midday.* Now when he has risen, he draws us into his own place.* Where? Clearly to the Father. For he came for the purpose of raising us from the world to heaven and saying: "When the Son of man has been exalted, he will draw all people to himself."* It is not surprising that the Son draws the believers to himself, since the Father himself also draws them to the Son. "For no one," he said, "comes to me unless the Father, who sent me, brings him."* Therefore that sun, which we said dies for some but is born for others, also set once for the patriarch Jacob when he left the holy land,* and rose again for him when he entered the land of the promise from Syria.* Also, when Lot left Sodom and came to the city to which he had been commanded to hurry, he ascended the mountain and "the sun came out over Segor."*

1.6 It goes to the south and whirls round to the north; the spirit goes whirling in whorls and returns to its circlings.

From this we can suppose that in wintertime the sun runs over* to the southern region and throughout the summer it is in the neighborhood of the north;* and that it does not start at the autumnal equinox, but rather when the west wind blows, when everything bursts forth into new life in the spring.*

In *the spirit goes whirling in whorls and returns to its circlings* he may have used "spirit" just for the sun (compare the poet's:

Meanwhile the sun revolves around its great year,*

and elsewhere:

And the year comes round on itself along its own track*),

on the ground that the sun is a living thing with breath and vigor, completing its annual cycle by motion of its own;* or else he may mean it as:

the spirit which nourishes also from within
the moon's bright globe and the stars, those Titans,
while Mind keeps the whole mass* in motion,
being commingled in its great body,
and infused throughout its members.*

In either case, he is talking here not about the sun's annual course, but about its daily paths.* For it makes its way by an oblique and broken line through the south to the north and in this manner it returns to the east.*

In another meaning, the sun is a closer neighbor of the earth when it runs through the south; when it passes over the north it is lifted high up.* And so, perhaps, the sun of justice is closer to those who are ring-fenced away from the chill of winter and of tribulations (for it is from the north that evils blaze out upon the earth),* but to those who live in the northern region and are deprived of the summer heat, it travels at a distance, and returns along its own orbits to where it started. Once he has drawn all things to himself,* and has lit up everyone with his own rays, the restoration of the beginning takes place, and God is "all in all."* Symmachus has translated this passage as: "It goes to the south and goes around to the north; the wind goes traveling about, and the wind returns through what it had traversed."

1.7 All torrents go into the sea and the sea is not filled. To the place from which the torrents go out, they return, so that they can go forth.

Certain people believe that the fresh waters that flow into the sea are either consumed by the blazing sun from above, or are nourishment for the brine of the sea. But look, our Preacher, and the founder of these waters,* says that they return through secret veins to the headwaters of the springs, and always bubble up from their source in the abyss to their own beginnings.

Preferable, though, is the Hebrews' view that the words *torrents* or *the sea* are meant as a metaphor for human beings, because they return to the earth from which they have been taken; and that they are called *torrents*, not rivers, because they soon die down,* and yet the earth is not filled with the great number of the dead.

Furthermore, if we ascend to higher things, it is correct that the roiled waters* return to the sea from where they arose. And if I am not mistaken, unless a qualifier is added, "torrent" is never read in a good sense. In the sentence "You will give them drink from the torrent of your pleasure,"* the word "pleasure" has been added to qualify "torrent"; but, to the contrary, the Savior is betrayed at the torrent Kidron,* and Elijah, during the time of persecution, hides near the torrent Cherith, which also eventually dries up.* Still, the insatiable sea is not filled up, just as in Proverbs the two daughters of the leech are not sated.*

1.8 A man will not be able to speak all troublesome discussions. The eye will not be satiated with seeing, and the ear will not be filled up with hearing.*

It is difficult to have knowledge about not only the natural sciences, but also ethics* as well. Speech cannot unfold the causes and natures of things, nor can the eye see as the worth of the object demands, nor can the ear, instructed by a teacher, attain to the height of knowledge.* For if now we see with a mirror in an enigma,* and we know in part and we prophesy in part,* it follows that our speech is unable to explain what it does not know; nor is the eye able to see where it is blind; nor the ear able to be filled where it is uncertain.

At the same time, this should be noted: all words are troublesome and are learned through great labor.* This stands against those who think that a knowledge of the Scriptures comes to them at their leisure, just by expressing wishes.*

1.9 What is there that has been? The same that shall be. And what is there that has happened? The same that shall happen. And there is not anything new under the sun.

It seems to me that he is now speaking collectively about the things he enumerated above: one generation and another, the mass of the lands, the rising and setting of the sun, the course of the rivers, the magnitude of the ocean, and all the things we know through thought, sight, or hearing; because nothing exists in the natural order that has not existed before.* For from the beginning of the world, men have been born and died, the earth has stayed balanced over the waters,* and the sun has risen and set. And, to avoid an exhaustive list, it was granted by God, the Designer, that birds should fly, fish swim, terrestrial animals walk, and serpents slither.

Something similar to this has also been expressed by the comic poet:

Nothing has been said that has not been said before.*

That is why my tutor Donatus,* when he was commenting on this line, said: "Curse those who have spoken our own thoughts before us!"* Because, if in talk it is not possible to say anything new, how much truer is this for the administration of the world, which from the beginning was so perfect that God was able to rest from his works on the seventh day!*

I have read in a certain book: "If everything that has been made under the sun existed in a former age before it was made, and man was already made at the founding of the sun, then man existed before he came into existence under the sun."* But this view is ruled out by the fact that, according to this explanation, beasts of burden, gnats, and every tiny and great animal would be said to have been created before heaven.* Unless, possibly, he were to reply that from what follows it is shown that what the Preacher was talking about was not the other animals but rather mankind, for he says: *There is nothing new under the sun* such that he could speak and say: "Behold, this is new," and that animals do not talk, but only mankind; because if animals talked, that would be new, and the view that there is nothing new under the sun would be vitiated.

1.10 Is there a word* of which it may be said "look, this is new"? It already existed in the ages that went before us.

Symmachus translated this less obscurely: "Do you think there is anybody who can say: 'See, this is new'? It has already happened in the generation that was before us." Nevertheless his translation agrees with the preceding assertions, that nothing new happens in the world, and that there is no one able to come forth and say: "Look, that is new," given that everything he thinks he is showing as new already existed in earlier generations.

Let us not think that the signs, portents, and the many new things that come from the will of God in the world were already performed in earlier ages; or that a place can be found for Epicurus,* who claims that the same things happen through countless periods, in the same[5] places and through the same people.* Otherwise Judas has betrayed Christ repeatedly, Christ has often undergone his passion on our account, and other things that have happened and will happen will recur in the same cycles.* But it must be said that, from the perspective of the foreknowledge and predestination of God, these things that will come have already happened. For those who were chosen in Christ, "before the foundation of the world,"* were already chosen in earlier ages.

1.11 There is no memory of former things, and even the final things that are going to be, they will not be remembered by those who are going to be at the end.

Just as in our case oblivion covers what is past, those who have yet to be born will not be able to know what is happening now or in the future, and all these things will pass away in silence and will be hidden as if they had never been. And that sentence will be fulfilled: *Vanity of vanities, all is vanity.* For again, the reason that the Seraphim veil the face and feet of God* is because the first and last things are covered.*

However, the Septuagint translators wrote: "The first people have no remembrance, and even those who are going to be last will have no remembrance among those that are going to be in the end."* So, according to them, the sense is the same as in the Gospel, that those who are first in this age are the last of all.* And because God, so benign and compassionate, recalls the deeds of even the least, and of everyone, he will not give as much glory to those who deserve to be last on account of their own fault, as to those who, humbling themselves, sought to be last in the world. And so he says the same thing in a later passage: *There is not memory of the wise with the fool for eternity.**

1.12 I, the Preacher, was king over Israel in Jerusalem.

The material to this point is a preface, as he has been discussing everything in general. From here on he reverts to himself, and explains who he was and how he learned all things through experience. The Hebrews say that this is the book of Solomon showing repentance for having placed his trust in his wisdom and wealth, and offending God with his women.*

1.13 And I gave my heart to investigating and considering in wisdom about all things that happen under the sun. God gave this evil occupation to the sons of men, so they would be occupied by it.

Aquila, the Septuagint, and Theodotion translate the word *anian* in the same way, as περισπασμόν.* A Latin interpreter* translated this

word as *distentio,* "a stretching out," on the grounds that the mind
of man is tortured by being stretched out into various worries. But
Symmachus translated the word as ἀσχολίαν, that is, "occupation."*
And so (because it is frequently mentioned in this book),* whether we
have used "occupation" or "stretching," or any other word, they are all
to be referred back to the sense suggested above.

Therefore the Preacher first of all gave his mind to the pursuit
of wisdom,* and, extending himself beyond what is permissible,
he sought to learn causes and reasons: Why are infants seized by a
demon?* Why do shipwrecks drown both the just and the wicked
equally? Are those events and things like them produced by chance,
or by the judgment of God? And if by chance, where is Providence?* If
by judgment, where is God's justice? "Wanting to know these things,"
he said, "I understood that unnecessary concern* was given to men
by God, and an anxiety, agonizing in all sorts of ways, such as to make
them desire to know what is not permissible to know."*

With the cause fairly set out in advance,* a "stretching" was given
by God, just as it is written in the Epistle to the Romans: "Therefore God
handed them over to disgraceful passions."* And again: "Therefore
he has surrendered them to a reprobate state of mind, so that they do
what they should not."* And then: "Therefore God handed them over
to the desires of their own hearts, to filth."* And to the Thessalonians:
"For that reason God will send the working of error to them."*

First the causes are shown for why they succumbèd either to
disgraceful passions, or to a reprobate state of mind, or to the desires
of their own hearts; or what they had done to receive the working of
error. Therefore the reason that God has also, for the present, given
"an evil stretching"* to mankind, so that they should be "stretched" by
it, is because in the past, they did this or that of their own accord and
of their own will.*

*1.14 I saw all the works that have been done under the sun, and behold: all
was vanity and presumption of spirit.* *

Necessity drives us to discuss the Hebrew words more frequently
than we want, as we are not able to understand the meaning unless we
learn it through the words. Aquila and Theodotion translate *routh**
as νομήν,* and Symmachus translates it as βόσκησιν.* However, the
Septuagint translators have not expressed the Hebrew language, but
rather the Syrian,* by saying προαίρεσιν.* Therefore, either νομή or
βόσκησις is a term from "pasture"; but προαίρεσις expresses "desire"
more than "presumption."*

What is being said is that everyone does what he wishes and

what seems right to him, and that people are led in diverse directions through their free will, and that everything under the sun is vain, while we fail to satisfy ourselves, in turn, on the definitions of good and evil.*

The Hebrew under whose tuition I read all the holy Scriptures told me that the above-mentioned word *routh* in this place signified "affliction" and "badness" more than "pasture" and "will"*—"badness" not in the sense in which "bad" is the opposite of "good," but in the sense given in the Gospel: "Sufficient to the day is its own trouble."* Which, more clearly, the Greeks call κακουχίαν,* and the sense is: I considered everything that happens in the world, and I discovered nothing more than vanity and troubles, that is, miseries of the spirit, by which the soul is afflicted with diverse thoughts.

1.15 The twisted man will not be able to be adorned; and a diminution cannot be counted.*

*The twisted man** will not be able to be adorned.* The straight receive adornment; the bent, correction. *Twisted* is not said except of one who has been distorted from the straight.* This is against heretics who introduce certain natures* that are incapable of cure.

And because a diminution, that is, something missing, cannot be counted, that is the reason why only the firstborn of Israel were counted, but women, slaves, children, and the rabble from Egypt, by no means an addition to the army but rather an immeasurable lessening, were omitted.*[6]

The sense may also be:* So much evil takes place in the fullness of this world, that the world is scarcely able to return to a pure state of goodness, and that[7] it cannot easily recover its order and perfection, the state in which it was first established.

Or in another sense: When everyone has been restored to wholeness through penitence, the devil alone will persist in his own error.* For all things that have happened under the sun have been ruined by the will of the devil and his spirit of malice,* while at his instigation sins are being piled on sins.

Finally: So great is the number of those who have been led astray and of those who have been snatched from the flock of the Lord by the devil* that it cannot be grasped by calculation.

1.16 I spoke with my heart, saying: "Behold, I have been made great and I have added wisdom above all who were before me in Jerusalem, and my heart has seen much wisdom and knowledge."

Solomon was not wiser than Abraham, Moses, or the other saints, but he was wiser than those who were before him in Jerusalem.*

We read also in the Books of Kingdoms[*] that Solomon was very wise, and that he had requested wisdom from God in preference to other gifts. Therefore the eye of his pure heart gazes upon much wisdom and knowledge, because he does not say: "I spoke much wisdom and knowledge," but rather, *my heart has seen much wisdom and knowledge.*[*] For we are not able to utter all that we perceive.

1.17 And I gave my heart to know wisdom and knowledge, errors and foolishness. I learned that even this is a grazing of the wind, or: presumption of spirit.

Contrasting things are understood from their antitheses:

The first principle of wisdom is to be devoid of foolishness.[*]

Still, a person is unable to be devoid of foolishness unless he has understood it. That is why a very large number of harmful things have been included in creation, so that in avoiding them, we may be educated toward wisdom.[*] Therefore the equal aim of Solomon's study was to understand wisdom and knowledge, and as a direct result, errors and foolishness, so that by seeking the former and avoiding the latter, his true wisdom could be attested. But in this too, as in other things, he said that he had grazed on the winds and had not been able to grasp perfect truth. Let the preceding discussion of "presumption of spirit" or the "grazing of the wind" suffice.[*] This is a phrase[*] mentioned often in this book.

1.18 Because in a multitude of wisdom, there is a multitude of madness; and he who adds wisdom, adds grief.

The more anyone has attained wisdom, the more he is angered at being subjected to vices and being so far away from the virtues that he is pursuing. Now because the powerful will undergo powerful torments, and from one to whom more is entrusted, more is demanded,[*] for that reason, he who adds wisdom adds grief, and is saddened by unhappiness in accordance with God's will, and feels pain over his faults. For this reason the Apostle says: "And who is there who gladdens me, except the person who is made sad by me?"[*]

Unless perhaps it should also be understood to mean that the wise man grieves that wisdom is hidden in such a secret and deep place, and that it does not present itself to our minds as light does to our sight, but is only forthcoming through, as it were, torments and intolerable labor, with constant meditation and study.[*]

Chapter 2

*2.1 I said in my heart: "Come now, I will test you in joy and I will see you in good"; and behold, even this was vanity.**

After I discovered that in a large amount of wisdom and the acquisition of knowledge there was grief and labor, and nothing else but a pointless and endless struggle,* I changed over to enjoyment, so as to overflow with luxury, assemble wealth, abound in riches, and seize passing pleasures before I died. But in this, too, I perceived my own vanity, as a pleasure once past gives no delight to a person in the present; once drained it does not satisfy.*

Not only physical joy, but even spiritual joy* is a temptation to the person possessing it, so that I need a goad* prodding me, and the angel of Satan to box my ears so that I will not be conceited.* That is why Solomon says: "Give me neither riches nor poverty."* And at once he adds: "Lest I become full, and a liar, and say: 'Who watches me?'"* seeing that the devil, too, fell through an abundance of good things.* Hence, in the Apostle, too, it is written: "He must not be swollen with pride, lest he fall into the judgment of the devil"*—that is, "into the sort of judgment in which the devil also fell."*

But we can also say this: that the reason spiritual joy, just like everything else, is now being judged a vanity, is that we see it with a mirror and in an enigma; however, when it is revealed, face to face, then by no means will it be called vanity, but rather, truth.*

*2.2 I said to laughter, "Folly!" And to delight, "Why are you doing this?"**

Where we read the word "folly," in the Hebrew text it has the word *molal,** which Aquila translates πλάνησιν,* that is, "error," and Symmachus has θόρυβον,* that is, "a commotion." But the Septuagint and Theodotion, as in many places, agree here as well, and translate this as περιφοράν,* which we, translating literally, can call "a revolution."*

So then, just as those who revolve with every wind of doctrine* are unstable and waver in varying directions; in the same way those who laugh with that laughter which the Lord in the Gospel said was to be changed to tears* are dragged off by the error of the age and the whirlwind. They do not comprehend the ruin of their sins or lament past vices.* To the contrary, they believe that these transitory good things are perpetual, and they exult in things that really call for lamentation.

It is possible, too, to understand this as about heretics, who promise themselves joys and prosperity while acquiescing in false doctrines.

2.3 I planned in my heart to plunge my flesh in wine, and my heart led me away to wisdom, and to persist in foolishness,* until I saw what was good for the sons of men that they should do under the sun in the number of the days of their lives.

I wanted to live out my life in delights and to lull my flesh, free from all cares as if by wine, into unconsciousness in pleasure.* But my thinking and natural reason, which God, the Author, has put even into sinners,* drew me back* and led me to search for wisdom and to trample on foolishness, so that I could see just what was the good that men can do in the course of their own life.*

Neatly, he compared pleasure to drunkenness, considering that it makes one drunk and destroys the vigor of his soul, and that if a person is able to exchange pleasure for wisdom and (as certain books have it) obtain spiritual joyfulness,* he will be able to arrive at the knowledge of what should be craved in this life, and what avoided.*

2.4 I made my works great; I built houses for myself; I planted vines for myself, and so on until the place where he says: *the eyes of the wise man are in his head, and the fool walks in darkness.*

Before I discuss individual details, I think it will be useful to cover all this in a short discussion, and to reduce the meaning, as it were, into a single unit, so that what is being said can be more easily understood.*

As king, and a powerful man, I had all things that are deemed good in this age.* I built palaces up to a great height for myself, and I planted hills and mountains with vines. And so that nothing should be less than luxurious, I planted gardens and orchards for myself, establishing various kinds of trees, to be irrigated by water collected into pools from above, so that the vegetation should be nourished from a distance by an unending supply of moisture.

And I had an uncountable number of slaves as well, whether purchased or born in my household, and many herds of four-legged animals, herds of cows, that is, and of sheep, more than any king had before me in Jerusalem. Uncountable treasures of silver and gold were also stored up, which the gifts of various kings and the tributes the nations had bestowed upon me. From this it also happened that I was stirred to greater delights by excessive wealth, and choirs of musicians performed for me with flute, lyre, and voice, and I was served by both sexes at my banquets.

Nevertheless, the more these things increased, the more wisdom fell short. For I rushed, unbridled and headlong, into whatever pleasure my enjoyment drew me. I imagined that the whole point of my labors was to be swallowed up in desire and luxury. At last, returning to myself and waking, as it were, from a deep sleep, I looked at my handiwork, and I saw that it was all full of vanity, full of filth, full of the spirit of error. For I could find[8] no good in anything deemed a good in the world.[*9]

Then, reflecting on what were the good fruits of wisdom and what were the bad fruits of foolishness, I subsequently burst out in praise of the man who pulls himself back after his vices and succeeds in becoming a follower of the virtues.[*] Obviously there is a great distance between wisdom and foolishness, and virtues are as far removed from vices as day differs from night. And so it seems to me that he who follows wisdom always raises his eyes to heaven, and has a face always turned upward, and contemplates the things that are above his own head; but he who has been given up to foolishness and vices walks about in the shadows and wallows in ignorance of reality.

I made my works great; I built houses for myself; I planted vines for myself.

The one who makes his works great[*] is he who is elevated into the celestial regions, after the image of the Creator.[*] He builds houses, so the Father and Son may come and live in them.[*] He plants vines to which Jesus may tie his donkey.[*]

2.5 I made gardens and orchards for myself; I planted in these every kind of fruit-bearing wood.

In the mansion of the wealthy man[*] there are vessels made not only of gold and silver but also of wood and clay.[*] And so gardens, too, are developed for the sake of everyone who is weaker or infirm, for the person who is infirm feeds on vegetables.[*] Trees are planted, not "all the fruit-bearing ones," as we have in the Latin manuscripts;[*] but "all fruits," that is, of different crops and fruit trees, because there are different gifts[*] in the church.[*] One is the eye, another the hand, another the foot, and those which are our more modest parts we clothe with greater honor.[*] Among these fruit-bearing trees, I consider the tree of life, which is wisdom,[*] to have primacy. Without that tree being planted in the middle, the other trees will wither.

2.6 I made pools of waters for myself to irrigate from them the woodland germinating the wood.[*]

Trees of the woodland, trees of the forests, those which are not for produce and do not bear fruit, are not nourished by the rain of heaven, nor by celestial waters, but by the water collected in the pools fed by streams.* For Egypt too, low-lying like a vegetable garden, is irrigated by water from an earthly source, coming from Ethiopia;* but the promised land,* which is mountainous and elevated, "awaits the early and later rain"* from heaven.

2.7 I purchased slaves and slave women, and I had homegrown slaves;* and also my holding of herds and sheep was numerous above all who were before me in Jerusalem.

If we want "the Preacher," as we said above,* to refer here also to the person of Christ, we can speak of his *slaves* as those who have a spirit of fear* in their servitude, and who desire, rather than have, spiritual gifts; whereas we can call *slave women* those souls who are still addicted to the flesh and world. We can also call those who are from the church *homegrown slaves;* they surpass the slaves and slave women,* about whom we have spoken, but still have not yet been given their liberty or nobility by the Lord.*

Still there are others in the household of the Preacher, like cows and sheep, on account of their tasks and simplicity, who labor, it is true, in the church, without reason and knowledge of the Scriptures, but have not yet attained a state where they deserve to be human beings and revert to the image of the Creator.*

Note carefully that no number is mentioned for the slaves, slave women, or homegrown slaves; but of the cattle and sheep it says: *And my holding of herds and sheep was numerous.*[10] That is because there are more cattle in the church than humans, and more sheep than slaves, slave women, or homegrown slaves.

But the phrase that comes at the end, *above all who were before me in Jerusalem,* is not a reference to the great glory of Solomon, meaning that he was richer than merely his own royal father; because under Saul the seat of the kingship was not yet in Jerusalem, and it was held by the Jebusites, who had settled in that city.* And we must therefore treat in a higher sense the question of what "Jerusalem" is, and in what way the Preacher was richer than all those who preceded him as king in Jerusalem.*

2.8 I gathered silver for myself, and gold, and the wealth of kings and provinces. I appointed for myself male and female singers, and the delights of the sons of men, wine stewards and stewardesses.*

Divine Scripture always puts silver and gold for speech and thought.* Hence also in Psalm 67 the dove, which is interpreted in the spirit, has wings silver-plated to the outward visible sight, but inwardly it hides a more secret sense in the pallor of gold.*

He *gathered together the wealth of kings and provinces,* or regions, into the assembly of believers; these are the kings[*] about whom the Psalmist sings: "The kings of the earth have made a stand, the princes have come together to one place";[*] and these are the regions to which the Savior ordered the eyes to be lifted, because they are now "white for the harvest."[*] The wealth of kings can be called the doctrines of philosophers and secular knowledge; carefully understanding these, the churchman arraigns the wise in their astuteness, and "destroys the wisdom of the wise, and rejects the prudence of the prudent."[*]

Male singers too, *and female singers,* are those men or women who sing the Psalms in the spirit, and sing them with intelligence. A cantor, as a man both robust and spiritual, sings about the higher things. But the cantrix still is immersed in materiality,[*] which the Greeks call ὕλην;[*] she is not able to raise her voice to the sublime. Consequently, wherever in the Scriptures we read "woman" or "the frailer sex" we must transfer this to understand it as meaning "matter." For this reason also Pharaoh did not want male children to be allowed to live, but only female, who are like matter.[*] To the contrary, none of the saints, except very rarely, are said to have had daughters; only Zelophehad, who was dead in his sins, produced all daughters.[*] Among the twelve patriarchs, Jacob is the father of one daughter, and because of her, he is placed in danger.[*]

Also *the delights of the sons of men* are to be understood as referring to wisdom, which, like paradise, has various fruits and multiple pleasures. And, concerning wisdom itself, it is laid down: "Delight in the Lord and he will give you the petitions of your heart."[*] And in another place: "You will give them drink from the torrent of your pleasure."[*]

Now on the "pourers" and "pouresses"[*] of wine (for my present purpose of making a distinction from the masculine, I decided to decline the word with a feminine ending, which Latin does not allow[*]) Aquila interprets something quite different from what is on the surface. For he has not called them "people," that is, men and women, but a type of small pots, labeling them κυλίκιον and κυλίκια[*], which in the Hebrew are *sadda* and *saddoth.* Finally, Symmachus, although he was not able to translate this word for word, is not far from this opinion, talking about "types of tables and serving at tables."

And so it must be supposed that Solomon had objects studded with gold and gems, whether pitchers, or goblets, or bowls, which are lined up in the course of serving at tables; that wine was drawn from one κυλικίῳ, that is, from a mixing bowl, and from the other κυλικίοις, that is, from smaller pots; and that the throng of wine-drinkers received it from the hands of the waiters. Therefore, because we interpret the Preacher in relation to Christ, and wisdom, in Proverbs, having mixed her wine bowl, summons to herself those who are passing by,* now we should take the large bowl as the body of the Lord. There is not undiluted divinity in it, as there was in the heavenly ones, but for our sake it was diluted with ordinary humanity,* and through the apostles, the lesser κυλίκια, the small goblets and bowls, wisdom has been poured out for those in all the world who are believers.

2.9 And I was made great, and I added above all who were before me in Jerusalem; and yet my wisdom stood for me.

It does not seem that the Preacher's being made great corresponds at all with our Lord,* unless perhaps we were to apply this to him: "He progressed in wisdom, age, and favor."* And: "Wherefore God exalted him."* However, in the words *those who were before me in Jerusalem,* he is talking about those who, before his arrival, governed the congregation of the saints and the church.*

If we are understanding the Scriptures spiritually, it is Christ who is richer than all others; if only carnally, this is better understood[11] of the synagogue than of the church. Therefore he took off the veil that was placed over the face of Moses* and caused us to see his face in full light.*

The sense of *wisdom standing* is that even when he was in the flesh, his wisdom remained with him.* One who makes progress in wisdom does not have wisdom standing still with him;* on the other hand, he who does not admit of progress and is not growing up by stages but is always in fullness, that person can say, *and wisdom stood for me.*

2.10 And everything that my eyes demanded, I did not take from them, nor did I hold my heart back from any joy, because my heart rejoiced in all my labor. And this was my portion from all my labor.

The eyes of the soul and the insight of the mind crave spiritual contemplation.* Because the sinner does not know this, he bars his heart from true enjoyment. And so the Preacher completely gave himself to this, and eternal glory compensated for the light weight of tribulation in this lifetime.* For this is our portion and our perpetual prize, if we labor here in the service of virtues.

2.11 And I looked at all my works, which my hands had made, and at the labor with which I had labored in making them.

The person who does everything with diligence and caution can say these things.

And behold, everything was vanity and a will of the spirit.

Just as in other passages, he regards everything under the sun as worthless and as different forms of caprice.*

And there is no abundance* under the sun.

Christ "pitched his tent in the sunlight."* Therefore Christ will not be able either to dwell or abound in the person who has not yet reached the brightness, order, and steadfastness of the sun.*

2.12 And I looked, that I might see wisdom and errors and foolishness, because who is there among men, who could go after the king, before his maker?

Above, I had included everything,* up to the place where the scripture says *the eyes of the wise man are in his head,* in a single discourse, because I wanted to point out the sense briefly, and for that reason I had also mentioned some points cursorily in the anagogical sense.*

Now, therefore, I should expound them in accordance with my original plan. Here, the sense is far removed from the Septuagint translation.* He is saying that after condemning delights and pleasures, he had returned to searching carefully for wisdom, in which he discovered more error and foolishness than true, unerring prudence. For man cannot know the wisdom of his Creator and King as clearly and plainly as he who is the Founder knows it. So, he says, even these things which we know, we suppose rather than comprehend; and we suppose, rather than know, what the truth is.

2.13 And I saw that an abundance of wisdom is above foolishness, just as an abundance of light is better than dark places.

Although, he says, I have perceived that the wisdom of men is itself blended with error, and cannot penetrate as clearly into our minds as it is in our King and Founder,* yet, even insofar as it does exist, I learned that there is a great difference between wisdom and foolishness, as far as day can be from night, and light from darkness.*

2.14 The eyes of the wise man are in his head and the fool walks in darkness. And I learned that they all have one outcome.

He who has arrived at the perfected state of a man and has deserved to have Christ as his head* will always have his eyes turned toward Christ,* lifting them to the heights, and he will never think about baser things. Given that this is so, and that there is so great a distance between the wise man and the fool that one is compared to day and the other to darkness, and one lifts his eyes to heaven, while the other lowers them to the ground, suddenly the thought crept up on me: Why is it that the wise and the foolish are confined by a common end? Why do the same plagues, the same outcome, the same death, and equal afflictions bear down on both?

2.15, 16 And I said in my heart, just as the outcome of the fool, so it will also come to me; and why have I become wise? And I said in my heart, that this too was vanity. For there will not be memory of the wise together with the fool in eternity, because look, in the days that will come suddenly, oblivion will overwhelm all things; and how will the wise man die together with the fool?

I said the wise man and the fool, the upright man and the impious, will die by the same destiny as each other, and they will endure all the evils in this age with a similar outcome; and so what good is it to me that I have followed wisdom and labored harder than the others? Thinking it over again and examining it diligently to myself in my mind, I discovered that my judgment was vain.* For the wise man and the fool will not *have similar memory* in the future, when the consummation of all things will come; and it is by no means a comparable end that will hold them, because one will go to consolations, while the other will go to punishment.*

The Septuagint translators rendered the sense of the Hebrew more clearly* in this place, although they did not keep close to the Hebrew wording: "And why have I become wise? Then I spoke excessively in my heart, since the fool speaks from excess, that 'this too is vanity, because there is no memory of the wise man together with the fool for eternity,'" and so on. That is, he is clearly demonstrating that his earlier opinion was foolish and testifying that he spoke unwisely and was wrong to take that earlier view.

2.17 And I hated life, because the work that is done under the sun is an evil over me, because all things are vanity and a grazing of the wind. *

If the world has been placed in the power of the evil one* and the Apostle groaned in this tabernacle,* saying: "Wretched man am I, who will free me from the body of this death?"* then quite rightly he regards everything that is done under the sun with aversion. Naturally, in comparison to paradise and the blessedness of that life,* in which we will enjoy[12] spiritual fruits and the delights of virtues, now it is as if we are in a holding pen for slaves, in jail,* and in a valley of tears,* eating bread by the sweat of our brow.*

2.18, 19 And I have hated all my labor that I have been laboring under the sun, because I am leaving it to the man who will come after me. And who knows whether he is a wise man or a fool? And he will have dominion over all my labor, at which I have labored, and in which I have become wise under the sun; but this also is vanity.

He does seem to be changing his mind about wealth and possessions, because, as the Gospel says, we do not know, if we are taken by an unexpected death, what sort of heir we will leave when we die,* whether the person who is going to enjoy our labor is foolish or wise. That happened to Solomon as well, for he had a son, Rehoboam, who was not like himself.* From this example we understand that not even a son, if he is a fool, deserves to inherit from his father.

But when I think about[13] it more deeply* he seems to be speaking about labor in a spiritual sense, on the grounds that the wise man labors in the Scriptures day and night, and composes books, and leaves behind a memorial of himself to future generations, and nevertheless these books fall into the hands of fools, who frequently, by the perversity of their heart, draw the seeds of heresies from them and misrepresent another man's works. For if the speech of the Preacher concerns material riches here, why was it necessary to say about labor and wealth: *And he will have dominion over all my labor, at which I have labored, and in which I have become wise under the sun?* What kind of wisdom is it to gather earthly riches?

2.20–23 And I turned to renounce my heart in all my labor that I labored under the sun, because there is a man whose labor is in wisdom, and knowledge, and virtue, and he will give his share to the man who has not labored. And this, too, is vanity and much wickedness. For what comes to a man in all his labor; and in the desire of his heart in which he labors under the sun? Because all his days of griefs, and of wraths and cares, and even at night his heart does not sleep. But this also is vanity.

Above he speaks about the uncertainty of his heir: that it is not known whether he will be a foolish or wise master of another's labors. Now he reverts to the same subject, but the sense here is different: that even if he is leaving his own property and labors to a son, to a relative, or to someone he knows, the matter still returns to the same circle: that another enjoys someone else's labor, and the sweat of the dead is the delight of the living.*

Let every single person consider himself, and he will see the labor involved in writing books:*

> The man who is going to write anything worth reading
> a second time must often reverse the stylus.*

And let him give his own share to the man who has not labored.[*] For what, as I have already said,[*] do wisdom, knowledge, and virtue, in which he has declared himself to have labored, have to do with the riches of the earth, when it is the mark of wisdom, knowledge, and virtue to trample earthly things underfoot?

2.24–26 There is not a good thing for man except[*] that he eat and drink, and show good to his soul in his labor. This too I saw, that it is from the hand of God. For who will eat and who will abstain without him? Because to the man who is good before him he has given wisdom and knowledge and happiness, and to the sinner he has given anxiety, so that he increases and gathers the things that are to be given to the good before the face of God. But this also is vanity and presumption of spirit.

After I examined all things and observed that there was nothing more unjust than to have another enjoy someone else's labor, it then seemed to me that it was the fairest thing, and almost a gift from God, that someone should enjoy his own work, drinking and eating, and saving the wealth he has amassed, as the time requires.[*] For it is the gift of God that an upright man should be given the view that he, himself, should use up what he has acquired through cares and sleepless nights,[*] just as, to the contrary, it is the effect of the anger of God against the sinner that by day and night he should gather wealth, and, without using it at all, should leave it behind to those who are upright in the sight of God. But, he also says, examining carefully and seeing that all things come to an end in death, I have judged this, too, to be the height of vanity.

This, though, is according to the literal sense, so that we should not seem to be completely ignoring the simple sense, and despising the poverty of the historical approach in our quest for spiritual riches.[*] What good is it, or what sort of gift of God is it, either to gloat over one's own riches, and, as it were, to snatch at fleeting pleasure, or turn another's work to one's own delight? Or to judge it a gift of God if we enjoy another's miseries and labors?

Consequently, what is good is to take the true foods and the true drink, which we find in the divine books concerning the body and blood of the Lamb.[*] For who is able either to eat, or, when necessary, to abstain, without God, who tells us that the sacred should not be thrown to the dogs,[*] and teaches how to give food to his fellow slaves at the proper time,[*] and in another sense, when one has found honey, to eat only as much of it as is sufficient?[*]

It is quite right, too, that God gives wisdom, knowledge, and happiness to the man who is good before him; for unless he has been good, and first reformed his character through his own will,[*] he does not deserve wisdom, knowledge, and happiness, according to what is said elsewhere: "Sow for yourselves in justice, reap in enjoyment of life, light the light of knowledge for yourselves."[*] Clearly the sowing of justice is to come first, and the reaping of enjoyment of life; and after this, the light of knowledge will be able to appear.

And so, just as God *has given wisdom* and the other things *to the man who is good before him;* in the same way, abandoning the sinner to his own will,[*] he has made him gather riches, and stitch together, from this side and that, pillows of perverse doctrines. When the holy man who is pleasing to God sees these things, he understands that they are vain, and composed out of *presumption of spirit.*

It is not to be wondered at that he said, *to the sinner he has given anxiety,* etc; this is to be referred to the sense that I have repeatedly discussed: the reason anxiety or distress has been given to him is that he was a sinner; and the cause of the distress is not in God, but in the man who, of his own accord, sinned before.

CHAPTER 3

3.1 There is a time for all things, and a time for every thing under the heaven.

In what precedes, he has taught that the state of the human condition is uncertain and subject to fluctuation; what he now wishes to show is that everything in the universe is self-contradictory, and nothing stands for ever, at least of things beneath the sky and within time: the other, spiritual beings are not confined by either sky or time.[*]

3.2 A time to give birth, and a time to die; a time to plant, and a time to pull up what has been planted.

No one doubts that both the birth and the death of human beings are known to God, and fixed; and that giving birth is the same as planting, and dying is pulling up what has been planted. However, we read in Isaiah: "From the fear of you, Lord, we have conceived, been in labor, and brought forth";[*] so this is to say that in a perfect man the birth which was brought forth from fear dies when once he begins to love God, since: "Perfect love casts out fear."*

The Jews understand this whole passage on contrasting times, down to *A time for war and a time for peace,* as referring to Israel. As there is no need to put their interpretation and view line by line, I shall summarize it briefly, leaving a broader commentary on it to the reader's intelligence: There was a time for giving Israel birth, of planting it, and a time for it to die, to be led into captivity; a time to kill them, in Egypt, and a time to set them free from Egypt; a time to destroy the temple under Nebuchadnezzar,* and a time to build it under Darius;* a time to mourn the destruction of the city, and a time to laugh and dance, under Zerubbabel, Ezra, and Nehemiah;* a time to scatter Israel, and a time to gather it together; a time for God to wear the Jewish people as belt and girdle, and a time for them to be led into the Babylonian captivity and to rot away there, across the Euphrates: read Jeremiah's passage on the girdle.*

A time to seek and save them, a time to ruin and reject them; a time to tear Israel apart, and a time to piece it together; now, in their Roman captivity,* a time for the prophets to be silent, but then, when even in an enemy land they were not without the consoling word of God, a time for them to speak; a time for the love with which he loved them before, under the patriarchs, and a time for his hatred, because they laid hands on Christ;* a time for battle now, when they are not showing repentance, and a time for peace in the future, when all Israel shall be saved as the fullness of the nations comes in.*

3.3 A time to kill, and a time to heal.

He[14] who says: "It is I who will kill and I who will make alive"* has both a time to kill and a time to heal.* He heals, by summoning to repentance; and kills,[15] in the sense of: "In the morning I killed all the sinners of the earth."*

A time to destroy, and a time to build.

We cannot build what is good without first demolishing what is bad, just as the word was given by God to Jeremiah that he should first uproot, demolish, and destroy, and then build and plant.*

3.4 A time to weep, and a time to laugh.

The time to weep is now; the time to laugh is in the future,* for: "Blessed are those who weep, because they are the ones who will laugh."*

A time to mourn, and a time to dance.

That is the reason for the Gospel's rebuke to those to whom the Lord said: "We wailed to you, and you did not mourn; we sang, and you did not dance."* We must mourn at present, so that afterward we may dance the dance which David danced before the ark of the covenant, when he displeased Saul's daughter,* but pleased God more.

3.5 A time to scatter stones, and a time to pick stones up.

I am surprised at a scholar's ridiculous comment* on this passage that Solomon is talking about house-building and demolition, on the grounds that people do sometimes demolish and sometimes build; some collect stones together to construct buildings, others demolish those that have been built, as in Horace's lines:

> He demolishes, he builds, he changes rounded
>   corners for square ones;
> he ebbs and flows; the whole tenor of his life is
>   inconsistent.*

I leave it to the reader to judge whether this comment is true or false.

As for us, let us follow the earlier line of explanation, saying that the time to scatter and to collect stones is in the sense recorded in the Gospel: "God is able from these stones to raise up children to Abraham";* that is, that there was the time to scatter the Gentile population, and a time to gather them back into the church. In one book* (but using the Septuagint version: "A time to throw stones and a time to pick them up") I read that the severity of the old law was tempered by the grace of the Gospel: that is, the law, stiff, unkind, and unmerciful, kills the sinner, but the grace of the Gospel has pity and summons him to repentance; and that is what the time for throwing stones or picking them up means, as they are thrown in the law, but picked up in the Gospel.* Responsibility for the correctness or otherwise of this comment should rest with its author.

A time to embrace, and a time to keep away from embracing.

The meaning is clear, in the straightforward sense, with the Apostle's agreement—"Do not hold out on one another, except perhaps temporarily by mutual consent, to give time for prayer"*—on the same point, that one must try to have children, but also try to be continent.

Alternatively, that there was a time for embracing, when the words "Be fruitful and multiply, and fill the earth"* were what was important; and then again a time to keep far from embracing, when it was superseded by: "The time is under constraint. It remains that even those who have wives should be as though they had not."*

However, if we wish to rise to the higher sense, we shall see that wisdom embraces those who love it—"Honor her," he says, "and she shall embrace you"*—and holds them in a tighter embrace within her arms and bosom. Further, the human mind cannot always be aiming at the sublime and thinking of higher, divine things, nor be constantly in contemplation of the heavenly, but must sometimes allow for physical needs; that is why there is a time to embrace wisdom and to hold her more tightly, and a time to relax the mind from the contemplation and embrace of wisdom, so that we may attend to the care of our bodies and to the necessities of our life, short of sin.*

3.6, 7 A time to gain, and a time to lose; a time to conserve, and a time to discard.

In different words, the sense is the same as it is above and below, where he says: *A time to destroy and a time to build,* and later: *A time to split, and a time to piece together.*

As the synagogue is destroyed so that the church may be built, and there is a split away from the law so that the fabric of the Gospels may be pieced together—which is what the individual evangelists have done, piecing together from the Law and the Prophets the evidences for the coming of the Lord*—so there was both a time for seeking out and conserving Israel, and a time for losing and discarding it;* or else, a time to seek out a people from the Gentiles, and a time to destroy the people of the Jews; a time to conserve the faithful from the nations, and a time to jettison the unbelievers[16] from Israel.

A time to be silent, and a time to speak.

I suppose it is from this passage that the Pythagoreans* drew the origin of their rule: their training is to observe five years without speaking, and to speak only then, after receiving their education.* So let us too learn not to talk[17] at first, so that we may open our mouth to talk later on; let us for a certain time say nothing, and attend to our instructor's discourse; let nothing seem right to us but what we are learning, so that after long silence we may be made into teachers instead of pupils.*

As it is, however, through the fault of our schools,[18] which are in daily decline, we are teaching in the churches things we do not know about;* and if we arouse the people's applause, by our style, or by the prompting of the devil—that furtherer of errors—we suppose (against our conscience) that we do know the matter of which we have succeeded in convincing others. We do not, in general, learn the arts without a teacher; it is this art alone that is so unvalued and easy as to need no instructor.[*]

3.8 A time to love and a time to hate.

A time to love, after God, our children, wife, and family; and a time to hate them, at our martyrdom, when we are stubborn for our confession of Christ, though assailed by an opposing loyalty.[*]

Or else: There was a time to love the law and its commandments—circumcision, sacrifices, the Sabbath, new moons[*]—and a time to hate them, when the grace of the Gospel came in their place.[*]

It can also be said that, as at present we see with a mirror, in an enigma, there is a time to love the present; and there will in the future come a time when we see face to face,[*] and, by progressing to something better, we shall begin to hate and despise the object of our love.[*]

A time for war and a time for peace.

As long as we are in this present world it is a time for war;[*] once we leave the world, the time of peace will come, for in peace is the place of God, our city Jerusalem—a word meaning "peace gained."[*] At present, then, no one should think himself out of danger; in time of war we must gird ourselves and, like the Apostle, take up arms,[*] so that eventually we may rest victorious in peace.

3.9–11 What profit is there for the workman in what he labors at? I have seen the occupation that God has given to the sons of men to be occupied in. He has made everything good in its own time, and yet he has put the age* into their hearts, so that man shall not discover the work which God has made from start to finish.*

I am not unaware of what has been said by several people on this passage, that the purpose of God's allowing even the teachers of perverse doctrines to be active in this age is to prevent men's minds from being sluggish through inactivity,[*] and that what God has made is good in its own time, yet all the same they cannot understand nature and scientific knowledge.

However, this is how it was expounded to me by the Hebrew who gave me my grounding in the Scriptures: As all things decline in their own time, and there is a time for destroying or building, weeping or laughing, being silent or speaking, and so on for the whole "a time" passage, why do we make futile efforts and struggles, and suppose that the hardships of our brief life are unending? We are not "content," as the Gospel says, "with the trouble of the day";[19] we should "not be anxious for tomorrow."* After all, what advantage can we gain by further labor in this life, in which all that has been granted by God to men is that, through their own various pursuits, they should have the means of educating and training themselves?

All that God has made is good—but good in its own time. It is good to be awake, and to sleep; but it is not good to be always awake, or always asleep: thanks to God's arrangement, every single thing is good in its turn, when it is required.* Also God has given mankind the world to live in, and to enjoy the variety of the seasons, not to enquire into causes of natural phenomena and the manner of everything's creation, or the reasons why he has made this or that grow, endure, and change, from the beginning of the world to its end.*

3.12, 13 I have learned that there is no good but to be happy and to do good in one's lifetime. Moreover, every man who eats, drinks, and shows some good in all his labor, it is by the gift of God.

The reason that man has been put as a settler, a visitor, in the world is so that he should make use of his brief lifetime and, with any hope of protracted living cut off, look upon all that he possesses with the perspective of one who is to move on to other things;* he should do what good he can in his life, without being racked by futile designs for accumulating wealth. He is not to think that he can make any more profit from his own labor than food, drink, and any part of his wealth that he spends on good works; this is all God gives. We are not invited, as some suppose, to use these gifts, like animals, for extravagance and self-indulgence, and for despair, according to Isaiah, "Let us eat and drink, for tomorrow we shall die";* but with the Apostle: "If we have food and clothing, with these we are content."* And whatever we can have above that, let us spend[20] it in feeding the poor and in generosity to the needy.

Furthermore, as the Lord's flesh is the true food, and his blood the true drink, on an anagogical level* all the good we have in the present age is to feed on his flesh and drink his blood, not just at the sacrament but also in our reading of the Scriptures; because the true food and drink, which is gained from the word of God, is knowledge of the Scriptures.*

Nor is anyone to think that Balaam's prophecy, "There will be no hardship in Jacob, nor grief in Israel,"* contradicts this,* as it is said to be God's gift if anyone *eats, drinks and shows some good in all his labor.* The tribulations of the upright are many, and it is of these the Apostle complains when he says he has sweated in hardship and grief;* but it is in the future, when the Lord has freed us from these tribulations, that "there will no hardship in Jacob, nor grief in Israel."* Just as we read: "Blessed are those who weep, for they are the ones who will laugh,"* and as our laughter will follow the words of Job's prophecy: "And the mouths of the true shall be filled with joy,"* so now we make use of our labor* in good works, by which we are constrained and weighed down, in order that afterward we may cease to labor.

3.14 I have learned that all things that God has made, they will be forever; nothing can be added to them, and nothing taken away from them. And God has caused them* to be afraid from his face.*

There is nothing in the world that is new. The sun's path, the changes of the moon and of the earth, and the withering or greenness of trees originated, and were jointly created,[21] along with the world itself; and the object of God's control of all things on fixed principles, and of his commanding the elements to serve human purposes, is that mankind shall see this and understand that Providence exists,* and so that they shall *be afraid from his face,* being aware from the even path and consistent order of things that there is a Creator; "For God's invisible aspects are understood and seen from what he has made, and so are his eternal virtue and divinity."*

If we wish to finish with the earlier interpretation, and reread *and God has caused them to be afraid from his face* as it were from the beginning, its meaning is: God has made all these things so that mankind should be afraid to veer away in a different direction from what he has once disposed. The inclusion *to be afraid from his face* is admirably fitting, because: "The face of the Lord is over the evildoers."*

3.15 What is it that has been? That which is; and what will be has already been. And God shall seek the man who undergoes persecution.

Everything we see, past, present, or future, both was and is, and shall be. The sun which rises now has existed before we were in the world and will go on rising after we are dead (we used the word "sun" so as to understand, from that, that everything else that has existed is the same).* Even though they appear to perish in the state of death, they do not perish, because they come to life again and regrow; nothing dies permanently, but is born again and comes back to life, as it were with a kind of interest. That is what *and God shall seek the man who undergoes persecution* is saying; it is better phrased in Greek as καὶ ὁ θεὸς ζητήσει τὸ διωκόμενον,* that is, what has passed, what has been driven out, what has ceased to be. Now, if this is said of everything in the world, there is no doubt that a dead person is to be reborn.

However, if it pleases anyone to read *and God shall seek the man who undergoes persecution* on a virtually literal basis, let him use it, during a persecution by pagans,* as evidence for consolation of one who is steadfast in martyrdom. Given that, according to the Apostle: "All who desire to live a godly life in this age suffer persecution,"* they are to have the consolation that *God seeks the one who suffers persecution,* just as "he requires the blood of the slain,"* and "comes to seek what had been lost,"* and "carried the straying sheep back to the flock on his own shoulders."*

3.16, 17 And still I have seen under the sun the place of judgment: there is impiety. And the place of justice: there is iniquity. I said in my heart, "God will judge the upright and the impious, because there is a time for all volition* and on every deed there."*

The sense is clear, but is enveloped in a cloud of interpretation. Under this sun, he says, I have looked for truth and judgment, and have seen that even on the very benches of the judges it is not truth that prevails, but bribery.*

Or else: I thought that there was some administration of justice in the present world, the godly man being rewarded in the present according to his own deserts and the impious being punished for his own wrongdoing, and I found the opposite of what I supposed: I saw both one who is upright enduring much suffering here, and one who is impious being rewarded for his wickedness with power.

Later, though, talking to my heart and thinking it over, I realized that God does not judge in part, one person at a time, but reserves his judgment for the future, so that all will be judged together, and will there be rewarded according to their volition and their works.* That is what *a time for all volition and on every deed there* means: that is, it is at the judgment, when the Lord begins to judge, that there will be truth; at present it is injustice that holds sway in the world. We read something like this in the Wisdom called Sirach: "Do not say 'What is this?' or 'What is that?' for all things will be required in their own time."*

3.18–21 I spoke in my heart about the utterance* of the sons of men, because God separates them in order to show that they are animals to themselves,* because the outcome of the sons of man and the outcome of cattle, there is one outcome for them. As is his death, so is their death also, and there is one breath for all, and there is nothing more for a man than for cattle, because all is vanity. All things go to one place; all things were formed from the ground, and all things will return to the ground. And who knows if the spirit of the *sons of men rises upward and if the spirit of cattle descends downward into the earth?*

As far as the worthlessness of their bodies is concerned, there is no difference between animals and a human being:[22] they have the same condition, of birth, and a single destiny, of dying; we come forth alike to the light, and disintegrate equally into dust. Considering that, it is not surprising that there is no distinction in the present life between the upright and the impious, and that virtues have no value, but that everything is floundering, with its outcome uncertain. If there does seem to be a distinction, that man's spirit ascends to heaven and the spirit of cattle descends down into the ground, on what certain authority do we know that? Who can know whether the hope is true or false?

He says this, not because he supposes that the soul perishes with the body, or that there is just the one place prepared for beasts and man, but because before the coming of Christ everything was being taken to Hades* together. Hence, even Jacob says he will go down to Hades;* Job, too, complains that both the pious and the impious are held in the nether regions;* and the Gospel gives evidence that Abraham also is in Hades with Lazarus, and that the rich man is in torment, though there is a gulf between them.* In fact, before Christ unbarred that fiery wheel,* the flaming sword,* and the doors of paradise, in company with the criminal,* the heavenly realms were closed,* and equal worthlessness confined the spirit of cattle and of man; even though one seemed to disintegrate and the other to be preserved, there was little difference between bodily death and imprisonment in the darkness of Hades.

Let us go back over the details, dealing briefly with them in their order, in clause-by-clause style. *I spoke in my heart about the utterance of the sons of men, how God picks them out.* The only difference that God wished there to be between humans and animals, he is saying, is that we talk, they are dumb; we express our will in language, they are sunk in silence.* Yet, though we differ from beasts just in language, we are nevertheless shown that, with regard to physical frailty, we are cattle. Just as an animal dies, so too does a human; breath, like the air that nourishes us, is one for all. That is what he says: *There is one breath for all, and there is nothing more for a man than for cattle.*

To stop us supposing that this saying includes the soul, he put in: *All things were formed from the ground, and will return to the ground:* it is only the body that was made from the ground.* Significantly, it is of the body that "you are dust, and to dust you shall return"* is said. Now, as to what looks like blasphemy: *Who knows if the spirit of the sons of man ascends to heaven and the spirit of an animal descends down into the ground?* he is not maintaining that there is no difference between animals and mankind with regard to the worth of the soul; by putting "Who" he wished to show the difficulty of the problem. In the holy Scriptures the pronoun "who" is always understood as not an impossibility, but a difficulty: for example: "Who will utter his generation?"* and in the psalm: "Lord, who shall ascend into your tent, and into your holy hill?"* and the rest that follows; and in Jeremiah (although it is different in the Hebrew): "And there is a man, and who knows him?"* So the sole difference between man and beasts is that the human's spirit ascends to heaven, and the animal's spirit descends into the ground and disintegrates with its body. However, if some churchman, a scholar in celestial subjects and confident on a supposedly doubtful point, should defend this assertion, <it would be safe to hold it, despite the difficulty>.[23]

So much for the literal interpretation; now for what concerns the spiritual sense of "Because the Lord shall save both man and beast,"* and elsewhere: "I was like a beast toward you,"* and what is said in all the prophets: that men and animals are to be brought safely to Jerusalem,* and that the promised land will be full of cattle and herds.* Who knows whether the saint, the one who deserves the appellation "human," is to ascend into heaven, and whether the sinner, who is being called "animal,"* is to descend into the ground? Given the uncertain, slippery condition of this life, it is possible both that the upright man may fall down, and that the sinner may rise up.* It sometimes happens that the more intelligent person, versed in the Scriptures, that is "a man," may live in an unconsidered way unbefitting his learning, and be taken to Hades, while any more unsophisticated, more uncultured person, called "an animal" in contrast to "a man," may live better, win the crown of martyrdom, and be a dweller in heaven.

3.22 And I saw that there is no good thing but that a man shall be happy in his work, because that is his lot. For who will bring him to see that which will be after him?

Instead of what we put as *to see that which will be after him,* Symmachus has a clearer translation: "to see those things which will be after these." So there is nothing good in this life but that a man enjoys his work of giving alms and preparing future treasures for himself in the kingdom of the heavens. This is the only portion we have that neither thief nor bandit nor tyrant can take away,* and which is to come with us after death;* for, once this life has disintegrated, we can no longer profit from our own labors, nor know what will happen afterward in the world.

Alternatively: Confused by my earlier mistake in thinking there was no difference between humans and beasts, I was led by unsound opinion into saying that I thought nothing good but making the most of present pleasure, as, once death has destroyed us, we cannot profit from what we are leaving ungratefully behind.* Others have referred *Who will bring him to see those things that will be after him?* to the sense that it is better for a man to enjoy his own labors, because that is all he can get out of his own property; once death comes, he does not know what kind of heir he will have when he dies: whether it will be one who deserves to enjoy the wealth that is his, or one who does not.*

CHAPTER 4

4.1 And I turned and saw all the oppressions that take place under the sun; and behold, the tears of those who endure oppression, and there is no one to console them, and strength is in the hands of those oppressing them; and there is no comforter for them.

After this thought, I turned my mind and eyes to see the oppressors who make false accusations* and the victims of oppression. And look, those who are wickedly harassed by the powerful bear witness with their tears—the only recourse open to them in their misfortune—to the vulnerability of their position, but they are unable to discover[24] a comforter. And to make their misery greater, and their grief inconsolable, they see the oppressors growing stronger in their own wickedness. This is the reason that they cannot be consoled. David develops this topic more fully in Psalm 72* and Jeremiah in his own book.*

4.2, 3 And I praised the dead, those who are now dead, more than the living, whoever are themselves alive until now. And better than both of those is the one who is not yet born, who has not yet seen the evil work that has been done under the sun.

In comparison with the miseries that weigh down mortals in this age, I judged the dead to be more fortunate than the living, following what Job says when he is discussing those in Hades: "In that place those weary in body have found rest, together with those who had been in bonds, now carefree, no longer hearing the voice of the taskmaster."* Nevertheless, better than these two (the living and the dead) is the person who has not yet been born; for one of those still suffers evils, while the other is like someone who has escaped naked from a shipwreck,* whereas the person who has not yet been born is more fortunate in that he has not yet experienced the evils of the world.*

But he says that, not because the person who has not yet been born exists before he is born, and is more fortunate in that he has not yet been weighed down with a body;* but because it is better not to exist at all, and to have no awareness of existence, than to exist, or to live, unhappily.* Just as also the Lord says about Judas, signifying his future torments: "It would have been better for that man not to have been born";* because it would have been better for him never to have existed at all than to endure eternal torments.

Others understand this passage as follows: those who have died are better off than the living, even if previously they were sinners. For the living are still in the battle, and, as it were, locked up and held in the prison of the body; but those who have died are now trouble-free and have ceased to sin.* In just the same way, John, than whom there is no one greater among them born of women, is less than he who is the least in the kingdom of heaven,* and who having been freed from the burden of the body, cannot say with the Apostle: "I am a wretched man, who will free me from the body of this death?"*

On the other hand, they say, the person who has not yet been born, who has not seen the evil things by which men are weighed down in the world, is better off than both of them. For our souls, before they descend to these bodies, dwell in the upper regions and are blessed for as long as they are kept among the celestial Jerusalem and the angelic choir.*

4.4 And I saw all labor and at the same time the whole virtue of working, that it is a man's envy of his neighbor; and this also is vanity and presumption of spirit.

I turned once more to other things and I saw all the strength and glory of those who labor, and I perceived that the good thing of one was the evil of another, as the envious man is tormented by another man's fortune and the boastful man is exposed to snares.* For what is more vain than for men, instead of weeping for their own miseries or deploring their own sins, to envy those who are better off? What is so like the spirit of worthlessness?

4.5 The fool has clasped his hands and consumed his flesh.

This is the man who is also described as lazy in Proverbs, wrapping his arms around his chest. To this man, "poverty comes like a fast runner,"* and he, on account of his great hunger (although the expression is hyperbolic), eats his flesh.* This person believes that it is better to have one handful of cheap flour and to live at leisure and listlessly than to fill both hands by laboring. However, the Preacher's whole point here is to show two things: that he who labors, and has something, is exposed to envy in this world;* and that, on the other hand, the man who wants to live free from exertion is oppressed by poverty. Each is miserable, since one is in jeopardy on account of his wealth, and the other is worn out with need because of his poverty.

A possible alternative explanation is that someone who envies another's happiness—seized as it were by a madness of the spirit, he allows envy into his breast and nurses it in his heart—is consuming his soul and flesh. For the happier he sees the man whom he envies, the more he himself wastes away and goes to ruin, and little by little drips with jealousy and spite.*

Another interpretation: "Hands" are frequently understood as meaning "works," just as in this verse: "The word of the Lord that came into being in the hand of Haggai"* (it might be Haggai's word, or any other prophet); because he has carried out such works that he proved worthy for the word of God to come into being in his work. The verse of David also agrees with this: "He trains my hands for battle."* And so *the fool clasped his hands,* that is, he folded them together and did not want to extend them,* and as a result he does not consume the labors of his hands, which he does not have, but his own flesh, living according to the wisdom of the flesh and feeding on the works of the flesh.

4.6 A full handful with rest is better than fullness of hands with labor; and with presumption of spirit.

It is better to have a small share that is just than the great riches of sinners.* The same thing is said in Proverbs: "A small amount received with justice is better than much produce with iniquity."* Elegantly, justice yields rest, iniquity yields labor. The singular number is always taken in a good sense, a double one in a bad sense:* for that reason, one handful has rest, while two hands are full of labor.

4.7, 8 And I turned and I saw the vanity under the sun. There is one man and there is not a second, and indeed there is a son, and he has no brother, and there is no end to all his labor. And indeed his eye is not sated with riches; and for whom do I work, and cheat my soul of goodness? But this also is vanity and a grievous strain.

I turned to other men and saw that they labored more than was necessary, gathering riches lawfully and unlawfully and not using what they had gathered, having everything, sleeping on their wealth, saving it for another, and not getting the benefit of their own labor; especially when they have neither son, nor brother, nor relative, so that their labor, stored up for their family, would seem a matter of duty.* And so I discovered that there is nothing more vain than the man who gathers riches, not knowing to whom he will leave them. We can, in fact, following the preceding interpretation,* also take this as referring to those who compose books and leave them behind for disdainful readers.*

Some interpret this passage, from *there is one man and there is not a second,* as referring to the Savior, because, alone and without any companion, he descended in order to save the world. And although there are many sons of God, and they are called his brothers through adoption,* still there has never been anyone worthy to be associated with him in this work. There is no end to his labor, as he bears our vices and sins, and grieves on our account; his eye *will not be sated with riches,* as he always desires our salvation, and the more he sees someone sinning, the more he urges him on toward repentance.

4.9–12 Two are better than one. They have a good recompense in their labor, because if they fall, one²⁵ will lift his partner. And woe to one man when he falls and there is not a second person to lift him up. And indeed, if two sleep, they will also have warmth; and how will one man be warmed? And if one man prevails over him, two will stand against that man, and a three-stranded cord will not easily be broken.

After the miseries of solitude which have seized the man who torments himself in procuring wealth without a certain heir,* the discourse now moves to companionship. What is being said is how good it is to have the fellowship of friends and the comfort of sharing, because the fall of one is supported by the help of the other, and the man who has a faithful friend copes with domestic cares, and even enjoys his night's rest, more than the man who sleeps alone²⁶ on top of the wealth he has amassed. But if any stronger enemy arises against one of them, the weakness of the one is supported by the comfort of his friend. And in the same proportion as two differ from one, if they are joined by love, so much more is a fellowship of three able to prevail. And as a matter of fact, with affection that is true and unstained by any jealousy, the more it grows numerically, the more it also increases in power. For the moment, take this in the literal meaning.

However, because above[*] we have taken the sense of certain passages as being about Christ, we must also discuss the rest on the same level. It is better for there to be two, side-by-side, than one, because it is better to have Christ living inside oneself than to be exposed alone to the traps of the adversary. Obviously the reward of fellowship is demonstrated at once in the actual value of companionship. For if one falls, Christ will lift[27] his partner. But woe indeed to him who, when he falls,[28] does not have Christ in himself lifting him up. Also, if one man falls asleep, that is, if he is broken up in death, and he has Christ with him, he will soon be restored to life, warmed and living. And if the devil, stronger in overcoming resistance, stands against a man, the man will stand and Christ too will stand up for his man, for his companion; not because the power of Christ alone is weak against the devil, but because man's will is left free,[*] and when we add our own efforts to his, Christ's war is waged with greater strength.

And if the Father, Son, and Holy Spirit too should come, that fellowship will not be quickly broken.[29] Not quickly broken; nevertheless it will sometimes be broken.[*] For even in the apostle Judas there was that threefold cord, but because: "After the bread, Satan entered into him,"[*] that cord was broken.

Now, as to the earlier words, *indeed if two sleep, they will also have warmth; and how will one man be warmed,* let us take an example from Elisha,[*] because he both drew himself close together to the boy and fell asleep and warmed his small body, and so revived the boy, who rose from death. Therefore we cannot receive the warmth of eternal life unless Christ has fallen asleep with us and slept in death.

4.13–16 A poor, wise boy is better than an old and foolish king who does not know how to take care for the future, because he goes out from the house of bondage to the kingship, and because even in his kingship, he was born a poor man. I saw all the living, who walk under the sun, with a young man following who will rise instead of him. There is no end to all the people, to all who were before them. And indeed the most recent will not rejoice in him; but this also was vanity and presumption of spirit.

Symmachus translated this passage in this way:

Better a poor man with wisdom than a king old and foolish, who did not know how to take precautions against change. For the one came from prison to rule; but the other, although he was born a king, was overwhelmed by poverty. I have seen all the living who walk under the sun, with a young man following, who rose instead of him. Endless were all the people, who were before both; and his successors will not rejoice in him. But this also was the air and a grazing of the wind.

My Hebrew, whom I frequently mention, when he was reading Ecclesiastes with me, testified that Bar Akiba,* the one whom they admire most of all, pronounced upon this passage as follows:

Better is the inner man who arises within us after the 14th year, the year of puberty, than the outer man, born from his mother's womb, who does not know to withdraw from vice, and who left the house of bondage (that is to say, his mother's womb) merely to be king among vices. Despite his power, he has become poor, by committing every evil. I have seen people who have lived in the earlier man and who subsequently spent their days with the second one (the one born in the place of the earlier one, his predecessor); and I have realized that they all sinned in the earlier man before becoming two men at the birth of the second one. These turned to better things and, after the philosophers' branching of the roads,[30] they too abandoned the left-hand path, and pressed on toward the summit on the right,* and followed the second (i.e. the latest man); such men will not rejoice in him—that is, in the earlier one.*

The Apostle also attests to the two[31] men,* and Leviticus is not silent either: "Man, man,"* if he meant some such thing.

The holy man, Gregory, bishop of Pontus,* a student of Origen, in his *Metaphrasis on Ecclesiastes*, understood this passage in this way:

But I prefer a young man, poor and wise, to a king who is old and foolish, to whom it has never occurred that it is possible that anyone of those whom he had imprisoned might leave prison and become king, and that he himself might then fall from his own unjust power. For sometimes it happens that those who have been under a wise young man are free from unhappiness, provided that they were under an old king before. For those who were born later, because they did not know the troubles of the past, are also unable to praise a young man who has risen to power later on; they are seduced by a perverse opinion and the impulse of an opposing spirit.*

The interpreter of Laodicea,* straining to express great matters in a brief discourse, in his usual manner also in this place said:

The Preacher is here talking of the change of good things into bad. He is trying to describe the foolish man, who, not considering what is to come, takes delight in present and perishable things as if they were great and lasting. Then, after the various things which ordinarily happen to men in their lifetime, and which are changeable, he produces what amounts to a general view about death: that the innumerable multitude dies and little by little is worn out and passes away; and everyone leaves someone else in his place, and then when this successor dies, another.*

Origen's view* was quite close to that of Victorinus,* starting with the general point, obvious to all, that a poor, wise, young man is better than an old, foolish king; and that it frequently happens that through his wisdom, the young man, even when he comes out of the king's prison, rules in place of a perverse lord, and a foolish king loses the power that he held. They have then interpreted this passage as about Christ and the devil, because they take the boy who is poor and wise to mean Christ. A boy, according to: "It is a great thing for you to have been called my boy";* and poor, because "he became poor though he was rich";* and wise, because "he increased in age and wisdom, and in favor with God and man."* He was born in the kingship of one who is old.* And for that reason he says, "If my kingship was of this world, my servants of course would fight for me, so that I should not be handed over to the Jews. As it is, my kingdom is not of this world."*

Therefore the best Child was born in the kingdom of that foolish old one, who showed him all the kingdoms of the world and its glory;* and from prison, about which Jeremiah spoke in Lamentations, saying: "So that he might humble all the prisoners of the earth beneath his feet,"* he advanced to the kingship, and went away to a distant region* and after some time, despite those who did not want him to be king, he returned as King.

And therefore, by a prophetic spirit, the Preacher saw all of the living who are able to be partners of the young man who says: "I am the life,"* and to dismiss the old foolish king and follow Christ. And at the same time, two groups from the people of Israel are signified:* the earlier, who lived before the coming of the Lord, and the later, who will receive the Antichrist in preference to Christ, because the earlier group has not been altogether rejected, as the first church was assembled from the Jews and apostles.* And at the end, it is the Jews who will receive the Antichrist in preference to Christ, who *will not rejoice* in Christ.

4.17 Guard your foot when you go into the house of God, and approach to hear. For a gift is a sacrifice of fools, because they do not know that they do evil.

He is giving rules for life, and he does not want us to offend when going to church. For it is not entering God's house that is praiseworthy, but entering it without stumbling. And if it were the characteristic of everyone in the church of God to hear the word, he never would have added: *And approach to hear.*

To make the point, it was Moses alone who used to come near in order to hear God; the others were not able to approach.* Because the foolish, not knowing that there is a remedy for sin, believe that they are able to satisfy God by an offering of gifts, and are unaware that it is also an evil, and a sin, to want to put right what they have done by gifts and sacrifices, instead of by obedience and good works.* That agrees with what is said elsewhere: "Obedience over sacrifice."* And: "I desire mercy, not sacrifice."*

CHAPTER 5

5.1, 2 Do not be hasty in your mouth, and do not let your heart be hasty to bring forth speech in the sight of God, because God is in heaven and you are on earth. Your words should be few, for this reason: that a dream will come in a multitude of anxiety, and the voice of an unwise person is in the multiplication of speeches.

Many think that what is enjoined in the present passage is that we should not make any promises lightly before God and make vows we are unable to fulfill, without reflecting on our powers,* because God is present here, and, though he is in heaven and we are on earth, he still hears what we say, and our folly is proved from *the multiplication of speeches.**

Others, however, with better understanding, maintain that what is being enjoined is that we should not, in either our speeches or our thoughts, hold any views about God that are beyond our powers. Instead, we should recognize our weakness, in that our powers of thought are as far apart from his nature as earth is from heaven, and that is why our words should be restrained. Just as someone with much to think about often has dreams about the subjects of his thought, so one who wishes to get into a long discussion about the nature of God will fall into foolishness.*

Another view is that the reason why our words should be few is that it is only with a mirror, and in an enigma,* that we see even the things we think we know, and only as a dream that we grasp the things we imagine we understand; when we have, as we supposed, said[32] a great deal, the end of our discussion is foolishness—for "from much talking we do not escape sin."*

5.3, 4 When you have made a vow to God, do not delay in paying it, because the volition is not in the unwise. * *Whatever you vow, pay it. It is better not to vow, than to vow and not pay it.*

The straightforward sense needs no interpretation: it is better to make no promises* than not to carry promises out, because those who do not fulfill vows are displeasing to God and count as unwise.

In the expression: *The will is not in the unwise,* "of God" is understood, as in the Apostle's: "In any case, it was not the will that I should come to you now."*

If, though, we wish in addition to say something more considered, the Christian is being commanded to fulfill his word in action, instead of being like the Jews, who worshiped idols,* despite giving an undertaking in the words: "Whatever God commands, we will do it all";* and after beating and stoning his servants, they finally murdered even the Father's Son himself.* So it is better to weigh up a doubtful remark for a long time than to be prompt in words and reluctant in action, for: "The servant who knows the Lord's will and will not do it shall receive a severe beating."*

5.5 You are not to give your mouth to make your flesh sin, and do not say in the sight of an angel* that it is ignorance, lest God be angry over your word and scatter the works of your hands.

My Hebrew took it as: "Do not promise what you cannot do, because what is said does not go off into the wind, but is at once delivered to the Lord by the angel present; every single person has one with him, close by.* And you, who think God does not know what you promised, are provoking him to anger, so as to have all your works scattered." But his exposition of the words *to make your flesh sin* was careless: he took it as if the words had been: "You are not to give your mouth, so as to sin."*

In our view the sense is different:* the people being reprehended are those who complain about the force of the flesh* and say that they are doing things against their will, under physical compulsion, as in the Apostle's: "For I do not do what I want, but what I do not want,"* and so on. So, he is saying: "Do not try to find vain excuses; do not give your flesh an opportunity to sin, and then say: 'It is not I that am sinning, but the sin which lives in my flesh.'"

Finally, where he says: *Do not say in the presence of an angel that it is ignorance,* Aquila's translation of the Hebrew *segaga* makes it ἀκούσιον, that is, "not of my own will"; if you say this, you are provoking God by making it seem that the sin is his fault,* so that he will be angry and take out of your hands any asset you seem to possess, or else, because you think that, give you over to your false view, so that you act inappropriately.

5.6 Because vanities, and also many words, are in a multitude of dreams. But fear God.

The Hebrews expound this passage, too, as: "Do not either do what has already been said above,* or[33] lightly believe dreams; when you have had various visions during your night's sleep, and your soul has been harassed by all sorts of terrors, or aroused by promises, spurn them—they are just part of your dream—and be afraid only of God. Someone who believes dreams is going to surrender himself to silly vanities."*

Alternatively: Because I said, and commanded, that you are not to *give your mouth to make your flesh sin** and try to find all sorts of excuses, I am now adding that in the sleep of this life—in the unreality, darkness, and cloud in which we live—we can find many things that seem plausible to us and seem to excuse our sins. That is why I am admonishing you that the one thing you must avoid is supposing that God is not there; that you should fear him and know that he is there, present at your every action; and that you are endowed with free will, and are doing what you are doing of your own volition, not under compulsion.

5.7, 8 If in the district you see the oppression of a poor man, and a plundering of judgment and justice, do not be surprised at the affair, because

a high one is on guard over a high one, and there is a higher one over them,
and a larger amount of land in them all. There is a king in the cultivated
land.

Christ's garment was woven throughout and could not be torn
by his crucifiers;* and the Savior commanded the man from whom he
had cast out the demons to go away wearing clothes belonging to the
apostles.* So let us, too, strive not to tear the clothes of our Preacher,
and not to stitch together pieces of our own notions higgledy-piggledy
just as we like, but to keep the unity of his argument and follow the
same sense and order.

Above, he had said: *Do not say in the sight of an angel that it is*
ignorance, lest God be angry at your word, and the rest.* It was against those
who denied that human affairs are governed by Providence that he had
said this.* Therefore, as questioning then began to arise, in opposition
to this command, about why the upright undergo oppression and
why wicked judgments take place all over the world, without God's
vengeance, he is now breaking down possible opposition by adding:
"If you see a poor man, who is declared 'blessed' in the Gospel,* being
oppressed, and affairs being conducted by force instead of justice, do
not be surprised, or think it is anything new." High over the high,
God sees this. He has set his angels over the judges and the kings
of the earth, and whatever happens, they can prevent injustice; they
are mightier on earth than any powers of men. But he is reserving
judgment to the end, and at the consummation of the world, when
the harvest is ripe and the reapers come, he is going to order the
grain to be separated and the weeds to be put into the fire.* That is
why at present he is waiting, postponing sentence until the field of
this world is fully cultivated. The interpretation of "field" as "world"
was explained by the Lord in the parable of the weeds and the grain.*

5.9, 10 The one who loves silver shall not be sated with silver, and the one
who loves wealth shall not enjoy it; but this too is vanity. For in a multitude
of goods there are many who consume them, and what is the strength for the
one who has them, but that he should see with his eyes?

Wherever we put "silver," it can, thanks to the ambiguity of the
Greek, also be replaced by "money": ἀργύριον* means either. (Cicero
tells us that originally "pecunious"* was used of those who had the
most *peculia,** the ancient word for *pecora;** gradually, by careless
usage, the word developed into the other meaning.)*

It is therefore a miser who is being described, as he is never sated
with wealth; the more he has, the more he wants. Horace agrees on
this point:

"The miser is always needy";*

and so does the aristocratic historian: "Greed is not decreased either by surplus or by shortage."* So the Preacher is saying that all the good that wealth does for its owner is merely that he can see what he owns. The greater his property, the more servants he will have to devour the wealth he has accumulated. All he can do is see what he has; he cannot eat more than one person's food.

5.11 Sleep is sweet to one working, whether he has eaten a little, or more. And the rich man's satiety does not let him sleep.*

The subject is still the rich miser; he is being compared to a working man who sleeps without anxiety. Thanks to the labor and sweat of his work, the working man digests any kind of food, whether his meal has been a large one or a small one, and enjoys *sweet sleep,* whereas the rich man, distended with feasting and torn in different directions by his thoughts, cannot sleep; his hangover surges back at him, and his undigested food seethes in his tight stomach.

Further, as "sleep" is used also of the departure of all of us from this life, the repose of the one who works in the present life and is saved because of his strength in good works will be better than the wealth of those of whom it is written: "Woe to you that are rich, for you have received your consolation."*

5.12–16 It is a grievous ill that I have seen under the sun, that riches are guarded by their owner to his harm, and the riches have perished in the worst manner of stress. And he was the father of a son, and there is nothing in his hands. Just as he left his mother's womb naked, he will return as he came, and take nothing of his labor to go in his hands. But this, too, is a grievous ill: that as he came, so also he goes. So what more will he have, that he toiled into the wind? And in all his days he will eat in darkness and in great resentment, and in weakness, and in anger.

Connect this, as a sequel, to what precedes: the Preacher is describing the rich man, who cannot profit from his own wealth himself* and frequently gets into danger because of it; nor can he leave what he has accumulated to his heir.* Both he and his son return, naked as they came, into the earth, and nothing from his own labors goes with them. Is it not *a grievous ill* to be tormented by thoughts about one's wealth, and with useless labor to acquire, at the cost of gloomy, resentful groaning, and litigation,* riches that perish without our being able to take them away with us when we die?

That, then, is the straightforward sense. To raise ourselves to a higher level, he seems to me to be talking about philosophers, or heretics, who to their detriment accumulate a wealth of dogma, the devisers of which can derive no use from them, nor bequeath any permanent profit to their followers. Instead, both they themselves and their disciples return into the earth and have their wealth destroyed by him who said: "I will destroy the wisdom of the wise, and the cleverness of the clever I will thwart."* Truly, indeed, they will labor in vain and go naked into the wind, just as they came from the womb of their mother—that is, their perverse church, the opposite of the one of which it is written: "But the Jerusalem above is free, and is the mother of us all."* They "are worn out searching with a search"* and "are carried about with every wind of doctrine";* they have no light, but eat their own sacraments in darkness; they are always in weakness, always in wrath, "storing up wrath for themselves in the day of wrath,"* and without God's favor.

5.17–19 Behold what good I have seen, which is the best thing: to eat and drink and look on delight in all one's labor with which he has labored under the sun in the number of his life's days that God has given him; for that is his portion. But also every man to whom God has given wealth and property, and allowed him to subsist on them, and to take his portion, and to be happy from his labor, this is a gift of God. For he will not recollect much of the days of his life, because God occupies his heart in happiness.

By comparison,* he is saying, the man who makes good use of what is present is better than the man who subsists on his wealth in the darkness of his worries, and who in great weariness of life amasses things destined to perish. In the one case there is pleasure, albeit a small one, in putting something to good use, but in the other there is nothing but a mass of anxieties. He is also giving reasons for its being a gift of God to be able to make good use of riches.

As to: *He will not recollect much of the days of his life,* that is because God distracts him, in the happiness of his heart; drawn away by his present happiness and pleasure, he will not be in gloom, nor be harassed by thought.* It is better, though, to take it, with the Apostle, of the spiritual food and spiritual drink given by God.*

Then: *To see goodness in all his labor* is because by huge labor and study we can contemplate what is truly good, and it is our portion to be happy in our own study and labor. Good though this is, it is still not fully good until Christ shall be made manifest in our life; and that is why God will not recollect much about the days of our life. It is to be noted also that περισπασμός* here is taken in the good sense of the "distraction" of true, spiritual happiness.

CHAPTER 6

6.1–6 There is an evil that I have seen under the sun, and frequent among
men. A man to whom God has given riches, wealth, and glory, and his soul
lacks nothing of all the things that he has desired; and God has not given him
the power to gain from it, but a stranger has devoured it. This is vanity and
a grievous ill. If a man should have sired a hundred children and lived many
years, and many were the days of his years, and his soul was not replenished
with good things, nor was there a tomb for him, I said that a stillborn infant
would be better than him, as he has come in vanity and departs in darkness
and his name will be hidden in the darkness; it has not seen the sun nor known
it, and indeed it has more rest than he does. And if he should live twice a
thousand years and not see goodness, do not all things hasten to one place?

He is describing a rich miser, and he claims this evil is common
among men, because a miser lacks none of the things that are
considered good in the world and nevertheless tortures himself with
utterly stupid parsimony, preserving what others are to devour.[*] And
furthermore, he also adds hyperbolically that, even if a man should
father one hundred children and live, not nearly one thousand years[*]
as Adam did,[*] but two thousand, with his soul wasting away through
greed and avarice, he would be in a much worse condition than the
stillborn child, who has died as soon as it seems to have been born.
For that child has seen neither evil things nor good; but that man,
although he possessed good things, has always been tormented by
gloomy thoughts, and the stillborn child would have more rest than
this long-lived miser; yet nevertheless, both are carried off by a similar
end, as both this man and that child are taken away by the same death.

This can also be taken as being about Israel, because God gave
that people the Law, the Prophets, the covenant, and the promise, but
the Savior said: "The kingdom of God will be taken from you and it will
be given to a people producing its fruits,"[*] so all these things are to
have been transferred to an unrelated, foreign people made up of the
Gentiles, and they see their good things without enjoying them. And,
he says, our condition is much better, we who were deemed stillborn
and newcomers by those who prided themselves on their antiquity,
boasting about their ancestors and saying: "Our father is Abraham";[*]

and nevertheless we and they are hurrying to the same place, that is, to the judgment of God.

As to his remark in the middle of this text: *Nor was there a tomb for him,* this either means that the rich man does not think about his own death, and despite all the things that he possesses, he is avaricious even over the construction of his sepulcher; or that often he is murdered by bandits, just because of his wealth, and his body is cast away unburied;[*] or that, what I believe to be the best answer, he has done no good by which he might gain for himself a reputation in posterity, instead of "passing through life in silence like cattle,"[*] despite having had the wherewithal to enable him to show that he had lived.

6.7, 8 All a man's labor is in his mouth, and yet his soul will not be filled. For what does a wise man have more than a fool? What does a poor man have, but to know how to encounter life?

Everything that men work for in this world is consumed in their mouth, ground down by the teeth, and passed to the stomach for digesting. It delights the appetite a little, but only seems to bestow pleasure for as long as it is held in the throat;[*] once it has passed into the bowels, there ceases to be any difference between foods. And after all this, the eater's soul is not satisfied: whether he again wants what he has eaten, and the wise man is just as unable as the foolish one to live without food, while the poor man seeks nothing but how he can support the organism of his own body and avoid dying of starvation; or because the soul attains nothing useful from the refreshment of the body, and food is common to both the wise man and the fool, and the poor man goes where he sees there is wealth.[*]

However, it is better for this to be understood as being about the churchman who, learned in the heavenly Scriptures, has *all his labor in his mouth and his soul is not filled,* as he always wants to learn. And what gives the wise man the advantage over the fool is that, though he knows himself to be poor (the poor who is called "blessed" in the Gospel[*]), he is hurrying to grasp the vital things. He is walking the constricted, narrow way that leads to life.[*] What he is poor in is evil works. He knows where Christ, who is life, dwells.

6.9 The sight of the eyes is better than one walking in soul. But this also is vanity and presumption of spirit.

Symmachus has interpreted this clearly, saying: "It is better to exercise forethought than to walk as one pleases." That is, it is better to do everything in accordance with reasoning, which is the eye of the soul,* than to follow the desire of the heart—that is what *walking in soul* means, just as Ezekiel said: "Those who walk in the desire of their own heart."*

Alternatively, he is finding fault with the proud, self-satisfied person and is saying that the man who foresees all things is better than one who is pleased by nothing but what he himself has done; than whom nothing is lower, and emptier than any wind.

On the other hand, here too Aquila and Theodotion have interpreted *presumption of spirit* as "grazing of the wind,"* where Symmachus has "an affliction of the spirit." Furthermore it should be realized that among the Hebrews both spirit and wind are denoted by the same word, namely *ruha.**

6.10 What is there that is to come? His name has already been called and known, because he is a man, and he will not be able to be judged with one stronger than himself.

This is a clear proclamation of the coming of the Savior, because he who will be was already called by his name* in the Scriptures before he could be seen in the flesh and known to the prophets and saints of God as being a man.* And in accordance with the fact that he is a man, he would not be able to compare himself with the Father, and would say in the Gospel: "The Father, who sent me, is greater than I."*

This is why it is laid down also in what follows that we are not to enquire further than what has been written for us about him; that a man should not want to know more than what Scripture has attested. For as we are ignorant about our own condition and our life passes by as a shadow, and future events are uncertain, it is not good for us to enquire into things too great for our capacity.

Some believe that what is signified in this place is that God already knows the name of all those who will exist and are to be clothed in a human body; and that man is unable to reply in the face of his maker, as to why he was made this way or that.* For the more we seek, he says, the more our vanity and useless words are displayed; and it is not that free will is removed by God's foreknowledge, but that there is an antecedent cause for each and every thing being as it is.

CHAPTER 7

6.11 Because there are many words increasing vanity.

7.1 What is there more for a man? For who knows what is good for a man in life, and the number of the days of his life of vanity? And he will make them as if a shadow, because who will announce to a man what is after him under the sun?*

A human being, he is saying, is unaware of his own condition,* and whatever he thinks he knows and discerns, he is seeing it not as the truth of the matter is, but in a mirror, in shadow, in representation;* he is ignorant of the future, and "in much speech does not escape sin."* He should impose silence on his mouth and believe that he of whom it is written has come, without enquiring into the magnitude, form, and manner of his coming.

7.2 A name is good above good oil, and the day of death is above the day of his birth.

Consider, O man, he is saying, your brief days; soon your flesh will disintegrate and you will cease to exist. Make yourself a lasting reputation,* so that your name will delight posterity, as a fragrance delights the nostrils with its scent. In the light of the fact that it is Hebrew usage to call good perfume "oil," Symmachus has translated this with clarity: "A good name is better than sweet-smelling perfume."

As to *and the day of death is above the day of his birth,* he is either pointing out that one's departure from this age, freed from tribulations and from the uncertain condition of life, is better than one's taking on all that, at one's entry into the world; or else that at our death our character is known, whereas at the outset, at our birth, it is not known what it will be. Another possible meaning is that birth fetters the freedom of our soul in a body, and death[34] releases it again.*

7.3 It is better to go to a house of mourning than to a house of entertainment, in which is the end of every man,* and he who is alive will give to his heart.

It is more beneficial to go to a funeral ceremony than to a house of entertainment, because there the presence of the corpse reminds us of our condition and of human frailty, whereas in the enjoyment of an entertainment we lose any fear we seemed to have. Symmachus's translation of the end of the sentence is clearer: "And he who is alive will mind his attitude."

This proves that above,* where he seemed to be approving of food and drink, he was not putting pleasure before everything else, as some wrongly suppose, but saying that in comparison with avarice and excessive parsimony, it was a positive thing, albeit brief, if someone enjoyed his own wealth even for the moment.* If he had thought that eating and drinking were of any importance, he would never have preferred the sadness of mourning to the entertainment of a festive occasion.

7.4 Anger is better than laughter, because the heart will be improved in the sorrow of the face.

Laughter relaxes the mind; anger rebukes and corrects it. We should be angry[35] with ourselves on any occasion when we sin, and we should also be angry with others.* "The mind will be improved by the sadness of the face," as Symmachus translates it. Hence: "Woe to those who laugh now, for it is they who shall mourn."*

7.5 The heart of the wise is in the house of mourning, and the heart of the unwise is in the house of happiness.

"Blessed," said the Savior, "are those who mourn, for it is they who shall be comforted."* Samuel mourned for King Saul all the days of his life;* Paul says that he is mourning over those who had refused to repent after all sorts of sins.* So the heart of a wise man should go to the house of the sort of man who will rebuke him if he does wrong, move him to tears, and prompt him to weep for his own sins, rather than going to the house of happiness, where[36] the teacher flatters and deceives him and is trying to gain his listeners' applause and congratulation, not their conversion. Such a teacher is praised:[37] rich in discourse, rich in words, he has had his fill, and that is how he is receiving his consolation.* The next sentences also agree with this explanation.

7.6, 7 It is better to listen to the rebuke of a wise man, more than a man listening to the singing of fools, because as the voice of thorns under a pot, so is the laughter of a fool. But this too is vanity.*

It is better to be rebuked by a wise man than to be deceived by the sweet talk of a flatterer. Similarly: "Wounds from a friend are better than ready kisses from an enemy."* Just as the *voice of thorns* burning under a pot produces an unpleasant noise, so too the words of a teacher who flatters his listeners, or urges them toward the cares of this world (rendered as "thorns"*), or prepares them for the fire which is to come, will be no good to them.

Where we put *as the voice of thorns under a pot, so is the laughter of a fool*, Symmachus translates: "For by the voice of the ill-informed, one is tied in bonds."* This gives the sense we put forward above, that at the voice of instructors like that a listener becomes further entangled, each being tied up in the bonds of his sins.

7.8 A false accusation distresses the wise man and will destroy the heart of his courage.

Understand here a wise man still in the course of progress, as in: "Reprove a wise man, and he will love you";* because a perfectly wise man needs no reproof, and is not distressed by any false accusation. Let us use this sentence on any occasion when we see a just, wise man undergoing false accusation* and being distressed by the injustice of a verdict, with no immediate help at hand from God. Where the Septuagint, Aquila and Theodotion have "destroy the heart εὐτονίας αὐτοῦ" (that is, "of his courage" or "vigor"), Symmachus, coupling the Hebrew word with his translation, has: "And *mattānâ,* a gift, destroys the heart"; this produces the sense written elsewhere as: "Bribes blind even wise men's eyes."*

7.9 The last part of a discourse is better than its beginning.

In making speeches, epilogues are better than the exordium,* as it is in the former that the speaker's anxiety comes to an end, and the latter is where it begins. Or else: The person who comes to the teacher and starts to hear his discourse is at the beginning, but the person hearing its conclusion has reached perfection and is the finished product.

It can also be understood as: While we are in this life, all we know is just the beginning; once "that which is perfect has come,"* we shall be among the final, finished products.

My Hebrew's comment, on this and the next sentence together, was: "It is better for you to consider the end of an affair than its beginning, and better to be patient than to be carried away by a frenzy of indignation."

We also learn from this short remark that there is no wisdom in people, as action is better than preambles; and that when the address is finished the hearer thinks over to himself what has been said, but when we have only just begun to speak he has so far received nothing useful.

*The patient man is better than one high in spirit.**

So that we should not suppose, from his concession above to anger: *Anger is better than laughter,** that it is passionate anger of which he is approving, he now comments that anger is to be done away with altogether. At that point he put anger as a means of rebuke for sinners, and of education for the young; here, though, he has curbed impatience. Patience, moreover, is not needed only when we are in difficulties, but in happier circumstances too, to prevent us from becoming unacceptably[38] elated. In my view the person now being called *high in spirit* is the opposite of the one called "poor in spirit"* in the Gospel, who is included in the Beatitudes.

7.10 Do not be hasty in your spirit so as to be angry, because anger rests in the bosom of fools.

The reason he is now saying *Do not be hasty in your spirit to be angry* is not that he is conceding that one is to be slower to anger, but that, by postponement, fresh, passionate anger is more easily calmed and can be dispelled. And, as anger is always coupled with overbearingness in its desire for retribution, he also said above* that *the patient man is better than one who is high in spirit* and who has now shown signs of a lack of wisdom: however powerful and wise someone is thought to be, he is proved unwise if he is bad-tempered, as *anger rests in the bosom of fools.*

7.11 Do not say: "What has happened, because earlier days were better than these?" For you did not ask wisely about this.

You should not prefer the past age to the present, because the one Creator of both is God. It is virtues that make the days good in one's lifetime, and vices that make them bad; so do not say that under Moses or Christ the days were better than they are now. Even in those days there were many unbelievers, and their days became bad; and nowadays there are many believers to be found, of whom the Savior said: "Blessed are those who have not seen, and have believed."*

Alternatively, you should live in such a way that present days are always better for you than past ones; otherwise, when you gradually begin to decline, you will be told: "You were running well; who hindered you from obeying the truth?"* And again: "Having begun with the Spirit, you are now ending with the flesh."*

Alternatively, do not say that the old times were better than now—the time of Moses than the time of Christ, and the time of the law than the time of grace. If you want to ask this question, you are acting unthinkingly, without seeing the difference between the Gospel and the Old Testament.

7.12, 13 Wisdom is good with an inheritance, and something more for those seeing the sun, because as is the shade of wisdom, so is the shade of silver; and what is more, knowledge of wisdom will give life to one who has it. *

A wise man with wealth has a greater reputation than one merely wise. Some lack wisdom, some wealth; one wise but not rich can admittedly give good teaching, but can sometimes not provide what is being asked for. That is why he says: *As is the shade of wisdom, so is the shade of money;* that is, money also sometimes gives protection, just as wisdom does. Then, so as not to seem to have been derogatory about wisdom by linking it to an incidental good (for ownership of wealth, which is often greater in the hands of the unjust, is not under our own control) he deliberately shows that wisdom is the greater, by saying: *And more: knowledge of wisdom will give life to the one who has it.* What makes wisdom greater than wealth, he is saying, is that, even without any wealth, it gives life to the person who has possessed it.

An interpretation some put on this passage is that, according to them, he has put "inheritance" for a good way of life, through which "we are heirs of God and fellow-heirs with Christ."[*] Hence, the Preacher wants to teach the difference between those who deserve to see the sun of justice,[*] and who have wisdom with a good way of life, and those who have merely applied their attention to life and how to live it, without wisdom. Daniel, too, shows this, with: "Those understanding my words shall shine, like the luminaries of heaven" (or, as Theodotion translates it, "as the splendor of the firmament"); "but those who have carried out my words, as the stars of heaven."[*]

For the anagogical sense, however, we should take *shade of silver* (or *of money*) in the sense in which the talents and minas[*] in the Gospel parables are understood; so that when we are under wisdom's shade, and under the shade of that kind of "silver," "the sun shall not burn" us "by day, nor the moon by night."[*] As our life on earth is just a shadow,[*] it can also be said: "And the breath[*] of our face is Christ the Lord, to whom we have said 'Under his shadow we shall live among the nations.'"[*] All our protection in this life is like shade, whether of wisdom or, as said above, of silver, "until the day breathes and the shadows flee away."[*] Symmachus, typically, is clearer in this passage too: "As wisdom protects, so, similarly, does money." Moreover, the next sentence is clearly an exhortation to the study of wisdom.

7.14 See the works of God, because who shall be able to set right one whom God has twisted?[*]

Here, again, is Symmachus's translation: "Learn the works of God, because no one will be able to put right what he has shattered." That is, the holy Scriptures, or else mere contemplation of the elements, are a sufficient source for you from which to know and understand what has happened,* though not to inquire into the causes and workings of why every single thing has happened as it did, or ought to have happened otherwise than it did.

To take an example, suppose someone wished to ask why God says to Moses: "Who made a man deaf, dumb, seeing, and blind; is it not I, the Lord God?"* and said: "Why are people created blind, deaf, dumb, and so on?" On this subject we must take evidence from Psalm 17, where God is addressed: "With the pure you will be pure, and with the crooked you will be perverse,"* and must say that the Lord is holy with one who is holy, and perverse with one who of his own will has already been perverse, as in Leviticus: "If they walk contrary to me, I too will walk contrary to them in my fury."* That will also be able to explain why God hardened Pharaoh's heart:* just as one and the same working of the sun is to liquefy wax and to dry mud, the wax liquefying and the mud drying according to their own nature, so the single working of God in the signs in Egypt* softened the heart of the believers and hardened the unbelievers. They, through their hard-hearted impenitence, were "storing up wrath for themselves on the day of wrath,"* from the miracles which they did not believe, despite seeing them happen.

7.15 In the day of goodness, be in good, and in the evil day, see! And moreover God has made this one like that one, in order to speak so that a man cannot find anything after him.*

I know I have heard these sentences expounded in church, by one regarded as having knowledge of the Scriptures, as follows:

> While you are in the present age and can do something in the way of good works, labor, so that later on, on the evil day—that is, the day of judgment—you may be free from anxiety when you see others being tortured. Just as God has made the present age, in which we can prepare a harvest of good works for ourselves in advance, so too he has made the age to come, in which no opportunity is offered for good work.

He did seem to be carrying his hearers with him on this; but in my view the sense is different, as in Symmachus's translation: "In the good day be in goodness; but contemplate the evil day, as God has made this one like that one, so that a man should find no ground for complaint against him." Endure both good and bad, he says, as each happens to you, and do not suppose that there are only good kinds of things, or only bad kinds, in the world. The world itself consists of opposites: hot and cold, dry and moist, hard and soft, dark and light, bad and good.[*] This is God's doing, so that there should be scope for wisdom, and so that man should be left free will in choosing the good and avoiding the bad, to preclude his saying that he has been brought into existence by God as senseless or stupid; in fact, the reason God made opposites is so that man could not complain of his own condition.[*] At the same time, this testimony will be linked, as a sequel, to the previous words *who shall be able to set right one whom God has twisted?*

7.16 I have seen everything in the days of my vanity. There is a just man perishing in his justice, and an impious man long-lived in his wickedness.

The Savior said something like this in the Gospel: "He who finds his life will lose it, and he who loses his life for my sake will find it."[*] The Maccabees,[*] in the cause of God's law and justice, appeared to perish in their own justice, and so did the martyrs who shed their blood for Christ; while, conversely, those who in those days ate pork, and after the Lord's coming sacrificed to idols,[*] appeared to live, in this age, and to remain long-lived on account of their own wickedness. But God's patience is hidden, both in bringing tribulation on the saints for the time being, so that they receive troubles in their lifetime, and in not coming down on the sinners for their wrongdoing,[*] but keeping them back, like sacrificial victims—his purpose in this being to reward the saints with eternal good, and to inflict eternal evil on the sinners.

The Hebrews surmise that *the just perishing in their justice* are the sons of Aaron, who thought that they were acting justly when they made an offering of inappropriate fire,[*] and say that *the impious man long-lived in his wickedness* is Manasseh, who was restored to his kingdom after the captivity and subsequently lived a long time.[*]

7.17 Be not just greatly, and do not ask more, lest you become bewildered.

If you see someone harsh and pitiless toward all the sins of his brethren, never pardoning anyone who makes a sinful remark or who from natural laziness is occasionally sluggish, you can be sure that he is being more just than is just. Given that the Savior's command is: "Judge not, so that you are not judged,"[*] and that no one is without sin even if his life lasts for only a day,[*] justice without forgiveness for the frailty of the human condition is inhuman. So *be not just greatly,* because: "A heavy weight and a small weight are an abomination to the

Lord."* In philosophy, too, virtues are placed in the middle ground, and every departure from that, whether above or below, is regarded as a vice.*

As to *and do not ask more, lest you become confused,* or *bewildered,* he knows that our mind cannot grasp perfect wisdom, and he tells us that we ought to know the measure of our frailty. Lastly, when someone asked Paul a question beyond man's ability to know: "Why does he still find fault, for who resists his will?"* Paul's answer was: "Who are you, man, to answer back to God?"* and so on. If the man presented as asking this had heard from the Apostle the issues involved in his question, he would perhaps have been numbed by bewilderment, and he would have found the favor he had received useless—there is, according to the same[39] Apostle, such a thing as a gift which does the recipient no good.*

The Hebrews interpret the command *be not just greatly* as referring to Saul, who had compassion[40] on Agag, whom the Lord had ordered to be put to death.* This sentence can also be applied to the slave in the Gospel whose master had let him off, as being *just greatly* in refusing to let his fellow slave off.*

7.18 Do not act very impiously, and do not be a fool. Why will you die at a time not yours?

God says: "I do not desire the death of a dying man; just let him turn back and live";* accordingly, let us stop at a single sin. We must pick ourselves up after a fall. If, according to those who discuss remedies, the swallow knows, unprompted, how to restore her chicks' sight by means of celandine, and wounded roe-deer go and find dittany,* why should we not be aware that the remedy of penitence is available for sinners?

As for *do not die at a time not yours,* we know that Korah, Dathan, and Abiram, for their rebellion against Moses and Aaron, were engulfed by a sudden earthquake* and a large number of people were judged, even in this life and before the day of judgment, for the rehabilitation of others. This, then, is like saying: Do not add sins to sins, so as not to provoke God into bringing judgment on you even in the here and now.

7.19 It is good that you should keep that; and from this, too, do not let your hand go: that he who fears God shall come out of everything.

It is good to do good to the just; but it is not unjust to do good to sinners as well. It is good to support those who are of the household of faith;[*] but we are also enjoined to provide for anyone who asks.[*] Someone who fears God and imitates his Maker, who rains alike on the just and the unjust,[*] makes haste to do good to all without discrimination.[*]

Alternatively, because the events of this wretched life have their daily changes, the just man's mind should be as well prepared for adversity as for prosperity, and he should ask for God's mercy to endure whatever happens with equanimity. A God-fearing person is neither overjoyed by success nor crushed by adversity.[*]

7.20, 21 Wisdom will strengthen the wise man more than ten men with power who are in the city; because there is not a just man on earth who does good and does not sin.

The reason that wisdom strengthens the just person and exceeds the help for him of all the chief men of the city is that, however just someone is, he is still subject, while in this flesh, to failings and sins; he needs greater protection.

Alternatively, the ten who have power and have their place in the city are angels, who have reached the perfect number, the decad,[*] and assist the human race; but if one considers all the sources of help, the greater help is that of Wisdom—that is, of our Lord Jesus Christ.[*] After the angels said: "We healed Babylon and she was not healed; let us leave her and go away, each to his country,"[*] the master physician himself came down and healed us by the touch of his hem,[*] when we were blood-spattered, soaked in the gore of our sins, and had spent all our property on doctors. It was *in the city,* that is, in this world, that he healed us, and *strengthened*—or as the Septuagint has it, "helped"—*the wise man;* for: "To any that has, it shall be given and added to him."[*] Wisdom came in person, because mankind, set in sins and stuck in deep⁴¹ mire, was in need of greater help.

Alternatively, he had said above that one must do good both to those of the household and to those outside it, so someone could have replied: "If I do want to do good to everyone, I have not the resources to do so. The just man cannot have that much wealth; it is sinners who are usually much better off." That is why he is now saying: Those you cannot help financially, help with advice, and soothe them with consolation, because for someone in difficulties wisdom can provide more than the greatest powers imaginable. And do even that sensibly; because the scales of justice are large <and can weigh up>⁴² for whom to make provision, of how much, for how long, and of what kind, whether financially, or by way of consolation.

7.22, 23 Also do not give your heart to all conversations which they will speak, because you will not hear your slave speaking ill of you. For your heart frequently knows that you, too, have spoken ill of others.

Do what has been commanded. Strengthened by wisdom's help, prepare your heart for either bad or good things; do not care about what enemies are saying about you, and about public opinion. Just as a sensible man does not listen to a grumbling slave, or put an inquisitive ear to what the slave is saying about him in his absence—because if he does, he will be permanently distressed and roused to anger at his slave's muttering—so a wise man follows wisdom's lead and takes no notice of vain gossip.

He also uses another example to show that a just man should take absolutely no notice of what people say: "Just as your conscience acknowledges," he says, " that you have talked about many people and often disparaged others, so you should excuse others' disparagement." At the same time, he is teaching that one should not make facile judgments, or talk about the fleck in someone else's eye when one has a beam in one's own.[*]

7.24, 25 I have tried all these things in wisdom, and have said: "I shall be made wise"; and it has become further from me, more than it was. And deep profundity, who shall find it?

He says, as the Books of Kingdoms also testify,[*] that he has sought wisdom further than anyone else, and tried to reach the limit of it; but that the more he sought, the less he found it: he was sunk in the midst of darkness, and hemmed in by the murk of ignorance.

Otherwise: the more an expert in the Scriptures begins to know, the greater is the obscurity in them that daily arises and confronts him.

Alternatively: The contemplation of wisdom in this life presents us with only a representation in a mirror; when, in the future, I reflect on the knowledge of wisdom then to be revealed face to face,[*] I shall realize clearly that I was at this time a long way from that knowledge.

7.26, 27 I and my heart went about to know, and consider, and seek wisdom and reason, and to find out the impiety of the fool and the error of the unwitting. And I find bitterer than death the woman whose heart is a snare and nets, and her hands are chains. The man good in God's sight will be rescued from her, and the sinner will be caught by her.

Where the Septuagint put "I and my heart went about to know," Symmachus translated it: "I traversed all things[43] in my thought to know, to discuss and to investigate."[*]

So, because the Preacher had said above[*] that he had thoroughly tried everything in wisdom, and the more he looked for it the further it shrank from him, he is now saying that there was something else he had looked for in his own wisdom: what was the evil above all evils in human affairs; what was it that held the chief place in impiety, folly, error, and madness. He found, he says, that the chief of all evils was Woman,* both because it was through her that death came into the world, and because she catches the precious souls of men—"they are all adulterers, their hearts are like a furnace"*—and makes young men's hearts fly out.

Once she has sunk into a poor lover's mind, she drags him headlong without letting him look where he is going; like *a snare and a net,* she entangles the young man's heart; *her*[44] *hands are bonds.* For this, Aquila translates: "her hands are tied" (the Hebrew word is *assurim**), because she can use persuasion, but not force; she cannot pull men to her against their will. The man who is just and good in God's sight will be rescued from her, but the sinner will be caught and taken off to his death. We are not to suppose that Solomon has given this view of the female sex without good reason; he is speaking from experience. That is just why he offended God: he was ensnared by women.*

So much for the literal sense. In the spiritual meaning, we either give all sin in general the name "woman" and "wickedness," because, in Zechariah, wickedness, in the shape of a woman, is sitting on a lead weight;* or we take "woman" as a metaphor for the devil, because of his feminized strength; or else for idolatry, and, to be more precise, for the heretics' church, which calls an unwise person gradually[45] to itself, to induce him to receive stolen loaves and stolen water*—that is, a false sacrament and polluted baptism.

7.28–30 See, this I have found, says the Preacher: one to one, to find the number that my soul still sought, and I did not find it. I found one person from a thousand, and I did not find a woman in all these. All I found was that God made mankind upright, and they themselves have sought many thoughts.**

Investigating everything carefully, he says, what I found was that in sinning little by little, and adding one offense to another, we produce a large sum of sins. All the translators are unanimous in putting λογισμός for *esebon;* the ambiguity of the Hebrew allows us also to put "number," "total," "reasoning," and "thought."*

Another question my soul asked, he says, was whether an upright woman was to be found; and though I could only find just a few who were good among the men, as few as one in a thousand, I was unable to find a single good woman, because they all led me into self-indulgence, not to virtue. Because the human heart is diligently disposed to wickedness from youth up,* and almost all have offended God, in this fall of mankind it is woman who is the more prone to fall.* As the Gentile poet has it:

> Ever fickle and changeable is woman;*

and the Apostle: "Ever learning, and never reaching a knowledge of the truth."*

So as not to appear to condemn the common nature of humanity, and to make God the author of evil in creating beings of a kind unable to avoid evil, he distinctly guards against that by saying that we were created good by God, but, let down by our free will, we slip by our own fault to the bad, while seeking after great things and entertaining all sorts of thoughts beyond our powers.

Alternatively: While taking daily account of every single thing, I could find no thought undisturbed by perverse external considerations. In a thousand men I found one true human being,[46] formed in the image of his Creator; and that not in an indiscriminate thousand, but in a thousand men—no woman could form part of that total—a thousand who had not gone near a woman, and who therefore remained entirely pure. All this, however, is to be taken metaphorically: that is, in a large number of studious persons perspiring in daily meditation, a pure thought, deserving of the appellation "man," is scarcely to be found. We can also take "thoughts" as "men," and "women" as "actions," and say that, with difficulty, a person's thought could be found that is pure; whereas actions, being physically controlled, are always mingled with some error.

The sentence translated above from Hebrew as *one plus one, so that the number may be found* was translated more plainly by Symmachus as: "to find the reckoning, one and one." Where we normally use an impersonal neuter pronoun "(*this* is what I looked for, *that* is what I wanted to find"), Hebrew expresses it in the feminine gender,* as in the Psalm: "One thing have I asked of the Lord, this will I seek after,"* with the same meaning as "one" in the neuter.*

CHAPTER 8

8.1 Who is as the wise man? And who knows the solving of a word?* The wisdom of a man will light up his face and the brave man will transform his appearance.

Above he had taught that it was difficult to find a good man, and he had struck out the ensuing counterquestion by saying that men are created good by God but fall into sins of their own volition.* Now he enumerates, almost boastfully, what kind of good thing God gave to man, namely, wisdom, reason, and insight, to know the hidden mysteries of God, and to enter into his secrets through the perception of the heart. Nevertheless, he is speaking obliquely about himself, because no one was as wise as he himself;* no one understood as he did the solving of problems,* and his wisdom was praised by all the people. This wisdom was not merely inward and concealed, but also it shone out on the surface of his body and the mirror of his face, and beyond all men he displayed sagacity of mind in his appearance.*

Where we have rendered: *Who is as the wise man,* the Septuagint translators put: "Who knows the wise?" And where we said: *And the brave man will transform his appearance,* they put: "And a shameless man will be hated for his face." In fact, there are many who profess wisdom, but it is difficult to discover anyone who can distinguish the wise man[47] from those who seem to be wise. And while there are very many who claim to be able to solve the hidden mysteries of the Scriptures, the person able to discover a true solution is rare indeed.

As for what follows: *The wisdom of a man will light up his face and the wicked man will be hated for his appearance,** we are able to explain it by employing the words of Paul: "However, we all, with unveiled faces, are contemplating the glory of the Lord,"* and of the Psalmist, who sings: "The light of your countenance, O Lord, has been marked upon us."* He does not here mean that the wisdom of man is different from the wisdom of God, which, although it is God's wisdom, begins to belong to one who has deserved to have it, as far as his capability allows. Every heretic and defender of false dogma has an impudent face; in fact, Marcion and Valentinus actually claim to have a better character than the Demiurge.* Even this would be to some degree tolerable, if what they were contending was that they hoped to achieve that, instead of claiming that they already had it.

8.2–4 I guard the mouth of the king and the speech of God's oath.* Do not hurry to go away from his face, and do not stand in an evil word,* because

he will do everything that he has chosen to do. Just as if a king; he holds the
power, and who says to him, "What are you doing?"

He seems to be teaching, like the Apostle,[*] that one must be obedient to kings and powers.[48] (This is especially the case with the Septuagint translators, who use the imperative mood: "Keep the commandment"); but I believe that what is meant here is the king about whom David says: "Lord, the king will rejoice in your strength."[*] And in another place, in order to signify the joint rule of the Father and the Son, the Scripture says: "God, give your judgment to the king and your justice to the king's son."[*] For the Father does not judge anyone, but he has given every decision to the Son.[*] The king, who is the son of God, is the son of the Father, the king. It is his commandments, therefore, that must be kept, and his will that must be carried out. This is also what is written in the Book of Tobit: "It is good to conceal the secret of the king."[*] He is especially warning us not to discuss the reason for every single command of God, but that the pious mind of a man should hurry to fulfill whatever he sees has been commanded. "Let his delight be in the law of the Lord."[*]

The Septuagint translated otherwise, saying: "From both the oath and the word of God do not hurry to walk away from the face of God." We are to know that the oath of God[*] is written in the divine books, and so we should not speak this oath, which by the word of God is sacred and secret, to just anyone, nor produce it in public, nor offer a quick opinion about it. And like Moses, you should not hurry to see the face of God, but hold back until he passes through and you may only see his back.[*]

Certainly, too, we should understand the next words: *Do not stand in an evil word,* etc., as being about a man who has been overcome by the error of heresy; or about a man who holds the faith of the church but nevertheless is overcome by sins, so that he is unfaithful. Do not persist in slander, nor in obscene language, in extravagance, avarice, or lust; if you do, the devil, the king of vices and sin, will work perdition in you, and will do whatever he chooses.

8.5 He who keeps the command does not know an evil word; the heart of the
wise man knows both the time and the judgment.

It must be noted that *he does not know an evil word* was used instead of *he will not allow an evil word,* or *there will be no evil word in him.* That is also the expression used about the Savior: "Who although he had not known sin, for our sake God made him to be sin."[*] In place of *word,* Symmachus has translated the phrase as: "He who keeps the command will not experience an evil thing."[*] What he has enjoined[49] is that the king's authority is to be maintained and that we should know what[50] he is ordering, and why, and when.

8.6, 7 Because there is a time and judgment for every matter. Clearly the affliction of man is great over him, because he does not know what will happen; for as it will be, who will announce it to him?

Although things may turn out differently, and the just man cannot know what will happen to him, nor learn the causes and explanations of individual events (for no one is cognizant of the future), nevertheless he knows that all things are made by God for the advantage of mankind, and that they are not put in place without his will. Yes, *the affliction of the human race is great,* because, as the poet says:

> The mind of man is unaware of fate and of future destiny.[*]

He hopes one thing, but something else happens; he awaits an enemy from one place, and is wounded by the javelin of someone else. Where the Septuagint and Theodotion have put: "Because the knowledge of man is great over him," the Hebrew reads "evil," not "knowledge"; because the Hebrew letters *resh* and *daleth* are similar except for a small corner,[*] they read *daath,*[51] "knowledge," instead of *raath,*[*] "evil."[*] One with an acquaintance of that language will be more aware of this.

Also, as for the last part of these lines, *Because he does not know what has happened; and who will announce to him what will happen after him?* we have now translated it word for word from the Hebrew,[*] so that we may understand it to have a second meaning: we clearly cannot know either what is past, or what is to happen as it will be.

8.8 For there is no man having power in the spirit to restrain the spirit, and there is no one powerful in the day of death, and there is no release in battle, and impiety will not save the one possessing it.

Our soul is not in our power to prevent its being taken away from us, and when the spirit is departing to the dominion of God, it is useless to shut our mouths and try to hold back the fleeing life.[*] When death, the opponent and enemy of our life, arrives, we can obtain no armistice. Nor can even kings, who once in the present age were, in their wickedness, devastating all we possessed, lift a hand against death. We shall disintegrate into dust and ashes. So we should not mourn if we cannot know the future and are often oppressed by the wicked, who are more powerful, considering that all things end in death and that the proud and powerful man, who has devastated all things, is unable to retain his soul when it is seized.

Alternatively: the Spirit, who manages all things, cannot be restrained by any human being and cannot accept any conditions governing its spiritual action.* On that, there is also what was said earlier: *The spirit goes whirling in whorls.** In the day of death we are not powerful; in the day of life the enemy is easily avoided. Similarly, he who is in a war and does not have "the peace of God, which transcends all understanding,"* will not be sent out, in the way spoken of to the spouse: "The shoots you send out are a paradise with the fruit of apples."* As for *impiety will not save the one possessing it,* piety will, directly. Impiety can be named the devil, and piety, our Lord Jesus Christ.

8.9–11 I saw all these things and gave my heart to every work that is done under the sun, and a man dominated a man so as to afflict him. And then I saw the impious buried; and they came and went out from the holy place, and they were praised in the city, because they had done this; but this also was vanity. For because there is no speedy rebuke for those who do evil, for that reason the heart of the sons of man is filled within them so that they do evil.

I gave, he says, *my heart,* to gaze upon everything that takes place under the sun, and especially the fact that man has received power against man, to afflict and condemn whomever he wishes. And so when I directed my mind toward the consideration of these things, I saw the impious with such a great reputation at their death, and buried in such style, that they were judged saints on the earth—men who in their lifetime were judged to be worthy of the church and the temple of God, and who, furthermore, walked in a puffed-up manner and were praised for their evil deeds. "For the sinner is praised in the desires of his soul and he who works iniquities is blessed."* The reason this happens is that no one dares to rebuke the sinners, nor does God punish their wickedness at once, but he defers punishment while he waits for repentance. However, the sinners persevere in their wickedness because they have not been convicted and rebuked immediately, and believe that there will not be a future judgment at all.

We can use this testimony against the bishops who have received power in the church and cause people to stumble, when they ought to have been teaching them and inciting them to better things.* These men are frequently praised in the church after their death, and are publicly pronounced "blessed," whether by their successors or by the people, for actions which did not deserve approval. And so this also is vain, because their reputation does not correspond with their actions, nor are they rebuked immediately as they sin, as no one dares to accuse a more important man. Therefore, in the guise of saints or of blessed men, walking in the precepts of the Lord, they redouble their sins. An accusation against a bishop is difficult, as even if he has sinned, it is not believed, and if he is convicted he is not punished.

8.12 Because the sinner does evil a hundred times and it is postponed for him, I learn from this that there will be good for those fearing God, those who will be afraid from his face. *

From the statement that God gives scope for repentance to the man who sins a great deal—that being what *a hundred times* means—and does not punish a man at once in his wickedness, but waits for him to turn back from his iniquity, I understand how kind and merciful God will be toward those who have a fear of him and tremble at his word.

Symmachus translated this verse in this way: "For the wicked sinner died, although patience was granted to him. Furthermore, I know that it will go well for those who fear God, who have been afraid from his face; however, the wicked man will have nothing good, nor will he survive for a long time, because he did not fear the face of God."* It is obvious what Symmachus was translating. Thus, it must be said that the Hebrew word *maath,** which the Septuagint translated "from then," and we have put as a *hundred times,* is translated by Aquila, Symmachus, and Theodotion as *he died,* making it: "He, who sinned and did evil, died." That is, "in that he sinned, he, at once, died."

However, if we follow the Septuagint translators and read: "From then" in place of *he died,* the sense, according to some, will be: The sinner is not sinning for the first time when he is seen to do a sin, but he has already sinned before: "For the sinners have been mad from the womb, they have gone wrong from the belly";* and they wonder how what follows, "they have spoken lies," can be explained; for the natural meaning—that little sinners tell a lie the moment they are ejected from the womb—does not seem to make sense.*

8.13 And let the impious man not have a good thing, and let him not prolong his days like a shadow, he who is not afraid from the face of God.

He calls down a curse on those who lack the fear of God, and he prays that they should not be kept waiting long for their punishment, but be at once taken away by death and receive the tortures that they deserve. The Apostle also says something similar: "If only they would be cut short, those who disturb you."* And elsewhere: "Alexander, the coppersmith, caused me much harm: the Lord will repay him according to his works."* It is questionable how merciful these remarks are.

This is an accurate rendering of the Hebrew sense, but the Septuagint translators (beginning from what seems a different sense), said: "And I recognize, that there will be good for those fearing God, so that they are afraid from his face, and the impious man will not have anything good, and he who is not afraid from the face of God will not prolong his days in the shadows." If one follows them, one will be able to say this: "Yes, what I have dealt with just above will happen; nevertheless, I recognize most clearly that it will be well for those who are afraid from the face of God: 'For the face of God is upon those doing evil things,'"* *and it will not be well for the impious man; for he is not afraid from the face of God and he will not prolong his days in the shadows*—that is, the days of his life, which are like a shadow to the living. It is not the case that those who live a great time *prolong their days;* it is those who make them great by the value of their good works. Hence, even Jacob, confessing himself as a sinner, said: "Few and evil are my days."* And the writer acknowledges this in the Psalm: "My days," he says, "have declined like a shadow and I have become like the hay of the field."* This is not because he sought long life in the present, in which our whole lifetime is brief, a shadow and an illusion: "For man walks in an illusion";* but because he is afraid about the future, that the length of his life, where the true life is, might be cut short.

8.14 There is a vanity that happens upon the earth, that there are the just to whom the deeds of the impious apparently apply, and impious men to whom the acts of the just apparently apply. I said that this also is vanity.
Among the other vain things that go on in the world with things turning out in different ways, I have also discovered that frequently things happen to the just that ought to have happened to the impious, and the impious live so fortunately in the world that one would believe them to be perfectly just. The Gospel will give the example of the rich man in purple and the poor man, Lazarus.* The 72nd Psalm* also treats the question of why sometimes bad things happen to the just and good things to the impious.

Where we have put: *There is a vanity that happens upon the earth,* the wording of Symmachus's translation is plain: *It is difficult to know what happens upon the earth.* The Hebrews infer that the sons of Aaron are the just to whom bad things happen, and that Manasseh* is the impious person, who gains the rewards of the just, because the sons of Aaron perished while sacrificing, and Manasseh, after so many evil deeds and captivity, was restored to power.

*8.15 And I praised happiness because a man has nothing good under
the sun, except to eat, and to drink, and to be happy. And that will be the
outcome with him from his labor in the days of his life, which God gave him
under the sun.*

We have interpreted this amply above,[*] and now we say, cursorily,
that he prefers the pleasure of feasting and drinking (albeit brief and
soon to be ended) to the distresses of the present age, and to the
things that seem to occur unfairly in the world; because all it seems
that a man can gain from his own labor is the enjoyment of some slight
refreshment.

However, this interpretation, if taken literally, will make
those who are fasting, starving, thirsting, and mourning, whom the
Lord calls "blessed" in the Gospel,[*] appear pitiable. So then let us
understand both the *food* and the *drink* spiritually,[*] and, as well as
those, the *happiness* as that which we are hardly able to discover in the
labor of our life. That these words should be understood as we have
said is shown by his words in the next sentence:[*] *I gave my heart that I
might see wisdom and activity,* because clearly men are active upon the
earth, and by day and night they are involved in meditation upon the
Scriptures, so that frequently sleep escapes their eyes in favor of the
investigation of truth.

*8.16, 17 For this reason I gave my heart to know wisdom and to see the
activity which has taken place upon the earth. Because both in day and in
night he is not seeing sleep in his eyes. And I saw all the works of God, that
a man will not be able to find the work that is carried out under the sun, at
which a man worked to seek it, and will not find it. Because even if a wise
man says that he knows, he will not be able to find it.*

He who seeks the causes and explanations of events, why this or
that has happened, and how the world is directed with its differing
outcomes—why one person is born blind and crippled, while another
has sight and health; why this man has poverty, that man has riches;
this one is noble, that one undistinguished—such a man achieves
nothing but to be merely tormented by his own investigation,[*] and to
have the inquiry acting as torment, yet still not find what he seeks; and
when he claims to have found out, he is then at the starting point of
his ignorance and is in deep error.

Nevertheless, he is incidentally pointing out that there are causes
for all things, and a just reason for the occurrence of every single
thing, but that these are hidden in mystery and cannot be grasped by
human beings.[*]

Chapter 9

9.1 I gave all this in my heart to consider things as a whole: that the just and the wise, and their works, are in the hand of God. Affection, too; and hate, too: there is not a man knowing everything in the face of them.

This is another passage more clearly translated by Symmachus, as: "I have set all these things in my heart to consider them as a whole, because* both the just and the wise, and their works, are in the hand of God. Further, man does not *know* about either friendships or enmities; in their view everything is uncertain, because similar things happen to everyone, just and unjust."

The sense, then, is: I have given my heart to this, too, and I wanted to know whom God loved and whom he hated. What I found was that, though the works of the just are in God's hands, they nevertheless cannot yet know whether or not they are loved by God; they waver in uncertainty as to whether it is for testing that they undergo what they undergo, or for punishment. Their knowledge, then, will be in the future, and everything is "in the face of them";* that is, knowledge about this is ahead of them, after they leave this life. Then is the judgment; now, it is the struggle. For the present it is an unsettled question whether anyone undergoing adversity is doing so through God's love, like Job, or through his hate, like so many sinners.

9.2 In all there is one outcome: for the just and for the impious, for the good and for the bad, both for the pure and for the unclean; both for the one who does sacrifice and for the one who does not sacrifice. The good man is as the sinner; the oath-taker as the one afraid of an oath.

Things neither good nor bad in themselves (called "indifferent" by secular philosophers,* as happening impartially to both the just and the unjust) worry all the unsophisticated: they wonder why these things happen as they do and so suppose there is no judgment, when in fact the decision on all matters is in the future, while everything here is uncertain.

In saying: *In all there is one outcome: for the just and for the impious,* the outcome he is referring to is that of suffering[52] or death. That is the reason why they do not recognize either God's love or hate for them.

The one doing sacrifice and the one not doing it, and the other pairs of opposites listed, are to be taken in the spiritual sense, as in: "A contrite heart is a sacrifice to God."*

*9.3, 4a This is the worst thing in everything that has happened under the sun: that there is one outcome for all. But also, the heart of the sons of men is filled with wickedness and there are errors in their heart, in their life, and after this to the dead. Because who is there who has fellowship toward all the living?**

Typically, Symmachus's translation of this is clearer: "But also the heart of the sons of men is filled with wickedness and with lewdness close to their heart in their life. But as to their last stages, they come to the dead; for who can remain alive for ever?" The text is repeating the same point that we dealt with just above: that although everything happens impartially to one and all, with no discrimination in their undergoing good or bad times—or, anyway, as we are removed from this world by an impartial death—we are nevertheless filled with errors, lewdness, and wickedness, and after all this are carried off by sudden death and can no longer have any association with the living.

Alternatively: shared sufferings oppress the just and unjust alike; this is why people are tempted to sin. Yet, after all the effort of their ignorant struggles, they go down to Hades.

9.4b There is ground for hope, since a live dog is better than a dead lion;

9.5, 6 because the living know that they are to die, and the dead do not know anything; there is no more reward for them, because their memory comes in oblivion. But both their love and their hate, and their zeal, have now perished; and there is no portion for them still in the age, in all that happens under the sun.

Because he had said earlier* that the heart of the sons of men is full of wickedness and lewdness, and that after all this everything is finished by death, he now completes and repeats the same point: while men are alive they can become just, but after their death no opportunity is offered for good work. A living sinner can be better than a just man who is dead, if he decides to change over to the just man's virtues.*

Or: Any utterly worthless pauper can be better than someone who used to vaunt his wickedness, power, and lewdness, and is now dead. Why? Because the living can, for fear of death, do good works, but the dead can add nothing to what they have once brought with them from life; and because everything is wrapped in oblivion, as is written in the Psalm: "I have been given over to oblivion, like one dead from the heart."* But their love, their hate, their rivalry, and all they could possess in the present age are ended by the coming of death. Then they can do no just action nor commit any sin; they can add neither virtues nor vices.

It is true that some counter this explanation by asserting that even after death we can both grow and decline: they understand[53] the words *they will have no portion still in the present age, in all that has happened under the sun* to mean that it is in this age, under the sun we see, that they have no fellowship; but under another age, the age of which the Savior says: "I am not of this world,"* under the sun of justice,* they do have such fellowship. They say that the view which argues that, after we have left this life, rational beings can still both commit offenses and earn merit is not excluded.

Alternatively, the Hebrew said that among his people the line *a dead dog is better than a live lion* is explained as meaning that someone still alive and teaching, however ignorant,[54] is better than a perfect teacher who is now dead. For example, he might take as a "dog" any ordinary teacher, and as a "lion" Moses,* or any of the other prophets.

We find this explanation unsatisfactory, so let us aim at higher things and apply the "dog" to the Canaanite woman who was told: "Your faith has saved you,"* and the "dead lion" to the people of the circumcision, as the prophet Balaam said: "Behold the people! It will rise up like a lion cub, and like a rampant lion."* Thus, it is we, from the nations, who are the live dog, and the people of the Jews, abandoned by the Lord, who are the dead lion. In God's eyes this live dog is better than that dead lion. We are alive and know the Father, Son, and Holy Spirit; they are dead and know nothing. They have neither promise nor reward to look forward to; their history is at an end. Neither do they themselves remember what they should have known, nor does the Lord any longer remember them. The love with which they once loved God has perished, and so has the hatred of which they boldly used to say: "Do I not hate those who hate you, O Lord, and did I not waste away over your enemies?"* Their zeal, too, which was shown by Phineas,* and which made Mattathias's knees shake,* has perished. It is evident, too, that *there is no portion of theirs in the present age;* they cannot say: "My portion is the Lord."*

9.7, 8 Go, and eat your bread in happiness, and drink your wine in good heart, because your works have now pleased God. Let your garments be white all the time, and let oil not be lacking from your head.

Before discussing details, we must briefly summarize everything down to *like fish that are held in a grievous catch, and like birds that are*

caught in a noose, similarly will the sons of men be caught in the grievous time
when it falls suddenly upon them,* so that the sense in which the whole
passage is meant can become clear.

In an earlier section he had already said that after their death
people fall from the hearts of the living,* and that no one held them
in either affection or hatred—compare the poet's:

> No strife is there with the dead, with those bereft of
> the air above*—

and that they can do no more under the sun. Now he stages a pres-
entation, as it were, of people's misguided habit of encouraging each
other to make the most of the good things of this world, putting on a
prosopopoeia* in the style of orators and poets: "Man," he says, "as

> there is nothing after death, and death itself is nothing,*

listen to my advice, and enjoy yourself while you're still alive: life is
short, have lavish dinners, drown your worries in wine, and realize that
it was all given you by God to use. Go about in smart white clothes; have
your head scented with fragrances; enjoy the embraces of any women
you like. Life doesn't mean anything—and it is short; career through
it in meaningless, short-lived pleasure. You won't have anything but
this to enjoy; grab anything you might find fun—and hurry, or it might
be over. You must not be frightened of the silly stories about having
to render itemized accounts in Hades of all the good and bad things
you've done, because there isn't any wisdom in death; there isn't any
consciousness, once this life has disintegrated."

"That," he says, "is what an Epicurus* would tell you, and
so would Aristippus,* the Cyrenaics,* and the rest of the herds of
philosophers; but I have gone over it all thoroughly for myself, and
I find that everything happens by God's decision, not haphazardly, as
some people mistakenly think, with fortune playing a game of chance
in human affairs."

A fast runner should not suppose that any running he does is
his own; the strong man is not to be cocksure about his own strength;
the wise man is not to suppose that being sagacious is the way to amass
wealth and resources, nor the eloquent scholar that he can find favor
with the public by eloquent scholarship; everything takes place under
God's management. If God does not rule everything by his own will,
and "build the house, those who build it have labored in vain; if he
does not guard the city, those who guard it stay on watch in vain."* So
it is not the case, as they believe, that there is only one outcome, and

that the condition of this life is a matter of chance. At a time when they are not reckoning on it,* they will be carried off by sudden death and come to the judgment. Just as fish are caught with hook and with nets, and as birds, with the freedom of the air, are tied unawares in a noose, so human beings will be taken off to the eternal punishment they deserve, once sudden death and judgment have come upon those who thought that everything was veering about at random.

That, then, is the general sense, in the brief summary we have chosen to make of the topic as a whole. We must now interpret it in detail, with the Preacher now speaking in his own person, not in the assumed character.

Go, eat your bread in happiness, and drink your wine in good heart, since your works have satisfied God.

As you have learned that everything is ended in death and there is no repentance in Hades, nor any access back to virtues, hurry while you are in this present age; make haste, repent, labor while you have time, for God is glad to receive repentance.

Alternatively, it is useful also when taken in the simple sense, as in: "Whether you are eating or drinking, or whatever you are doing, do it all in the name of God";* and elsewhere: "Drink wine sensibly."* One who overuses created things has no true *happiness* or *good heart.*

Better, though, is to take it in the sense: One whose works have been satisfactory in God's sight[55] will never lack the true bread* and the wine trodden from the vines of Sorek.* We have been given the instruction: "You desired wisdom; keep the commandments, and God will provide it for you."* So, let us keep the commandments, and we shall be able to find spiritual bread and wine, both. However, one who does not keep the commandments, and boasts of his plentiful supply of bread and wine, is told by Isaiah: "Also, lest you should say 'I know it,' you have neither found it out, nor do you know it, nor from the beginning have I opened your ears. For I know you are utterly contemptuous."* What is said in the Septuagint version: "Come, eat your bread in happiness," is the voice of the same Preacher who in the Gospel also says: "Anyone who thirsts, let him come to me and drink,"* and in Proverbs: "Come, eat my loaves and drink my wine."*

Let your garments be white all the time, and let oil not be lacking from your head.

Be personally clean,[56] he is saying, and be merciful. Or else: There should be no occasion on which you do not have white clothes— be sure you are never dressed in dirty clothes. The sinful people are described as wearing dark clothes for mourning;[*] but you, put on light,[*] not the curse written about Judah: "Let him wear a curse, as a garment."[*] Put on "bowels of compassion, kindness, humility, meekness and patience."[*] And: "When you have been stripped of the old man with his works, put on the new man who is renewed"[*] from day to day.

As for: *and let oil not be lacking from your head*, one must know that the nature of oil is both to feed a lamp, and to relax the labor of the weary. There is a spiritual oil, the oil of exultation described in the Scripture: "Therefore God, your God, has anointed you with the oil of exultation above your fellows."[*] With this oil, our countenance is to be made glad;[*] with it, the fasting man's head is to be anointed,[*][57] something the sinners cannot have. To them is said: "There is no liniment to put on, nor oil, nor bandages";[*] they have the opposite kind of oil, which the just man detests, in the words "The oil of the sinner shall not smear my head."[*] This is the oil the heretics have, and they want to pour it over the heads of those they have deceived.

9.9 See life with the woman whom you have loved in all the days of your vanity, which have been given you under the sun in all the days of your vanity, because this is your portion in life and in the labor in which you labor under the sun.

Pursue wisdom and knowledge of the Scriptures, and link that to you in the marriage spoken of in Proverbs: "Love her, and she shall keep you safe; embrace her and she shall encircle you."[*]

Days of vanity means "days of this wicked age," on which the Apostle also has something to say.[*]

As for: *See life with the woman whom you have loved*, it is said with two meanings, either: "Both yourself, and your wife with you, see and consider your life"—because you will not be able to see life on your own, without such a wife—or: "Consider and see them both—your life and your wife—in the days of your vanity."

His command to seek, during *the days of our vanity*, the true life wedded to wisdom, was an apt one: if we should be able, during this shadowy life, to find the life that is true, that is our portion, and the fruit of our labor.

9.10 Everything which your hand finds to do, do it with your valor; because in Hades, to which you go there, work, thought, knowledge, and wisdom do not exist.

Do whatever you can now, and labor, because when you go down to Hades there will be no scope for repentance. Something similar is also enjoined by the Savior: "Work while it is day; night will come, when no one will be able to work."* On *in Hades, to which you go there,* note that you are to believe that even Samuel, truly, was in Hades,* and that before the coming of Christ everybody, however saintly, was held under the law of Hades.* However, we have the Apostle's testimony that after the Lord's resurrection the saints are certainly not held in Hades; he says: "It is better to be set free and to be with Christ,"* and one who is with Christ is certainly not in Hades.

9.11 I turned and saw under the sun that the race does not belong to the swift, nor the battle to the strong, nor bread to the wise, nor wealth to the sagacious, nor favor to the learned; because time and the outcome confront them all.

One who is chained in iron fetters and weighed down with heavy bonds of lead—"because wickedness is sitting on a lead weight"*—and who says, in the Psalm: "They are loaded down on me like a heavy load,"* is not fit for the race spoken of in "I have finished the race, I have kept the faith."* However, even an unencumbered person, whose soul is not weighed down is still unable to reach the finish line without God's help. When the battle with the opposing powers takes place,* the one meant in the Scripture "Sanctify war,"* he will not be able to win by his own powers, strong though he may be. Even one who is perfect and wise among the sons of men will not be able to have the living bread of heaven* except at the summons of Wisdom: "Come, eat my loaves."* There are riches of which the Apostle says: "To become rich in good works,"* and elsewhere: "You have become rich in all discourse and in all knowledge";* so we must know that the sagacious man cannot amass these riches without having received them from God, whose riches they are. This wealth is also what is mentioned elsewhere in "The ransom of a man's soul is his real wealth."* Grace, too: however learned a man is, he will not be able to find grace unless it has been granted by God as a concomitant of his learning. Knowing this, Paul, too, said: "I have labored more than all; though it was not I, but the grace that is in me,"* and again: "His grace in me was not without effect."* At the end, man does not know when the time is to come at which the differing outcome and end of everyone is to ensue.*

This was in the anagogical sense.* To expound it in a simpler way, this passage agrees with the Epistle to the Romans: "Because it is not a matter of one's will, or one's running, but of God's mercy."*

The words *The wise do not have bread* are borne out daily by the example of the many who lack the necessities, despite their great wisdom.

The learned do not have favor: in the church, one may see all the most totally ignorant men flourishing. Because they have cultivated an unabashed expression and achieved glibness of tongue without considering what they are saying, they think they are sagacious and scholarly—especially if they have a following with the public, which mainly enjoys, and is affected by, less serious talk. To the contrary, one may see a scholar in obscurity and disregard, suffering persecutions—not merely without popular favor, but wasting away in poverty and want. This happens because everything goes on in an undetermined condition, and the reward for one's deserts is not in the present but in the future.

9.12 And also man does not know his time. Like fish that are held in a grievous catch, like birds that are caught in a noose, similarly the sons of man will collapse in the bad time, when it has fallen suddenly on them.
We have said already above[*] that either sufferings or death come upon people unawares. In addition, we must know, with the parable, that "The kingdom of the heavens is like a net cast in the sea";[*] and, on the other hand, that heretics have a net by means of which they catch fish for destruction.[*] Their net is affable conversation, a smooth way of talking, pretended or put-on fasting, unimpressive clothes, and assumed virtues. But if they start discussing higher things as well, lifting their face upward and seeking the heights of God, they are setting their noose up high. Just as fish and birds are quickly caught in such a net, and in a noose like that, so will it be[58] when "wickedness is multiplied and many men's love has grown cold,"[*] and "signs and portents happen, such that, if possible, even the elect are led astray."[*]
We must know that even the churchmen called "sons of men," who are of limited faith, can fall quickly. Also to be noted is that throughout the book, wherever the expression "sons of men" is used, the Hebrew has "sons of the man," that is, sons of *Adam.*[*] Almost all Scripture is full of this idiom, calling the whole human race "sons of Adam."

9.13–15 But I have also seen this wisdom under the sun, and it is great with me: there was a small city and few men in it, and a great king came to it and surrounded it and built a great siege-engine against it; and he found in it a poor and wise man, and this man saved the city in his wisdom; and man has not remembered that poor man.
Although others say that everything is uncertain and that the just person has no advantage over the unjust, here is another way in which I have confirmed that wisdom is the most important thing.

It frequently happens that there is a small city and there are few inhabitants in it, and it is besieged by an enemy force too big to count. The people inside are starving to death in the siege, when suddenly, against anyone's expectation, an obscure, poor person is found who has greater wisdom than all the rich, great, powerful, proud people who are panicking at the danger they are in from the siege. This man thinks, investigates, and discovers how to rescue the city from its troubles. Alas for men's ingratitude and forgetfulness! Once they are freed, once their imprisonment is over and liberty is restored to their country, no one remembers that poor, wise man, and no one thanks him for saving them; instead, they all honor the rich who could do nothing to help them in their peril.

The Hebrew put a different interpretation on this passage: The small city is a human being, called a "smaller world" by philosophers too.[*] The few men in it are the members comprising the man himself. When the great king—the devil—comes against it and tries to find a point through which he can break in, there is found inside it, obscure, wise, and tranquil, the thought of the inner man; and that saves the city, which was hemmed in and besieged by the enemy. Once the man is rescued from danger of persecution, sufferings, or whatever adversity or sin it may be, the outer man, who is no friend to the poor, wise man, does not remember his inner man and no longer puts himself under his advice but enjoys his own independence again.

Alternatively: The small city and its men, few in comparison to the whole world, is the church. The devil, the great king—not that he *is* great, but that he vaunts himself to be so—keeps making war on it and hemming it in by siege, consisting of either persecution, or some other kind of pressure. In it, the devil finds a poor, wise man: our Lord Jesus Christ, who for us became poor,[*] and who is Wisdom itself;[*] and that poor man, in his wisdom, sets the city free. How many times have we seen the lion[*] sitting in ambush with the rich, that is, with the senators and princes of this world, contriving against the church but brought down by the wisdom of that poor man? When this poor man is victorious and the city has been restored to peace, hardly anyone remembers him or takes any notice of his commandments; they just give way entirely to extravagance and pleasures, and to the pursuit of wealth, which is not what sets them free in the hour of need.

9.16 And I said, wisdom is better above courage, even the wisdom of a poor man, which has been despised, and his words, which have not been heard.

No one remembers that poor, wise man when everything is happy, but instead they all, in a body, admire power and wealth; but I (in line with all the above interpretations) give greater honor to the wisdom they despise, and to words to which none of them thinks fit to listen.*

9.17 The words of the wise are heard in quietness, more than the clamor of one having power among fools.

Whenever you see anyone loud-mouthed in the church, stirring applause, raising a laugh, and working his hearers up into a happy mood by means of a kind of meretricious charm of language, take it that that is a sign of senselessness on the speaker's part, as well as on that of the audience.* *The words of the wise,* that is, *are heard in quietness,* in a restrained silence. A senseless person, however influential, with an uproar about him (whether that of his own voice, or from the acclaim of the public), is talking among the senseless.

9.18 Wisdom is better above equipment of war, and one man sinning will destroy much goodness.

Here, again, he is putting wisdom above courage, and saying that it is worth more in battles than the weapons of the men fighting; and if there is a single senseless person, however slight a nonentity, his folly frequently subverts great resources and wealth.

However, the Hebrew may be taken as reading *and he who commits one sin will destroy much goodness;** in that case we are also to understand this as meaning that because of one sin many acts of justice fall back into perdition, followed in turn by virtues; he who has one virtue has them all,* and he who has sinned in one thing is at the mercy of all the vices.*

Chapter 10

10.1 The flies of death pollute the oil of a compound; precious above wisdom and glory is a small foolishness.*

This is an example he has given of the comment above,* in which he said that through one stupid person many good things can be overthrown, because a bad man, mixed with good people, contaminates many, in the same way that flies, if they die in perfume, destroy both its scent[59] and its color. And because often wisdom is mixed with cunning and prudence contains malice, he teaches that we should search for simple wisdom and that it should be combined[60] with the innocence of doves;* we should be prudent toward what is good but simple toward what is bad. This means that it is more fitting for a just man to have a little bit of simplicity and to seem foolish, because of his great patience, while he is reserving vengeance for the Lord, than to employ malice by taking revenge right now, under the covering of prudence.

Alternatively: The flies that, according to Isaiah, rule a portion of the Egyptian river,* destroy the sweetness of the oil, leaving behind, in everyone who believes, the odor and traces of their filth. It is from these flies also that the prince of demons, Beelzebub,* was named. His name means either "the idol of flies," "a man of flies," or "one who has flies."

10.2, 3 The heart of a wise man is in his right hand and the heart of the foolish man is in his left. But even on the road, when the fool walks, his heart is diminished, and he says: "Everyone is unwise."

In the Gospel, too, it is taught that a wise man's left hand should not know what the right hand is doing.* When we are struck on the right cheek, we are not commanded to present the left cheek for striking, but the other cheek;* for the just man does not have a left side in himself, but there is only the right in him.* When the Savior comes to judge, the sheep will stand on the right but the goats on the left.* Also, it is written in the prophet: "The Lord knows the right-hand ways, but the perverted ways are to the left."* And so, the wise man always thinks about the coming age, which leads to the right. The unwise person, however, thinks of the present age, which is placed on the left. Following the same idea, the philosopher poet says:

> The right-hand road, which leads to the walls
>   of great Dis,
> on this is our road to Elysium; but the left road sets
>   working
> the punishments of the wicked, and sends them to
>   impious Tartarus.*

Our Firmianus,* recalling the fork in the road[61] in his splendid work *The Institutes,* is also mindful of the literal sense and has a very full discussion of the right and the left, that is, of virtues and vices.* Nor should we regard this remark as opposed to the saying "Do not deviate to the right nor to the left."* In our present context, "right" is taken as meaning "good," whereas in that context, what is being criticized is not so much the right-hand side as a deviation to the right. We are not to be wiser than it is necessary for us to be, because the virtues lie on the middle path and every excess is in the direction of vice.[*]

In the next sentence, where he says: *But even on the road, when the fool walks, his heart is impoverished, and he says, everyone is foolishness* or *foolish*, the meaning is: the foolish man hopes that all people will sin in the same way as he does, and he judges all men on the basis of his own character. Finally, Symmachus has translated it as: "But even when the fool is walking in the road, the unwise man himself suspects everyone of being fools." The Septuagint, however, turned the sense into: "Everything that the unwise person thinks is entirely vain."

10.4 If the spirit of one having power comes up over you, do not relinquish your place, because healing makes great sins rest.

The text now indicates the prince of this world, the ruler of darkness and of those working in the sons of unbelief, whom the Apostle also mentions.[*] If he comes up into our heart and our mind receives the wound of an evil thought, we should not give it any further room, but rather should fight against the wicked thought and be liberated from the greatest sin of completing the thought by action.[*] For it is one thing to sin in thought, but another to sin in action. There is also a text in a Psalm about this great sin: "If they do not master me, then I will be unstained and I will be purified from the greatest fault."[*]

Everyone else has translated the Hebrew word *marphe* alike as ἴαμα (that is, "health" or "healing"), but Symmachus rendered it to fit the sense,[*] with: "If the spirit of the prince assaults you, do not leave your position, because purity checks great sins." That is, if the devil should titillate your mind and incite you to lust, do not pursue the wicked thought and the alluring pleasure, but stand strong and inflexible and extinguish the flame of pleasure with the chill of chastity.

On this passage, my Hebrew here supposed some such sense as: If you receive a position in the world and are given a higher rank among the congregations, do not relinquish your earlier works, and do not start to neglect your former virtues and abandon your earlier labor, because the cure for sins comes from good living, and not from a swollen-headed, excessive self-importance.[*]

10.5–7 There is an evil that I have seen under the sun, like ignorance coming out from the face of a powerful man: a fool being set in great heights, and the wealthy sitting in a low place. I have seen slaves on horses and princes walking on the ground like slaves.

Where we have put: *Like ignorance coming out from the face of the powerful*, Aquila, Theodotion, and the Septuagint translated: "Like an

unintentional deed (that is, ὡς ἀκούσιον*) from the face of a prince."
Symmachus went on: "A foolish person put in great loftiness, whereas
the rich sit in low places."

He is remarking, then, that in this world he had also observed
the inequity that the judgment of God seemed to be unjust, and that
either through lack of awareness, or without his will, it is often the case
that (whether among the powers of the world, or in the leadership of
the church) those who are rich in speech and wisdom, and who are
also rich in good works, sit in low status, and it is all the unwise men
who hold the leadership in the church. This happens *from the face of the
one who holds power* in this world; he suppresses all the able and learned
men and does not permit them to appear among the congregations,
but promotes in the churches those whom he knows to be imprudent,
so that the blind are led by the blind into the pit.*

What follows is also to the same effect: *I saw slaves on horses and
princes walking on the ground like slaves.* Because those who are slaves of
vices or sin, or are so lowly that they are counted by people as slaves,
are puffed up with sudden status by the devil and wear down the public
highways with their fast ponies,* while all the noble or sensible people
are oppressed by poverty, and walk, traveling like slaves and serving.

My Hebrew expounded the powerful one and *the prince, from whose
face lack of awareness seems to come,* as God, because men believe, from
the unfairness of things, that he is not judging justly and equitably.
Others, again, think this should be linked with the previous passage,
so that the powerful one is the same as the one mentioned before
these two sentences: *If the spirit of one with power comes up over you, do
not relinquish your place.* Therefore we should not be saddened, if in
this age we are perceived as low-ranking people, knowing that it is by
the face of the devil that both fools are elevated and the rich are flung
down, and that slaves wear the insignia of masters, and princes walk
along in the low position of slaves.

We should note that here, as elsewhere, *horse* is taken in a good
sense, as in: "And your riding is salvation."*

*10.8 He who digs a ditch will fall into it, and he who demolishes a wall, a
serpent will bite him.*

The meaning of this sentence is partly simple and partly
mystical. Solomon himself also says elsewhere: "He who sets up a snare
will be caught in it."* And in Psalm Seven: "He has opened a cistern
and excavated it, and he will fall into the pit which he has made."*
The tearing down of the wall and its masonry are the doctrines of

the church and the teaching founded by the apostles and prophets. Anyone who dismantles them and wishes to pass by them is struck by a serpent in the very place which he is disregarding. Amos has written about this serpent: "If he descends into Hades, I will command a serpent and it will bite him."[*]

10.9 He who removes stones will be hurt by them, and he who splits pieces of wood will be endangered by them.

In Zechariah, too, there are sacred stones being rolled on the earth.[*] They do not stand firm in that position, but go past and hurry to depart from here, always striving for higher places. It is from these living stones that the city of the Savior is built in the Book of Revelation;[*] and the apostle also talks of the church being built of them.[*] So if any perverse person, through heretical ingenuity, takes away these stones from the building of the church, he will afterward suffer torments. Hence both Aquila and Symmachus, where we put: *He who removes stones will be hurt by them,* expressed it clearly as: "The person transferring stones will be torn to pieces by them; afterward, he will suffer torments."

However, the text simply says: *he who removes stones,* or, *he who transfers stones,* without adding the good or bad ones. Therefore it must also be understood in an opposite way: If a churchman, that is, a bishop or priest, following the Levitical code, takes away a stone from the house of a leper to be crumbled into dirt and ash,[*] he will feel pain even as he does so, because he is being compelled to take away a stone from the church of Christ.[*] He will say, following the Apostle: "Weep with those weeping, mourn with those mourning";[*] and: "Who is weakened and I do not burn?"[*]

Second, *He who splits pieces of wood will be endangered by them.* The timber of a heretic is unfruitful and his woodland is without useful fruit.[*] For this reason it is prohibited for a grove to be planted in the temple[62] of God,[*] and the useless scrap of shade from its leaves— that is, from words that are nothing but noise—is rejected. And so, however prudent and learned the man may be who chops up these trees with the sword of his speech, he will be imperiled by them, unless he takes great care; especially if what follows happens to him: *If his ax is blunted, and he has spoiled its edge*[*]—that is, if his argument has been found too weak, and it does not have a sharp edge with which to cut down all the opposing arguments, but in fact the core of his heart has been blunted—he will cross over to the opposite side and a perverse strength will reinforce him. This is the point of the Septuagint translation: "And he will be strengthened in his strength,* and the strong man's wisdom is excessive." He is saying: "He will begin[63] to have a strength and a wisdom that is excessive and does not help the person possessing it."

10.10 If his ax is blunted and is not as it was earlier, but spoiled, it will be reinforced with virtues, and the residue of strength is wisdom.

If, he says, someone sees that he has lost his knowledge of the Scriptures through negligence, and if his natural acumen has become dulled and confused,[64] he will by no means have remained the sort of person he had begun to be.

It does sometimes happen that when someone has a modest amount of knowledge, he becomes puffed up with pride; then he stops learning and reading, and, because nothing is being added to him, he gradually suffers diminution. Thus his mind is devoid of training,[65] and *his ax,* which had been sharp, *is blunted.* For leisure and idleness are a kind of rust to wisdom. So if there is anyone to whom this has happened, let him not despair of a curative remedy, but rather let him go to a teacher and again be instructed by him. Then, after labor, industry, and copious sweat, he will succeed in recovering the wisdom that he had lost. And this is what is said more clearly in the Hebrew: *He will be reinforced with strengths;* that is, by labor, sweat, industry, and daily reading he will achieve wisdom, and his strength will gain its end of receiving wisdom.

10.11 If a serpent bites in silence, there is also not more for the one having a tongue.*

This is the simple sense: A serpent and a detractor are equal. Just as the former, biting in secret, inserts venom, so too does the latter: disparaging someone in private, he pours the venom of his heart into a brother and is no better than a serpent. For while a human tongue* was created for blessing and for the edification of those close to one,* that man, by misusing his virtues in a perverse manner, makes his tongue like a serpent.

Otherwise: If the serpent, the devil, secretly bites anyone, and, unobserved, infects that man with the venom of sin, and if the person who was struck stays quiet and does not repent, and refuses to confess his wound to a brother and a teacher, the brother and teacher, who have the tongue for curing him, will not easily be able to help him.* If a sick man is embarrassed to confess a wound to his doctor, medicine does not heal what it is unaware of.

*10.12   The words of the wise man's mouth are grace, and the lips of an
unwise man will throw him down.*

Foolishness would do less harm if it were satisfied with its own
lack of education. As it is, though, it wages war against wisdom and
does not accept whatever good sense it sees in a learned man, because
it is stung by jealousy. For the wise person speaks words of knowledge,
words of grace, which can render a service to his listeners, but the lips
of the fool do not receive what is said in the way in which it was said. To
the contrary, they try to trip up the thoughtful man and make him the
same as themselves. In fact, the wise man really is thrown down head
first when he speaks in the ear of the thoughtless one, and his words
vanish in the depths of the abyss, so to speak. For this reason, blessed
is the man who speaks to a listening ear.*

*10.13, 14   The beginning of his words is unwisdom and the last word of his
mouth is grievous error. And the fool multiplies his words. Man does not know
what it is that has happened, and who will proclaim to him what will happen
after him?*

The discussion is still about the fool whose lips throw down
the wise man, or, according to another interpretation, make the
fool himself fall down. For the beginning and end of his discourse
are foolishness and grievous error (or, as Symmachus translated: "A
commotion and a certain inconsistency of words"). Without sticking
to his opinion, he believes that through the multiplication of talking
he is able to escape sin.* He does not remember the past and does
not know the future, but tosses about in ignorance and darkness,
promising himself false knowledge. He believes that if he multiplies
his words, that makes him learned and wise.

It is also possible to take this as being about the heretics, who,
instead of taking hold of the sayings of thoughtful men, prepare
themselves for confrontational debates and envelop the beginning
and ending of their speaking in vanity, commotion, and error. Since
they know nothing, they talk about more than they know about.

*10.15   The labor of fools will damage those who do not know how to go into
the city.*

Attach these lines, also, to what precedes. His point is either,
generally, about all the fools who do not know God, or, more
particularly, about the heretics. Read Plato, peruse the subtleties of
Aristotle, look carefully at Zeno and Carneades, and you will prove
the truth of the saying: *The labor of fools will damage them.* Those men

did seek truth with all earnestness, but because they did not have a guide and a pathfinder for the journey, and thought they could grasp wisdom through the human senses, they totally failed to reach the city about which it is said in the Psalm: "O Lord, you will scatter their likeness in your city."* For in his city, the Lord will scatter all the shadows and the various illusions and pretenses that they have put on in their various doctrines. About this it is also written elsewhere: "The rush of the river gladdens the city of God."* And in the Gospel: "The city placed upon a mountain cannot be hidden."* And in Isaiah: "I am the firm city, the city that is attacked."* All the wise men of this world, and the heretics also, try to attack this city of truth and wisdom, even though it is firm and strong.

What we have said about philosophers we must also think about the heretics, because they labor in vain and are crippled in their study of the Scriptures, since they walk in the desert and are unable to find the city. The Psalmist also mentions their error, saying: "They have lost their way in the desert and the waterless place, and they have not found the road to the city and to his abode."*

10.16, 17 Woe to you, O land whose king is a young man and whose leaders eat in the morning. Blessed are you, O land of which your king is the son of freeborn people and whose leaders eat in time, in strength and not in confusion.

He seems to be rejecting the leadership of the young and to be condemning extravagant judges, on the ground that in the first wisdom is weak on account of their age, and in the others even their mature age is weakened by pleasures. And, by contrast, he seems to be commending the leader of good character and liberal education, and to be proclaiming that judges are people who never put pleasure before the affairs of their fellow citizens, but are just compelled to take food as a necessity, only after much labor in the administration of the state.

However, to me, something holier seems to be concealed under the literal meaning. In Scripture, "young" is used to denote those who, in revolt from ancient authority and contempt of the hoary precepts of their parents, neglect the command of God and wish to establish traditions of men. In Isaiah, too, the Lord threatens the Israelites on this, because they did not want the water of Shiloh, which flows silently,* but diverted the old pool,* choosing for themselves the river of Samaria and the currents of Damascus.* "And I will make," he said, "young men their leaders, and mockers will be their masters."*

Read Daniel and you will find God called "the ancient of days."[*] Read the Apocalypse of John and you will discover[66] that the head of the Savior is white as snow and like white wool.[*] Jeremiah too is forbidden to call himself a young man because he was wise, and it was gray hair[67] that was reckoned as wisdom.[*]

And so woe to the land whose king is the devil, who is always eager for revolution, who in the case of Absalom rebels even against a parent,[*] who has, as his judges and leaders, those who love the pleasures of this world and, before the day of death comes, say: "Let us eat and drink, for tomorrow we will die."[*] In contrast, blessed is the land of the church, whose king, Christ, is the son of free parents, descending from Abraham, Isaac, and Jacob, and from the line of the prophets and all the saints. In them, sin was not the master, and for that reason they were truly free.[*] From them a virgin was born, even freer, the holy Mary, who had no shoot, no bud from her side, but her entire fruit burst forth into the flower[*] that says in the Song of Songs: "I am the flower of the field and the lily of the valleys."[*] The church's leaders also are the apostles and all the saints, who have as their king the son of free parents, the son of a free woman, not engendered from the slave-woman Hagar, but from the liberty of Sarah. They do not eat early or quickly, for they do not seek pleasure in the present age, but they will eat at their time, when the time of retribution has come, and they will eat *in strength, and not in confusion.* All the good of the present age is confusion; the good of the age to come will be everlasting strength. Something like this is said also in Isaiah: "Behold, those who serve me will eat; you, however, will hunger."[*] And again: "Behold, those who serve me will rejoice; you, however, will be ashamed."[*]

10.18 In laziness the floor will be brought down, and through weakness of hands the house will leak.

If we are lazy and tardy in doing good works, our house, the one that was built during our human condition, will be brought low; and so will the residence that we have in heaven. Every floor, which ought to support the high rooftop, will collapse to the ground and crush its occupant. When the aid of hands and virtues grows sluggish, all the storms from above burst forth upon us with a whirlwind of rain clouds.[*]

Additionally, what we have interpreted as referring to one person can be better taken as relating to the church, on the ground that through the negligence of its leaders all the height[68] of it collapses;

and it is just where there was thought to be a protective covering of virtues that there are temptations to vice.

10.19 They make bread in laughter, and wine so that the living can feast. And all things obey silver.

I consider that this is connected with the above as a continuation of it. Through the laziness and apathy of teachers, the church is brought low and the ridge of its roof collapses,* and its planks leak, as we explained above. Now, therefore, he is speaking about the same teachers. He had previously seemed to reproach them by asking: Why are they silent? Why do the bishops and priests appointed in the church not discharge their duty as teachers? Why do they not labor in the word and in instruction as Titus is admonished to do,* and as Timothy is told not to "neglect the grace which he had received through the laying on of hands"?* Instead, they consider that the point of their being priests and bishops is so that they can receive salaries, and so that dumb[69] teachers can gain the double honor that is due to those laboring in instruction and in preaching the word.

Now, by contrast, he is accusing those who do speak in the church and teach their congregations, but teach what the congregation is delighted to hear, because it flatters the sinner in his vice and excites a buzz from their hearers. Does it not seem to you that, when someone starts talking alluringly in church and promises the multitude blessedness and the kingdoms of the heavens, he is *making bread in laughter* and mixing wine for the joy of those drinking? This is either because those who teach are gaining wealth, food, and resources by promising delights; or because they are using gladness and joy to make the church's bread, which is the bread of those mourning, not laughing. "Blessed are those who are mourning, because it is they who will laugh."*

The next words, *all things obey money,* or *silver,* are to be taken in two ways: either that these learned men, after being enriched by flattery, hold absolute power over the congregations; or else, because silver is always taken to mean speech*—"For the utterances of the Lord are pure utterances, silver tested in the flame of the earth, purified seven times"*—what he is asserting is that the common herd is easily won over by the kind of eloquent speech that is composed in leafy language.

Alternatively: Those who have the bridegroom with them, and for that reason are forbidden to mourn and to fast,* *make bread in laughter.* Isaac received his name from this laughter,* and it is for the joy of those who drink it that they prepare wine. And so every holy man who, as Christ commanded, is a teacher of the church,* makes bread in laughter and joyfulness, and serves chalices of wine with rejoicing. The silver too, *which all things obey*, is the head of the household's five talents from the Gospel, and the two, and the one;[*] and the ten minas[*] entrusted to the servants for trade.

10.20 In your mind do not curse the king, and in the solitude of your bedroom do not curse the rich man, because the birds of the sky will carry your voice, and one having wings will announce your word.

Even the simple command edifies those hearing it: we are not to be overcome by anger and fury, and break out into cursing and slandering of kings and leaders, because it sometimes happens, against our expectation, that our words are reported to those whom we cursed, and we run into danger through our intemperate speech. The words *A bird of the sky will carry off your voice, and one having wings will announce your word* should be understood hyperbolically, just as we often say that even the walls themselves know what we say and will not hide what they hear.[*]

But it is better to understand the command in such a way as to know that we are commanded not only to say no chance word against Christ, but also not even to think any blasphemy or impious thought in our hidden hearts, whatever kinds of tribulation may grip us. And because we owe also to our neighbor the love that we show to Christ— "love the Lord your God," but also, "your neighbor as yourself"[*]—it is also commanded that, after our King, we should not lightly disparage the saints either. Nor should we slander with biting tongue those whom we see enriched with knowledge, wisdom, and the virtues, because the angels, who go around the earth and are the ministering spirits,[*] say in Zachariah:[70] "We circled the earth, and behold all the earth is inhabited and silent."[*] Like birds, they deliver our own words and thoughts to heaven.[*] What we think secretly is not hidden from God's knowledge.

Chapter 11

11.1 Let your bread go on the face of the water, because in multitude of days you will find it.

This is an encouragement to almsgiving:[*] one must give to everyone who asks, and do good without making distinctions. Just as one who sows on watered land awaits the harvest of his sowing, so one who is generous to the needy is sowing an actual loaf of bread, not just a grain of seed, in anticipation of its increase. It is a kind of investment: when the day of judgment comes, he will find much more than he had given.

Alternatively: In the case of anyone in whom you see the water referred to in "Rivers of living water shall flow from his vitals,"* you should not be reluctant to provide the bread of wisdom, reasoning bread, the bread of the word. If you do this frequently, you will find that your casting of the seed of teaching has not been in vain. There is also something similar, I think, in Isaiah: "Blessed is the man who sows over water where ox and ass tread,"* meaning that the teacher who sows on the watered heart of his listeners, in a congregation of people gathered from Jews as well as from Gentiles, is to be considered deserving of blessedness.

11.2 Give a portion to seven and even to eight, because you do not know what evil there will be on earth.

In Ezekiel, too, we read of flights of seven and eight steps up to the temple.* After the ethical Psalm, the one hundred and eighteenth,* there are fifteen step Psalms,* by which we are first educated in the law, and then, after completing the number seven, climb to the Gospel by way of the ogdoad.* This teaching, then, is that we should believe with equal veneration in both covenants, the Old as well as the New.

The Jews *gave a portion to seven,* with their belief in the Sabbath, but not to eight, because of their denial of the resurrection on the Lord's day. The reverse is true of the heretics Marcion,* Mani,* and all those who use their rabid mouth to rip up the old law: they give a portion to eight, by accepting the Gospel, but deny it to seven, by eschewing the old law. We, therefore, are to believe in both covenants; at this stage, we cannot yet imagine the deserved tortures, the deserved punishment in store for those—that is, the Jews and the heretics—who, while on earth, deny one or other of the two.

The Hebrews' understanding of this passage is: Keep both the Sabbath and the circumcision,* lest unexpected trouble come on you if, maybe, you fail to do so.

11.3 If the clouds are full they will pour rain on the earth. And if timber falls southward or northward, in the place where the timber has fallen, there it will be.

Keep the commandments that you have been set above, so that the clouds will pour their rain on you. Wherever you prepare your place and your future abode, whether to the south or to the north, that is where you will stay when you are dead.

Alternatively: The reason why we said above, *Let your bread go on the face of the water* and give to all who ask you, is that clouds, too, when they are full, bestow their riches on mortals; and that, like timber, however long you live, you will not live for ever. You will be uprooted by the sudden storm of death, like that of gales, and wherever you fall, that is where you will stay permanently, whether the last time finds you stiff and harsh, or mild and merciful.

Alternatively: "Your truth," it says to God in the Psalm, "is up to the clouds";* and in Isaiah, God threatens the sinful vineyard: "I will command the clouds not to shed rain on it."* Clouds, then, are the prophets and any holy man who has gathered several branches of learning in his heart and will then be able to rain down the precepts of his teaching, and say: "May my discourse be awaited like rain,"* and: *They will pour rain on the earth*—the "rain" being explained by: "Let the earth hear the words of my mouth."*

For the next words, *If timber falls southward or northward, in the place where the timber has fallen, there it will be,* let us take the parallel from Habakkuk: "God will come from Teman,"* for which other translators have given: "God will come from the south."* As far as my judgment goes, "south" is always taken in a good sense: hence, in the Song of Songs, there is the saying: "Get up, north wind"—that is, "withdraw, go away"—"and come, south wind."* So timber that has fallen in this life and been axed by its state of mortality has either sinned earlier, while it was standing, and will then be put[71] to the north; or, if it has produced fruit deserving the south, it will lie in a southerly direction. There is no timber which will lie neither north nor south. The text "I will say to the north wind 'Bring,' and to the south-west wind 'Do not hinder'"* has this same meaning; south and east winds are never commanded to "Bring," because those who are subsequently to be taken eastward and southward must be at the other points. Thus, the north wind takes its dwellers southward; and the south-west wind, eastward. Should they remain in their original positions, they cannot thrive.

11.4 He who watches the wind does not sow, and he who looks at the clouds will not reap.

He who considers whom to benefit, instead of giving to anyone who asks him, often misses one who deserves to receive.

Alternatively: He who preaches the word of God only at a time when the congregation is glad to listen, and when the breeze of acclaim is blowing favorably, is a slack sower and a lazy farmer. Even while things are going well, troubles mount without our being aware of them. The word of God is to be preached "in season and out of season,"* in its own course; and by faith's timing, a storm of opposing clouds is not to be taken into account. This is what the saying in Proverbs is about: "As rain that is violent and useless, so are those who abandon wisdom and praise impiety."* Heedless of clouds, unafraid of winds, we must sow even at the height of storms, and must not say: "That is a suitable time; this one is useless," because we do not know the way and the will of the all-controlling Spirit.

11.5 In the same way as you do not know what is the way of the breath, and like the bones in a pregnant woman's womb, so you will not know the works of God, who will do all things.

You are unaware of the way of the breath,* and of the soul, as it enters the baby, and you do not know the changes of the bones and the blood vessels in a pregnant woman's belly: how the human body develops from a worthless element into different forms and limbs, with one part (the fleshy areas[72]) growing soft, another hard (the bones), another pulsating (the blood vessels), and another connecting (the tendons), all from the same seed. In the same way, you will not be able to know the works of God, the Maker of all things.

From this he is teaching that one must not be afraid of things that are against one, nor make ill-informed decisions about the winds and clouds that we have mentioned above,* because the sower has to keep on in his own direction and course, reserving the outcome for the Lord's decision. "It is not a matter of wanting, nor of running, but of God's mercy."*

11.6–8 In the morning sow your seed, and at evening do not let your hand drop, because you do not know which is pleasing, this one or that. Yet each, as if one, is good: both sweet is the light, and good it is for the eyes to see the sun; because if a man lives many years, let him be glad in them all, and let him remember the days of darkness, that they will be very many. All that is to come is vanity.

Do not pick and choose to whom to do good; but even when you have done good, you are never to desist from the good work. Let the evening find the morning's justice, and the sunrise heap up the evening's mercy. It is not certain what work is more pleasing to God, and from what the harvest of your justice is stored up; it can happen that not just the one thing, but both, are pleasing to God.

Alternatively: your labor should be as great in your old age as in your youth. You are not to say: "I labored while I could; in my old age

I should have a rest," because you do not know whether it is in your youth or your later years that you are pleasing to God. Thrift in youth is no good if old age is spent in extravagance, because on the day when the just man strays, his previous acts of justice will be unable to free him from death.[*]

However, in either interpretation, if you always do good, keeping on an even course at all stages of your life, you will see God the Father, the *sweetest light;* you will see Christ, the "sun of justice."[*] Further, you may live many years and have all good things, or perform good works; but provided that you know that you are always going to die, and that you have the coming of the darkness always before your eyes, you will despise the present as being unstable, fragile, and fleeting.

Symmachus translated the end of this sentence as: "If a man lives many years and is glad in them all, he should also remember the days of darkness, because they will be many, in all of which it will come that he ceases to be."

Alternatively: In another passage of Scripture, God promises: "I will give you seasonal rain, and the late rain"[*]—that is, the Old Testament and the New—and I shall water you with the rain of each. Hence we are now also being admonished to read the old law without despising the Gospel, and to seek the spiritual meaning in the old covenant without supposing that in the evangelists and the apostles the literal sense is all there is to hear.[*] We are being told that we do not know in which covenant it is that knowledge and grace are the more bestowed on us; and that fortunate is the man who allies them both together and makes them as it were a single body. He who succeeds in this will see the light; he will see Christ, the "sun of justice."[*] If he has more years of life, he will spend them in the greatest joy and delight, possessing knowledge of the Scriptures, and will be impelled all the more to this labor by recollection of the judgment to come; because the endless time of darkness will arrive, and eternal punishments will be in store for those who have not sown *in the morning and at evening,* but have utterly failed to link them together. They have not seen the light, nor the Sun who is the source of that light.

CHAPTER 12

11.9, 10 Be glad, young man, in your youth, and let your heart be in good in the days of your youthfulness, and walk in the ways of your heart and in the seeing of your eyes. And know this: that God will bring you to judgment on all these things. And banish anger from your heart and remove wickedness from your flesh, because youth and folly are vanity. *

12.1 And remember your Creator in the day of your youth, before the days of evil come and the years approach in which you will say: "I have no will in them."*

In this section everyone's explanation has been different; there are almost as many opinions as there are people.* Hence it would be a long task—in fact it would take practically a whole book—to review everyone's suppositions and explain the arguments by which they have wanted to recommend their views. The judicious should find it enough for me to indicate the views, as one might depict the positions of the countries on a small map, showing the huge extent of the entire world and its surrounding ocean,* in a limited abridgment.

The Hebrews regard the command as relating to Israel. Israel is being told, they say, to enjoy its wealth before the time of captivity comes to it, and before it exchanges its youth for old age. It is to make full use of whatever seems delightful or pleasant to its heart as well as its eyes while it is available, but on the condition that it recognizes that it is to be judged on everything. It is to shun evil thoughts as well as desires, knowing that folly is associated with youth, and it is always to remember its Creator, before the coming of the days of its Babylonian and Roman captivity,* in which it will be unable to have any *will.*

The whole passage from *Before the sun darkens, and the moon, and the stars* down to the point where the text has *and the dust will turn into its earth, as it was, and the spirit will return to God, who gave it,** is explained by the Hebrews as being on the state of their own existence. This all being, as we said above, bitty and long-winded, we shall touch on it only briefly and summarily.

So: Be glad, Israel, in your youth, and do so-and-so (as said above), before the captivity comes and your own honor and glory leave you; before you are deprived of your judges and your holy men (which is what they want *sun, moon, and stars* to mean); before Nebuchadnezzar* comes, or Titus son of Vespasian,* summoned by the prophets, and before their prophecies are fulfilled,* on the day when the *guardian*-angels of the temple leave, and all the mightiest men in your army are thrown into disarray, and the utterances of your teachers are useless, and the prophets, who used to receive the illumination of their visions from heaven, go into darkness; when the *doors* of the temple *will be closed,* and Jerusalem will be brought *low,* and the Babylonians will come, summoned by Jeremiah's words* as by *the call of a bird,* and when the *daughters of song* (the choruses of psalm-singers in the temple) will fall silent. Then will be the time when even your enemies, as they come to Jerusalem, will be terrified of God's greatness and hesitate *on their way,* fearing the death of Sennacherib* (this is what they think was meant by *And they will fear from high places, and will be afraid on the way*). In those days *the almond tree* (the rod and stick which Jeremiah saw at the beginning of his prophecy*) *will blossom,* and the *caper berry* (God's love for Israel) *will waste away.* The meaning of the "caper berry" will be explained more fully once we begin to go into details.

All this is going to happen to Israel because *the man is going to go away into the house of his eternity,* and return from the protection of God into the heavenly realms; and when he goes away into his tent* *they will go about in the street weeping and lamenting,* walled round by the siege of the enemy. Therefore *be glad,* Israel, *in your youth, before the silver cord is broken* (that is, while your glory is still with you); *before the golden band runs back* (that is, before the ark of the covenant is removed); *before the pitcher is shattered at the well, and the wheel is tangled up over the cistern* (that is, while the precepts of the law and the grace of the Holy Spirit are still in the holy[73] of holies); before you return to Babylon, from where you came forth in the loins of Abraham,* and begin to be *shattered* in Mesopotamia, from where you once emerged; and before all the grace of prophecy with which you had once been inspired *returns to its Giver.*

That is the Jews' exposition of these words to this day, taking the meaning of this section as applying to them personally. Now, though, we shall revert to the plan of the preceding discussion, and try to explain the details.

Be glad, young man, in your youth and let your heart be in good in the days of your youthfulness, and walk in the ways of your heart and in the sight of your eyes. And know that God will bring you to judgment on all these things.

He had said* that the light of this world was very sweet, and that a man should be glad in the days of his life and seize pleasure with full enthusiasm, because the everlasting night of death is coming on, when one is not free to enjoy what one has amassed and when everything we had passes away like a shadow. Now, therefore, he is encouraging the man: Young man, before old age and death come upon you, be glad in your youthfulness and grasp whatever seems good in your heart and pleasant in your sight; enjoy the things of the world as you like. Then again, so as to avoid giving the impression, by saying this, that he is inciting the man to be extravagant and to fall into Epicureanism,* he has obviated that idea by adding: *And know that God will bring you into judgment on all these things.* Enjoy the things of this world, he is saying, but only in the knowledge that at the end you are to be judged.

And banish anger from your heart and remove wickedness[74] from your flesh, because youth and folly are vanity.

In *anger* he includes all disturbances of the mind; by *wickedness of the flesh* he means physical pleasures as a whole. He is therefore saying: Enjoy the good things of this present age, but without committing offenses, either of desire or physically. Give up the old vices by which, in your youth, you were a slave to vanity and foolishness, because youthfulness is associated with folly.

And remember the One who created you, in the day of your youthfulness, before the days of evil come and the years approach in which you will say: "I have no will in them."

Always remember your Originator. Tread the path of your youth, though without forgetting the death at the end of it, before the time comes when all that is grim supervenes.

12.2 Before the sun darkens, and the light, and the moon, and the stars; and the clouds return after the rain.

If we take this section as being on the universal end of the world, it agrees with the Lord's words: "There will be tribulation and distress such as there has not been since the beginning of creation, no, nor shall be....For the sun will darken, the moon will not give its light, the stars will fall from the sky, and the powers of the heavens will be moved."* The "powers of the heavens" are the *guardians of the house;* thus *the house* is to be understood as this world, and the *strong men* are those deceived by error, and the opposing strengths, which are to be shattered.

If, however, it is taken as the individual end of each particular person at the close of this life, then it is for the dead person that sun, moon, stars, clouds, and rain will cease to exist.

Alternatively: Be glad, you Christian people (*young man*) and enjoy the good things granted you by God, and be aware that in all of them you are to be judged by God. You are not to think yourselves carefree, just because the original branches have been broken and you have been grafted into the sound olive tree.*

Banish anger from your heart and pleasures from your body; abandon your other vices and *remember your Creator, before the day of evil comes* on you, the irremediable day on which eternal punishment is in store for sinners. Otherwise, when you sin, *the sun* of justice will set for you at midday, *the light* of knowledge will die, the brightness of *the moon* (that is, of the church) will be taken away, and *the stars* will set. Those are the stars of which the Scripture says: "Among whom you shine as luminaries in the world, having the principle of life,"* and elsewhere: "Star differs from star in glory."*

Before the clouds return after the rain is so that the prophets, who have watered the hearts of the believers by their own voice (their own rain),* do not discern that you are unworthy of their rainwater, and return to their abode, that is, to the One by whom they were sent.

12.3 On the day when the guardians of the house have been moved, and the men of strength have perished.

The guardians of the house means either the sun, the moon, and the troop of the other stars, or the angels who preside over this world. *The men of strength* (or "strong men," as Symmachus translates it) who will *perish* (or, in Aquila's version, will "go wrong") implies the demons, who themselves acquire the epithet "strong" from the devil, who is strong; but the Lord conquers the devil, binds him, and plunders his house, as in the Gospel parable.*

Alternatively: there are those who relate everything in this text to the human body.* They suppose that *the guardians of the house* means the ribs, because it is by them that the inward parts are walled in and all the softness of the belly is kept safe. They reckon *the strong men* as the legs; they fit *sun, moon, and stars* to eyes, nostrils, ears, and the sense organs of the head as a whole. Their reason for this is that, further on, they are unavoidably compelled to understand what follows* in terms of parts of the human body, not of angels and demons, sun, moon, and stars.

And the grinding-women will cease, because they have decreased; and the women looking in chinks will grow dark.

It is at the end of the world, when the love of many grows cold,* and when the teachers' souls, which can provide the bread of heaven* to believers, decrease and are translated to the heavenly realms, that those who in this life had a partial insight into the light of knowledge will begin to be enveloped in darkness. If Moses is told: "I shall put you in a chink of the rock and in that way you will see my back,"* how much more is it through a chink, through some kind of dark caves,* that each individual soul sees the truth?

Alternatively: There are two women grinding, and the Gospel is heard to say that one is snatched away and the other left.* When *their number is diminished* and *they have ceased,* inevitably all the light of knowledge will be taken from their eyes.

Alternatively: They suppose that *ceasing to grind because they have decreased* refers to teeth, because in extreme old age the teeth, which grind up the food and pass it on to the stomach, either become worn or fall out.* They think *those looking in chinks going dark* are the eyes, because in the very old sight becomes dim, and their vision is impaired.*

12.4 And they will close the front doors on the street, in the lowness of the voice of the one grinding. And he will get up at the call of a bird, and all the daughters of song will grow dumb.[75]

When *the voice of one grinding* is weakened and the teaching of the teachers ceases, everything will cease accordingly, including the door on the street being closed, so that, as with the silly girls in the Gospel,* everyone will have his street doors closed and they will be unable to buy oil.

Or else, while the silly girls are walking about in the street, those who went in with the bridegroom will close the door of his room. If the way leading to life is restricted and narrow, and the way leading to death is wide and spacious,* it is right that, as the love of many grows cold,* the door of all teaching is closed on the streets.

The next sentence, where it says *and he will rise at the call of a bird* (or, *of a sparrow*), is one we shall use appropriately on any occasion when we see a sinner rising to his feet in penitence at the voice of his bishop or priest.

Exceptionally, although we would not be following the context of the section, this can also be taken of the proper resurrection, when the dead will rise again at the call of the archangel.* It would not be surprising for us to compare the archangel's trumpet to the call of a sparrow, given that any voice is feeble compared to that of Christ. As far as I am able to call to my mind, I know of no occasion when I have read of *sparrow* being used in a bad sense. In the tenth Psalm, the just man says: "I trust in the Lord; how do you say to my soul, 'Cross over, like a sparrow, to the mountain?'"* Also, elsewhere: "I was awake, and became like a lonely sparrow on the roof,"* and again, in another place: "Even the sparrow finds itself a house."*

Alternatively, they want *the doors closed on the streets* to be taken of an old man's impaired gait,* because he is always sitting down and cannot walk. They understand *the lowness of the voice of the one grinding* to refer to his jaws, as being unable to chew the food,* and to his breathing as being so restricted that a feeble voice can only just be heard.* His *getting up at the call of a bird* indicates that, as the blood cools and the fluid dries, which is what conduces to sleep, he wakes up at a slight sound and hurries to get up in the middle of the night,* at cockcrow, being quite unable to keep turning over any more on his bedding. *The daughters of song going dumb,* or better, as in the Hebrew, *going deaf,** means the ears, because hearing in the old grows harder, and they cannot distinguish any differences between words, or enjoy music—just as Barzillai says to David when declining to go across the Jordan.*

12.5 But they will fear from high places, and will be afraid on the way.*

That is, they will not have the strength to go on steep places, and even on a level stretch they will sway about with tired knees and unsteady tread, afraid of stumbling.

And the almond tree will blossom, and the locust will be fattened, and the caper berry will waste away, because the man will go into the home of his eternity, and they will go about mourning in the street.

The Preacher is still talking metaphorically about parts of the person. With the onset of old age, the hair will go gray, the feet will swell, desire will go cold, and the man will be destroyed by death. Then he will *return to his earth,* into *the home of his eternity,* his tomb, and at a properly performed funeral a crowd of mourners will go[76] in front of the body. The *almond blossom,* which we have put as gray hair, is interpreted by some as the sacrum, because the sacrum grows prominent (*blossoms*) as the flesh of the buttocks shrinks.*

At *the locust will be fattened,* one must be aware that the Hebrew word for which our books read "locust" is *aagab,* a word ambiguous in that language: it is translatable both as "locust" and as "heel." This is like the opening of Jeremiah,* where the word *soced,* with a change of pronunciation, means both "nut" and "wakefulness."* There, Jeremiah's answer to the question: "What do you see, Jeremiah?" was: "A nut," to which the Lord replies: "You have seen well, because I shall be wakeful over my people,[77] to do so-and-so."[78] The fact that God will be "wakeful," and assign his people what it deserves, does have a verbal connection with "nut." So here, too, the point of the words lies in the double sense of *aagab,* which, by its verbal link, indicates old men's legs, swollen and weighed down with gout.* (Not that this is a universal condition in the old, but it is a common one and is applied by synecdoche from the part to the whole).

Now where we have *caper berry,* the Hebrew has *abiona,* another ambiguous word, translatable as "love," "longing," "desire," or as "caper berry."* What is meant, as we said above, is that old men's libido grows cold and their sexual organs waste away.* All this is because these ambiguous words develop by a figure of speech from their basic meanings "almond," "locust," and "caper berry" into other, derived meanings applicable to old people. One must also be aware that the actual word for what the Septuagint translators put as "almond" is *soced*, as in the opening of Jeremiah; but there it has been translated "nut," here as "almond tree."

On this passage Symmachus has some idea producing a very different translation: "And, as well as these things, they will also see from a high place, and there will be a straying on the way, and the one who is awake will go to sleep, and the bravery of the spirit will be dissolved. For the man will go into the home of his eternity, and they will go about mourning in the street." The Laodicean,[*] by following that rendering, can please neither the Jews nor Christians, because he is a long way away from the Hebrews, and is also disdaining to follow the Septuagint translators.

12.6–8 Before the silver cord is broken, and the golden ribbon runs back, and the pitcher is shattered over the well, and the wheel is broken over the cistern, and the dust returns into its earth as it was, and the spirit goes back to God who gave it. "Vanity of vanities," said the Preacher, "everything is vanity."

He returns to what he said before. After inserting the huge hyperbaton[*] beginning: *And remember your Creator in the day of your youth...before the days of evil come...and before the sun and moon grow dark, etc....and when the guardians of the house are moved,*[79] he now brings the sentence he had begun to a similar conclusion, with *before the silver cord is broken, and* so-and-so happens.

By *the silver cord* he is indicating this bright life[*] and the breath[*] granted us from heaven; by the *running back of the golden ribbon* he means the soul running back to where it came down from.

The next two clauses, about the *shattering of the pitcher over the well* and the *breaking of the wheel over the cistern*, are metaphorically veiled allusions to death. The shattered pitcher ceases to draw water, and if the wheel by which water is raised from a cistern or from wells is broken (or as the Septuagint translators prefer, "is tangled in its own rope"), the supply of water is interrupted. Similarly, when *the silver cord is broken* and the river of the soul *runs back* to its source, the person will die. The sequel makes this clearer: *The dust will return into its earth from which it was taken, and the spirit will turn back to God, who gave it.* This makes pretty good fools of those who think souls are sown with bodies and are generated by their parents' bodies instead of by God.[*] Given that *the flesh reverts to the earth and the spirit goes back to God, who gave it,* it is obvious that the parentage of souls is divine, not human.

After his description of human mortality, he appropriately goes back to the opening of his book,* with "*Vanity of vanities*," *said the Preacher,* "*all is vanity.*" All mortals' labor, which is what has been discussed in the whole book, reaches its end with the *dust going back into its earth* and the *soul going back* to where it was drawn from. Thus, it is serious vanity to be laboring in this present age over acquiring nothing that will be of any use.

12.9, 10 And, more than that the Preacher became wise, he further taught the people knowledge and made them hear. And, contemplating, he composed proverbs. The Preacher sought much to find words of will and to write words of truth correctly.*

Here, at the end of his little work, Solomon again proclaims the wisdom in which he excelled the whole human race.* Not content with his education in the old law, he plunged on his own initiative into profound researches, and, to teach his people, he composed proverbs and parables with a core meaning different from what they offer on the surface. In the Gospels, too, we are taught that the message of proverbs is not their written text: the Lord spoke to the public in parables and proverbs, but gave his apostles the solution to them in private.* That makes it obvious that the commands in the Book of Proverbs, too, are not self-evident, as the unsophisticated suppose; their divine sense has to be more deeply investigated, like searching for gold underground, or for the kernel in a nut, and for the hidden fruit in the hairy outer shells of chestnuts.

Additionally, he puts in that he wanted to find out the causes and natures of things, and God's providential system. Hence, he wanted to know why and how every single thing happened. What David hopes he will find on returning to heaven after the separation of body and soul, in the words "I shall see the heavens, the works of your fingers"* Solomon has striven to discover here and now, with the aim that a human mind, walled inside the barrier of the body, could grasp a truth known only to God.

12.11 The words of the wise have been given by one shepherd,[80] as goads, and are fixed like nails into the depth, for those having assemblies.

This is to avoid his appearing to be a sudden upstart, issuing commandments subsequent to God's law and claiming for himself teaching that even Moses—with whom God was angry at first;   God inspired him only later—had not undertaken voluntarily.* What he is saying is that his own words are those of the wise. Like goads, they correct offenders, and by their sharp stinging they set mortals' sluggish steps in motion. They are as firm as nails deeply and solidly fixed and are uttered not just on one person's authority, but with the consultation[81] and agreement of all teachers. To avoid its being condemned as merely human wisdom, he says it was granted *by one Shepherd;* that is, though there are numerous teachers, the sole origin of all the teaching is God.

This passage counters those who deem the God of the Gospel to be different from the God of the old law:[*] it is a single Shepherd who has instructed the consultation[82] of the prudent, and the prudent include the prophets as well as the apostles.

It is also to be noted that the words of the wise are said to sting, not to caress with flattery or to arouse wantonness with a soft hand. They inflict a painful wound on those who stray and who are, as we said earlier,[*] slow to repent. Thus, anyone's discourse that has no sting in it, but instead gives pleasure to the audience, is not the discourse of a wise man, because *the words of the wise are as goads.* These words challenge the offender to conversion. They are the words that are firm, given by the consensus[83] of the holy ones, *granted by the one Shepherd,*[*] and founded on a solid base. It was by this goad, I suppose, that Paul (when he was still Saul, not yet Paul) was stabbed on the road of error and heard the words "It is hard for you to kick against the goad."[*]

12.12 And, my son, beware of more than these things. Of making many books there is no end; and very much meditation is a labor of the flesh.

You are to do nothing, and claim nothing for yourself, apart from the words *given by the one Shepherd* and uttered on the consultation and agreement of the wise. Follow the footsteps of your predecessors and do not diverge from their authority. Otherwise, if you do try to find out many things, you will encounter an infinite number of books to distract you into error and cause you to labor in vain over your reading.

Or else he is teaching that one should aim at brevity, following the sense rather than the words, as against the philosophers and professors of this present age who try to assert the falsehoods of their own dogmas by varying and multiplying their discourses. Divine Scripture, on the other hand, is confined within a small compass, as limited in language as it is wide in what it has to say; "for the Lord has made his word complete and concise on the earth,"[*] and "his word is close by, in our mouth and in our heart."[*]

Alternatively: Frequent reading and daily meditation are usually a labor more of the soul than of the flesh. Anything that is done manually, physically, is brought to completion by manual, physical labor; equally, what is involved in reading is primarily a labor of the mind. That makes me think that the above saying, about the large number of books, should be understood differently from what is generally supposed. Although the Scriptures comprise a number of books, it is customary to speak of them as a single volume, on the principle that they are on the same subject, and not mutually contradictory. In the same way "Gospel" is used in the singular, despite there being more than one Gospel, and so is "the commandment of the Lord is pure, converting souls,"* though the law contains numerous commandments. Analogous are the sealed "book" in Isaiah's discourse,* "all Scripture is divine,"* and Ezekiel's and John's eating one section* of a book.* The Savior, too, who was foretold in the words of all the previous holy men, says: "In a section of the book it is written of me."*

I think, then, that this is the sense in which it is here being commanded that there should not be a plurality of books; for whatever one says, as long as it relates to the One "who was in the beginning with God,"* God the Word, it is one volume, just as innumerable books are referred to in the singular as "the law" and "the Gospel." If, on the other hand, you argue divergently and discrepantly, and apply your mind in different directions with excessive curiosity, even if in only one book, that constitutes *many books*. Hence the saying: "From much talking you will not escape sin."* That, then, is the kind of book of which *there is no end*.

Everything that is good, including the truth, comes to a definite conclusion; it is wickedness and falsehood that are endless, and the more they are pursued, the longer the series of them that comes into being. That is where study and *meditation is a labor of the flesh*—of the flesh, I say, not of the spirit. Spirit does have its labor, as in the Apostle's "I have labored more than them all; though it was not I, but the grace of God which is with me,"* and in the Savior's "I have labored, clamoring."*

12.13, 14 The end of the entire discussion is very easy to hear: Fear God and keep his commandments. That is the whole man, because God will bring every action to judgment on everything hidden, whether it be good or bad.

The Hebrews[84] say that it might seem that this book of Solomon's, like other writings of his that have become obsolete and are no longer on record,* should also be deleted,* because of his assertion of the vanity of God's creations, his regarding of the sum of things as worthless, and his preference of food, drink, and transitory pleasures to everything else. Yet, despite that, they say, it earns its authoritative place in the canon of the divine books on the strength of this one section, in which he has compressed his entire argument and its whole list of contents. This précis, as it were, is: The end of my discourse is completely accessible to hear and contains nothing difficult. It is that we should fear God and do what he tells us. The purpose for which mankind was created is to be aware of its Creator, and to worship him in fear and respect, and in fulfillment of his commandments. When the judgment time comes, whatever we have done is subject to the Judge and awaits the long-undecided verdict that is handed down to each, according to whether his actions have been good or bad.

Where we have put *on everything hidden, whether it be good or bad,* Symmachus and the Septuagint have translated: "on everything despised"[85] or "overlooked," on the ground that we are going to render an account on the day of judgment even for an idle word uttered unwittingly, without intent.

Alternatively: "Fear is servile; perfect love casts out fear";[*] and fear in divine Scripture has a twofold usage, according to whether it is used of those who have reached perfection, or of those who are only just beginning. Hence I regard "fear" here as applied to one being perfected in the virtues, as in: "Those who fear him have no lack."[*] Or else, because he is still human and has not yet received the name of God, the principle he has for his existence is that while in the body he should fear God. God brings every action into judgment; that is, he brings all humans into judgment on every matter on which their view has diverged, in whichever direction, from what he has laid down and has said. "Woe," then, "to those who call evil good and good evil."[*]

COMMENTARY ON THE TRANSLATION

PREFACE

Paula: Paula was a wealthy Roman widow and a member of a group of women whom Jerome had taught in Rome. The mother of five children, including Eustochium and Blesilla (see following notes), Paula left Rome when Jerome was driven out in 385. After a tour of the Holy Land and a visit to Egypt in order to meet famous monks (Hier. *Ep.* 108.14), Paula and Jerome moved to Bethlehem, where Paula used her money to build two monasteries. She died in 404 and was the subject of a lengthy eulogy written by Jerome (Hier. *Ep.* 108). For further biography, see Cloke, *Female Man of God,* 35–36, 93–94; Kelly, *Jerome,* 91–103.

Eustochium: Julia Eustochium was Paula's third daughter, a girl who shared her mother's interest in the ascetic life. When Jerome was driven out of Rome in 385, she accompanied her mother to Bethlehem. Eustochium was the recipient of one of Jerome's most famous letters (Hier. *Ep.* 22), a treatise that discussed the proper way to live as a female ascetic. After her mother died in 404, Eustochium assumed the leadership of the Bethlehem monastery (Hier. *Ep.* 108).

Blesilla: Paula's oldest daughter (see preceding notes), Blesilla was widowed after only seven months of marriage (Hier. *Ep.* 22.15). After the loss of her husband she continued to maintain an aristocratic lifestyle, spending too much time on her appearance, dress, and luxuries (Hier. *Ep.* 38.4). Finally, a serious fever broke through her vanity and drove her to embrace an ascetic form of Christianity. Blesilla became famous for her prayer, fasting, and Bible study, mastering Hebrew in only a few months (Hier. *Ep.* 39.1). Quite possibly her extreme mortification of the flesh shortened her life, for she died three months after the renunciation of her earlier life. At her funeral, the crowds muttered darkly about the ill effect Jerome and his fellow monks were having on the Roman women, with some saying that the

135

monks should be cast into the Tiber or driven out of the city (Hier. *Ep.* 39.6).

more august: The oldest extant manuscript reads *augustiore* ("more august"), while most later manuscripts have *angustiore* ("less spacious," "narrower"). Considering that Jerome had arrived in Bethlehem after having been driven out of Rome (see Introduction) the former reading is probably to be preferred, a case of sour grapes that seems quite in character for Jerome. Rome had been the highlight of his career to this point, and now he was forced to make the best of existence on the periphery of Christian political life. This interpretation is supported by his comment in the preface to his translation of Didymus's *On the Holy Spirit:* "the place which gave birth to the Savior of the world (Bethlehem) is to be regarded as far more august than the place which gave birth to the murderer of his brother (Rome, referring to the fratricide of Romulus)."

Septuagint...Hebrew text: At the time Jerome was writing, the Septuagint (the Greek translation of the Hebrew Bible) was the church's standard version of the Old Testament. Despite its many flaws and errors, the Septuagint enjoyed the same status among late antique Christians that the 1611 King James Version currently commands among some modern readers. After the *Commentary on Ecclesiastes* was finished, Jerome came to doubt the accuracy of the Septuagint translation (see Hier. *Ruf.* 2.35), and he made a fresh Latin translation of the Hebrew Scriptures (a work that ultimately became the Vulgate). This new translation met considerable resistance from Jerome's contemporaries (e.g., Ruf. *Apol.* 2.32–35; Aug. *Ep.* 28.2).

Aquila, Symmachus, and Theodotion: Earlier Greek translators of the Hebrew Bible. See Introduction for a discussion of these writers as sources for Jerome's work.

Chapter 1

1.1

Solomon: The Hebrew etymology for this name is not entirely clear. In 2 Sam 12:24 it is recorded that David named his newborn son Solomon, a name that is most likely based on the root of the Hebrew word שלום (*šālōm*, "peace"). This view is supported by the prophecy in 1 Chr 22:9, which states that God will give David a son who will be a man of peace. It is also possible, however, that the name Solomon is taken from the word that is derived from the same stem שלם (*šillēm*, "to recompense" or "make payment"), implying that God had given David a replacement for Bathsheba's first son, who had died (2 Sam 12:15–18).

Ididia: ידידיה (*yĕdîdĕyâ*, "Jedidiah" or "Yahweh's delight"). After his second son was born and David had named him Solomon (see previous note), God sent the prophet Nathan to tell David to call his son Jedidiah (2 Sam 12:25). In his discussion of Hebrew names (Hier. *Nom. Hebr.* 4 Reg I–M), Jerome noted: "*Ididia* means 'attractive to the Lord.'"

Coeleth: קהלת (*qōhelet*, "preacher") is a nominal form of the Hebrew verb קהל (*qāhal*, "to assemble"). *Coeleth* (also spelled Qohelet) usually refers to the leader of an assembly, although it can also mean a teacher or speaker.

Ecclesiastes...in the Greek language: From the Greek verb ἐκκλησιάζω (*ekklēsiazō*, "to hold an assembly").

church: Cf. Or. *Cant.* Prol. 4.18: "The word 'Ecclesiastes' is derived from 'to gather the church.'"

rouser: A *concionator* is "a person who addresses a public meeting." Although a *concionator* can be a good thing, it also has a negative connotation: "a person who stirs up a mob." Augustine, for instance, stated that the Temple of Concord had been erected in the Forum so that it would be in plain view of those speaking on the rostrum, a check on their rabble-rousing rhetoric (Aug. *Ciu.* 3.26). Jerome's use of the word suggests that Solomon was a teacher who stirred up the people and made them think.

speaks to the people: In 1 Kgs 8:14–53, Solomon is said to have addressed the assembly (ἐκκλησία [*ekklēsia*]) of Israel.

one who assembles the gathering...world at large: The title of the book offered Christian exegetes room for fruitful speculation about the intended audience for this work. Jerome, in considering the significance of the title "Ecclesiastes," suggests that the Preacher's message is directed to the whole world, and not (as he develops later in this chapter) to the Jewish people alone.

Gregory of Nyssa takes a different line. Noting that this is the only book read in ecclesial assemblies to have the title "Ecclesiastes" attached to it, he suggests that this must have a special significance. In fact, Ecclesiastes is unlike other books of the Bible because it is directed to the church alone and is intended to give instruction in the practices that would lead a Christian into the life of virtue (Gr. Nyss. *Hom. 1–8 in Eccl.* 1.2).

Gregory Thaumaturgos also suggests that the book is directed toward the whole church of God (Gr. Thaum. *Eccl.* 1.1).

reign: Solomon ruled Israel from ca. 970 to 930 BC.

Psalms 44 and 71: Psalms 45 and 72 in English translations. Jerome cites psalms throughout this work based on the numbering found in the Septuagint, which divides the text slightly differently from the Hebrew Bible. When referring to one of the psalms in this work, we shall cite the numbering system of the Septuagint first, followed by the English reference number in brackets (e.g., LXX Psalm 44 [Psalm 45]).

For Psalms 44 and 71...beloved and peacemaker: LXX Psalm 44 [Psalm 45] has "Of the beloved" in the title, and offers an extended panegyric to the king and describes his wedding banquet. LXX Psalm 71 [Psalm 72] is dedicated to Solomon, which Jerome here takes in the sense of "peacemaker," as he did in the first line of his commentary on this verse; it is a prayer for the prosperity of the king. This is in accordance with the literal interpretation of the text.

In his commentary on Psalms, Jerome noted that although this psalm was dedicated to Solomon, it also referred to Christ: "Solomon naturally was the peacemaker, and the peacemaker is Christ" (Hier. *In. Psal.* 71. 1). Since LXX Ps 71.5 [Ps 72.5] states: "He persists with the sun and before the moon, generation by generations," the psalm clearly pointed beyond Solomon (who did not live forever) to Christ, who has no end (Hier. *In. Psal.* 71. 5). For earlier patristic claims that LXX Ps 71.5 referred to Christ rather than Solomon, see Just. *Dial.* 34.

according to history: Jerome, like most patristic readers, believed that the biblical text contained meaning on several levels. What he has just offered is the literal interpretation, a reading intended to extract historical details about past events. Below he will discuss the spiritual sense of the verse, developing the hidden meaning immanent in the text. For a discussion of Jerome's reading strategies, see the Introduction; for general introductions to patristic exegesis, see Kannengiesser, *Handbook*, 167–269; and O'Keefe and Reno, *Sanctified Vision*.

Proverbs...Song of Songs: In the patristic period, these three books were commonly attributed to Solomon (see Or. *Cant.* Prol. 1.1; Prol. 3.1). Modern biblical scholars do not believe that Solomon was responsible for any of the books. The Book of Proverbs consists of several proverb collections that were brought together by an unknown compiler, probably after the Israelites returned from the Babylonian exile (see Whybray, *Proverbs*, 6–7). Although the Song of Solomon is ascribed to the king (an identification that was widely accepted until the advent of textual criticism in the late nineteenth century), scholars doubt its claim to Solomonic authorship (for a discussion of authorship and dating, see Pope, *Song*, 21–33); as for Ecclesiastes, despite the claim that the author was David's son and a king over

Jerusalem (Eccl 1:1), modern scholars believe that the book was not written until the postexilic period and is concerned more with a critique of kingship than with the experience of having been a king (see Murphy, *Ecclesiastes*, xx–xxi).

teaching a young person...duties through maxims: Or. *Cant.* Prol. 3.6–8 advances two ideas about the function of the Book of Proverbs. The first is that the proverbs are a set of rules or guidelines for life, a legal code written in concise maxims. Origen's second idea springs from the words of Jesus: "I have spoken to you in proverbs; the hour will come when I will no longer teach you in proverbs, but will speak plainly about the Father" (John 16:25). This verse, according to Origen, proved that the proverbs are sayings that appear to express ideas openly, but, in fact, conceal a mystery.

Jerome, who knew Origen's views from the two books of the *Commentary on the Song of Songs* he had translated into Latin for Pope Damasus in the years 383–384 (Kelly, *Jerome*, 85–86), adopted Origen's first idea, that the proverbs are a legal code. They are the foundational guidelines for an upright life, and once the externals of life have been correctly channeled by the code, the reader is ready to move on to the teachings of Ecclesiastes. This formulation is explicit in his advice to a Roman matron named Laeta about the education of her daughter: "Let her be educated for life from the Proverbs of Solomon" (Hier. *Ep.* 107.12).

Gregory of Nyssa, on the other hand, saw the maxims contained in the Book of Proverbs as a series of twisted and obscure ideas, riddles intended to exercise the mind. Once the reader has mastered these riddles, acquiring an intellect that has been honed through its engagement with these puzzles, he or she is then ready to tackle the greater problems served up in Ecclesiastes (Gr. Nyss. *Hom. 1–8 in Eccl.* 1.1; cf. Meredith, "Homily I," 145–46); see also Gregory's account of his sister Macrina's early education, which was based on the wisdom of Solomon, especially Proverbs (Gr. Nyss. *V. Macr.* 3). The proverbs, for Gregory, were the mental equivalent of the training exercises a wrestler undertook before competing in athletic contests.

world is perpetual: Or. *Cant.* Prol. 3.14 states that the second division of Christian education, after the learning of morals through Proverbs, is the discipline of natural knowledge. This area of study teaches a person to know the causes and natures of the material world and to recognize that this vanity of vanities must be rejected before one can make the ascent to spiritual realities.

In Proverbs...underfoot: Jerome offers a similar plan of Bible reading in his advice to Laeta (Hier. *Ep.* 107. 12). He suggests that Laeta's daughter, Paula, should first memorize the Book of Psalms, learn the lessons of life from Proverbs, and then read Ecclesiastes in order to discover how to tread the things of this world underfoot. Only after mastering the rest of the Bible was the girl to turn her attention to the Song of Songs, for only then would she be able to read it safely, recognizing that the sensual language of the book is intended to express spiritual truths.

This characterization of the Song of Songs is drawn from Or. *Cant.* Prol. 1.5, where Origen claimed that if the spiritually immature tried to read the Song of Songs before they had passed through the earlier works, they would receive no nourishment from the book. In fact, they might actually be harmed. The book was to be understood spiritually, and a reader who lacked maturity and discernment might be encouraged to pursue the physical pleasures of the flesh described in that work.

relinquished our vices—arrival of Christ: For both Jerome and Gregory of Nyssa (following Or. *Cant.* Prol. 3.15), the Preacher's denigration of the material world and his demonstration of the futility of mortal pursuits were intended to turn a person toward the virtuous life and the contemplation of higher realities (see Gr. Nyss. *Hom. I–8 in Eccl.* 1). This reformation of life, coupled with an intellectual and upward focus on the transcendent, represents a fusion of Platonic ideals with the Stoic emphasis on the search for moral perfection (Meredith, "Homily I," 146–47).

Let him kiss...mouth: Cant 1:2.

Philosophers too...theological study: This tripartite division of philosophy can be traced back to the Stoics (Meredith, "Homily I," 147 n. 6). Seneca, for instance, wrote: "The majority of leading authorities said that philosophy has three divisions: moral, natural, and rational. The first division settles the mind; the second investigates natural events; the third weighs properties of words, both structure and arguments, so that false ideas do not creep up in place of the truth" (*Ep.* 89.9).

Origen developed this sequence of education in the prologue to his *Commentary on the Song of Songs* (Prol. 3.1). Here he equated Proverbs, Ecclesiastes, and the Song of Songs with the three patriarchs, Abraham, Isaac, and Jacob (Prol. 3.17–20). These three men, in turn, symbolize moral philosophy, natural philosophy, and theology. Jerome repeats Origen's schematization here but omits his explanation of these divisions.

author's name...in the three books: Jerome appears to have drawn much of the following explanation from Origen's discussion of the three names (Or. *Cant.* Prol. 4.15–35). Origen noted the differences in the names found at the beginning of each of these books and suggested that the variations signaled Christ's different aspects or roles (Prol. 4.15–19). For an extended account of Origen's analysis of these names, see King, *Origen on the Song*, 221–26.

The Proverbs...king of Israel: Prov 1:1.

The words...king of Jerusalem: Eccl 1:1.

Israel, wrongly found...manuscripts: Jerome offers no support for his belief that the word "Israel" was erroneously present in the Greek and Latin manuscripts he was using. It is possible that his Hebrew manuscripts omitted it, but modern critical editions of the Hebrew text do contain this word. Origen's citation of this verse also has the word "Israel" (Or. *Cant.* Prol. 4.15).

is here unnecessary: Presumably because Jerusalem is in Israel, so the name of the country is redundant (see previous note). Cf. Eccl 1:12: "king over Israel, in Jerusalem"; a more satisfactory arrangement that goes unremarked.

Song of Songs...Songs of Solomon: Cf. Or. *Cant.* Prol. 4.27.

For just as...heavenly things: Jerome uses the schema applied above to individual progression in the spiritual life as an interpretive key to describe the historical development of God's people. The twelve tribes of Israel represent God's initial plan for training humans, followed by the Christians who dwell in a spiritual Jerusalem, and then the perfect (ascetics) who have renounced the world and focused their hearts and minds on God.

fear...by love: A possible allusion to 1 John 4:18.

teacher is an equal: This interpretation, that the titles "son of David" and "king of Israel" have been omitted because the fully trained disciple is the equal of his teacher, is taken from Or. *Cant.* Prol. 4.28.

spiritual sense: Throughout this commentary, Jerome will vary his interpretation between a literal/historical reading of the text and a spiritual/allegorical reading in which he makes Christ the Preacher who directs these words to the church. He will usually, as here, indicate when he is shifting between these interpretive modes. For further discussion of these exegetical strategies, see Introduction.

Christ: An identification made by Origen in *Cant.* Prol. 4.18–20.

Gregory of Nyssa developed Origen's identification with two arguments: (1) the true Ecclesiast is the one who gathers together things that have been scattered and assembles them into one body (as Christ did in creating the church); (2) Nathaniel identifies Christ as the king of Israel in John 1:49: "Rabbi, you are the Son of God! You are the king of Israel!" If the words of Ecclesiastes are the words of the king of Israel, and Jesus is both the Son of God and the king of Israel, then Jesus must be Ecclesiastes and the author of this text (Gr. Nyss. *Hom. 1–8 in Eccl.* 1.2; 2.1; for discussion, see Meredith, "Homily I," 147–48).

Evagrius Ponticus simply identified Christ as Ecclesiastes, without providing any justification for this view (Evagr. Pont. *Schol. Ecc.* 1), while Gregory Thaumaturgos did not make this connection, claiming that the Ecclesiast was King Solomon (Gr. Thaum. *Eccl.* 1.1). **dividing wall...made both one:** Eph. 2:14–15. According to Paul, Christ's sacrifice has removed the dividing wall between the Jews and Gentiles, abolishing hostilities and making them one people united in a single church.

My peace...leave with you: John 14:32.

This is my beloved...listen to him: Matt. 3:17.

multitude of nations: Jerome now develops the spiritual sense of the office of *concionator* (see note above), suggesting that Christ stirs up not only the Jewish people, but the entire world.

living stones: An allusion to 1 Pet 2:5: "And like living stones be yourselves built into a spiritual house, to be a holy priesthood, to offer spiritual sacrifices acceptable to God through Jesus Christ." Jerome's metaphor evokes the image of a city composed of spiritual houses (Christians), a new Jerusalem that replaces the old.

Jerusalem, Jerusalem...prophets: Matt 23:37.

behold your house...desolate: Matt 23:38.

because...city of the great king: Matt 5:35.

son of David: A view that is also found in Gr. Nyss. *Hom. 1–8 in Eccl.* 1.2, although Gregory supports his argument with a reference to Matt 1:1.

have mercy...son of David: Matt 9:27.

Hosanna to the son of David: Matt 21:9.

Finally, the Word...other powers: Unlike the other prophets, who were inspired by the Holy Spirit, the identification of the Preacher with Christ on a spiritual level means that he is the Holy Spirit. Consequently there is no need for an external force to inspire this work. Gregory Thaumaturgos, in his translation of this verse, asserted that Solomon was both a king and a prophet (Gr. Thaum. *Eccl.* 1.1), evidently intending to suggest that Solomon's authority transcended that of an earthly king (Jarick, *Thaumaturgos' Paraphrase*, 7–8).

Concern about the inspired quality of the Preacher's text is evident also in the Jewish reluctance to include the book in the Hebrew canon. Its status was debated in Judaism and early Christianity, primarily because the book's apparently secular conclusions led many to doubt its divine inspiration. Belief that the book had been written by Solomon was a strong argument for its inclusion in the canon, as was a recognition of the quality of the work (cf. 12.13, 14). For a full treatment of the book's status in Judaism and early Christianity, see Christianson, *Ecclesiastes,* 89–94.

their voice has gone...ends of the earth: LXX Ps 18:4 [Ps 19:4].

1.2

Vanity of vanities: Heb.: הבל הבלים (*hăbēl hăbālîm*]; for a discussion of the Preacher's use of this key phrase, see Fox, *Ecclesiastes,* xix.

Jerome has translated *hebel* with the Latin word *uanitas.* An English translation of the Latin is problematic. Its semantic domain covers a wide range of meanings, including "futility," "pointlessness," "falsity," and an "unsubstantial or illusory quality." "Vanity," the traditional English translation of the Latin, no longer triggers these associations in the minds of modern readers; to the contrary, a vain person, someone who exemplifies vanity, is a person who takes excessive pride in appearance or character.

Although "vanity" no longer conveys what the Preacher meant to express, the expression "vanity of vanities" is so embedded in our Western consciousness that exchanging it for something like "futility of futilities" simply does not sound right. Consequently, we have opted to translate *uanitas* with "vanity," following the sound judgment of Murphy, *Ecclesiastes,* lviii–lix.

everything that God made...very good: See Gen 1:31.

vanity: Jerome does not offer a satisfactory definition for the Hebrew word הבל (*hebel*), which he has translated with *uanitas* ("vanity"). Gregory of Nyssa suggests three possible definitions: it is either a meaningless word, an action that cannot possibly be realized (such as shooting arrows at the stars), or work that is thwarted by an obstacle, thus proving fruitless (Gr. Nyss. *Hom. I–8 in Eccl.* 1.3).

Gregory also suggested (*Hom. I–8 in Eccl.* 1.10) that this life could be compared to the sand castles a child builds at the seashore. Power, riches, and ambition are all sand. One day we shall get away from this beach, where the ocean always threatens our sand castles with its storms and breakers, and when we do, we shall have only the memory of the things we once desired.

Origen suggested that the Preacher labeled this life "vanity" because transcendent human souls have been subjected to the burden of a corporeal body (Or. *Princ.* 1.7.5).

magnitude of this vanity: A similar idea, that the repetition signifies an intensification of the thought, is found in Or. *Cant.* Prol. 4.1, which is followed by Gregory of Nyssa (*Hom. I–8 in Eccl.* 1.4), who echoes

Origen's arguments by examining the same phrases: "work of works" (Num 4:47) and "holy of holies" (Exod 26:33–34). This is certainly the correct understanding of this Hebrew idiom.

Nevertheless...entirely vanity: LXX Ps 38:6 [Ps 39:5]. This is a particularly apt citation for Jerome, as this psalm considers many of the themes developed by the Preacher, including the shortness of life, the transient nature of human existence, and the folly of acquiring riches that cannot be enjoyed by the person who earns them.

Moses' face...unable to look at him: An allusion to Exod 34:30–35. When Moses came down from Mount Sinai with the tablets of the law, his face shone because he had been speaking to God. The Israelites were afraid to approach him; after giving them God's commandments, Moses veiled his face to conceal his appearance.

For what was glorified...superior glory: 2 Cor 3:10. Jerome echoes Paul's argument: the dispensation given to Moses and the Jewish people was good, but it was a transitory glory, meant to be supplanted by the glory of Christ. Likewise, the things of this world are good, but they are thin shadows when compared to the ultimate reality of God and the world to come.

good in themselves...are as nothing: Like Gregory of Nyssa, Jerome faces a potential problem (signaled in the first line of this chapter) with his interpretation: if God created the material world, how can it not be good?

Gregory argued that God's creation parallels human nature. A human consists of both body (transient) and soul (eternal), just as creation has a material component (transient) and a spiritual, unseen component (eternal). Both bodies and the material world are a vanity, in that they pass away while the eternal components endure. The vain nature of creation is a teacher or a signpost, intended to turn our minds to the higher good which is not vain and does not pass away (Gr. Nyss. *Hom. 1–8 in Eccl.* 1.5).

Jerome, somewhat less satisfactorily, draws a distinction between the world we now experience and the eternal reality to come, and states that when the two are compared, what is experienced in this life appears vain and futile. This comparison, when pondered by a thoughtful person, might have an educative element, but the argument does not receive the careful development found in Gregory. Nor does Jerome attempt to address the question of why God made the world to be a vanity.

Despite this apparent shortcoming, Jerome's discussion of this verse inaugurated an extremely influential way of reading this passage. His treatment of material good as something to be eclipsed by the coming greater good leads naturally to a *contemptus mundi* ("contempt of the world") that was picked up by his medieval successors (see discussion in Christianson, *Ecclesiastes*, 100–106; and the relevant section in the Introduction to that work).

small flame...sun rose: This analogy bears a strong resemblance to an illustration found in Or. *Princ.* 1.1.5. Origen suggested that humans were unable to grasp the incomprehensibility and magnitude of God's nature, being like a man with an eye disease who can barely tolerate the dim flicker of a small lamp; this man would be completely overwhelmed by the full power of the sun, just as our minds, able to grasp only the dimmest flickering of understanding about God, would be incapacitated should we ever gaze upon the fullness of God's nature. Consequently, we must restrict ourselves to asserting that God's nature surpasses our limited ability to understand it.

Septuagint: The Septuagint has the phrase ματαιότης ματαιοτήτων (*mataiotēs mataiotētōn*, "vanity of vanities") in Eccl 1:2.

ἀτμὸς ἀτμίδων or ἀτμὸς ἀτμῶν: *atmos atmidōn*, lit. "vapor of vapors," or *atmos atmōn*, lit. "vapor of odors."

creation has been subjected...sons of God: An allusion to Rom 8:22–23.

now we understand...prophesy in part: 1 Cor 13:9.

perfect comes: An allusion to 1 Cor 13:10.

1.3

begins with men...constructing buildings: Here Gregory of Nyssa (*Hom. 1–8 in Eccl.* 1.7) and Jerome both offer short summaries of the Preacher's argument that will be developed over subsequent chapters. They differ, however, in their emphasis. Jerome focuses attention on the futility of a person's life, the endless pursuit of gain in this world that is ultimately lost at death.

Gregory, on the other hand, develops Solomon's discussion of the futility of the cycles observed in the material world: the endless repetition of the sun moving across the sky and the insatiable hunger of the sea as it swallows the endlessly flowing streams that empty into it. What is likely to be the state of a person who immerses himself in a material world that is trapped in endless, futile cycles? The vanity of these cycles should serve as an example for humans; they should not lose themselves in material toil that is unprofitable, but should work for things that confer an advantage upon the soul.

foolish man...prepared: Luke 12:20.

naked to the earth...taken: An allusion to Job 1:21.

1.4

age: The Latin word *saeculum*, which we have translated "age," has a wide range of meanings including "human lifetime," "generation," "this present world," or "future age"; here it means "for a long (defined) period of time."

benefit of man: The implication of Gen 1:26–31 is that God had created the world as a good thing, and that this world was intended to be a blessed place for humans to live. After the Fall, however, sin entered the world and it was cursed, becoming a place of trial and suffering (Gen 3:17–19; Aug. *Symb.* 2).

crumbles into dust: An allusion to Gen 3:19.

Gentiles followed: Jerome now turns from a literal/historical reading of this verse to offer an allegorical interpretation. He repeats his earlier assertion that the gospel had supplanted the covenant that God had made with the Jews (cf. 1.2, where he discusses the glory of the Mosaic law passing away, eclipsed by the gospel). This was a common patristic argument, found in apologetic writing aimed at both pagan adversaries who charged Christians with forsaking the religion of their ancestors (a good example of this line of attack in a pagan writer may be found at Juln. Imp. *Galil.* 43A) and the Jews (cf. Just. *Dial.* 11).

When the gospel...end will come: An allusion to Christ's prediction of the end that will come once the gospel has been preached throughout the entire world (Matt 24:14).

will pass away: An allusion to the prophecy of the passing of the old heaven and earth followed by the creation of a new heaven and earth, recorded in Rev 21:1.

in the age: The present earth belongs to the age that will be brought to a close with the last judgment.

ages of ages: Based on his exegesis of *vanity of vanities* (1.2), Jerome surely intends his readers to understand an age that transcends all ages. For further discussion of this phrase, see Aug. *Ciu.* 12.20, who argues that it does not support the view of the philosophers who thought that the ages recur in cycles, repeating themselves *ad infinitum.*

1.5

sun...light to mortals: For the idea that the earth was made for the benefit of humanity, see note at 1:4 (benefit of man).

transience of the world: Gregory of Nyssa (*Hom. 1–8 in Eccl.* 1.7) suggests that the cyclical motion of the sun points to the transience of human life; a person rises in birth, journeys through life, and then sinks into the earth.

set forth: The belief that the sun, moon, and stars revolved around a fixed, spherical earth was a staple of ancient cosmology (see Plin. *Nat.* 2.2.5–3.6).

bursts forth from its own chamber: LXX Ps 18:6 [Ps 19:5].

common edition: By this phrase, used in contrast to the three other versions he is about to mention, all of which are Greek, Jerome presumably means the Septuagint, the most widely familiar Greek version of the Old Testament. For an extended discussion of Jerome's sources, see the Introduction.

Aquila: Aquila of Sinope. For the first time, Jerome refers to some of the other Greek translations he has consulted in producing his work. The texts of the three named translators, Aquila, Symmachus, and Theodotion, were all included in Origen's Hexapla, the undoubted source for Jerome's work. For a discussion of Aquila as one of Jerome's sources, see the Introduction.

εἰσπνεῖ *eispnei*, "breathes into": Aquila's rendering is the closest to the literal meaning of the Hebrew word שׁאַף (*šōʾēp*, "breathes hard," here "hurries").

Symmachus: A second-century Jewish translator who made a Greek translation of the Old Testament that was included in Origen's Hexapla. See Introduction for further information on Symmachus and his importance as one of Jerome's sources for this work.

Theodotion: Another second-century Jewish translator of the Hebrew Scriptures. His Greek version of the text, as with Aquila and Symmachus, was included in Origen's Hexapla. See Introduction for further information on Theodotion and his importance as one of Jerome's sources for this work.

sun of justice…wings is healing: An allusion to Mal 4:2, which refers to the sun of justice rising with healing in its wings. In ancient Near Eastern cultures, the sun was commonly portrayed as a winged disc. The Mesopotamian god Shamash, linked to the sun, was associated with law and justice. Wings are also used metaphorically in the psalms as a place of refuge, symbolizing God's protection of his people (see Pss 17:8; 36:7; 57:1; 63:7; 91:4). The writer of Malachi seems to have fused these images in his picture of Yahweh, rising like the sun to dispense justice for his people (see Petersen, *Zechariah 9–14*, 225; Glazier-McDonald, *Malachi*, 239).

The rabbis also made a connection between these two verses in the Midrash Rabbah, stating that in the hereafter the sun of justice would rise with healing in its wings, benefiting the upright and punishing the wicked (*Qoh. Rab.* 1.5.2).

rises with people fearing him: An allusion to LXX Ps 71:5 [Ps 72:5]. Jerome is here much closer to the meaning of the Hebrew text, "May they fear you while the sun endures," than to what is found in the Septuagint: "And he will endure, along with the sun."

false prophets at midday: An allusion to 1 Kgs 18:1–40; here Elijah competed with the prophets of Baal to determine whose god was greater. The prophets called upon Baal until midday, after which Elijah called upon Yahweh, who responded. Having lost the contest, the false prophets were killed by the people. Neither the sun, which people fear (see preceding note), nor the false prophets have any apparent connection to Jerome's argument.

he has risen...his own place: Jerome here takes the sun of justice as a reference to Christ, who rose (from the dead) to draw all people to his Father.

When the son...people to himself: John 12:32.

For no one...sent me, brings him: John 6:44.

left the holy land: An allusion to Gen 28:11, in which Jacob rested at Bethel after he left Beer-sheba.

land of the promise from Syria: An allusion to Gen 32:31, in which the sun rose on Jacob as he passed Penuel.

the sun came out over Segor: Gen 19:23. Segor is rendered Zoar in English Bibles.

1.6

can suppose...sun runs over: Jerome's interpretation of this verse is based on a Septuagint mistranslation of the Hebrew text (for the LXX error, see Jarick, *Thaumaturgos' Paraphrase*, 12). In the Hebrew version, it is the wind, not the sun, that goes to the south and circles to the north. Since Jerome had not seen this, he was compelled to explain how the sun moved north and south and why it was here called a "spirit."

north: The ancients realized that the length of day and night altered as the sun moved north and south in its equinoctial plane (cf. Plin. *Nat.* 2.17.81). Augustine has the same basic idea about the sun's track through the sky. In *Litt.* 1.10.21 he states that when the southern part of the sky has the sun, it is daytime there, while still night in the north. When the sun moves into the north, night falls over the southern part of the sky and it is day in the north. Tacitus notes that during the British summer, the sun is said not to set, but only to cross the heavens in the north (Tac. *Ag.* 12).

Gregory of Nyssa suggests that the sun's orbit lay in a flat plane that bisected the spherical earth. It passed over the southern half of the globe while it was visible, and then, after setting, moved across the northern half (Gr. Nyss. *Hom. I–8 in Eccl.* 1.7).

it does not start...spring: The ancients realized that the sun moved north in the summer and south in the winter, thus accounting for the lengthening and shortening of the days. Like modern scientists, they recognized four basic points in the sun's motion, the vernal and autumnal equinoxes, when the sun is directly over the equator, and the summer and winter solstices, when the sun reaches the northern- and southernmost points of its track (Plin. *Nat.* 2.17.81). Jerome's point is that the annual motion of the sun is cyclical, and that the starting point of this cycle is the spring equinox, when the sun, heading north, passes over the equator. See also Pliny (*Nat.* 2.41.108), who asserts that at the midwinter solstice the sun has completed its cycle.

Meanwhile...great year: Ver. *Aen.* 3.284. The verse describes the cyclical motion of the sun through the seasons of the year.

and the year...track: Ver. *G.* 2.402. The poet is describing the endless round of tasks associated with the cultivation of a vineyard as the year moves through its annual cycle.

living thing...motion of its own: Are the heavenly bodies (the sun, moon, and stars) living creatures? Augustine raised the question in *Litt.* 2.18.38, but then declined to answer it. Opinions were divided among the ancient philosophers; Origen, one of the most important influences on Jerome, thought that the heavenly bodies were infused with their own souls (Or. *Princ.* 3.5.4; Or. *Or.* 7), but Basil rejected this idea as an old wives' tale (Bas. *Hex.* 3.9). For an exhaustive survey of ancient views on the stars as living beings, see Scott, *Origen,* passim.

whole mass: That is, the universe.

the spirit...throughout its members: Ver. *Aen.* 6.725–27. Jerome adapts line 725 of this poem, writing *lunae lucentem globum et astra Titania* in place of Vergil's *lucentemque globum lunae Titianiaque astra.* The verses come from the portion of the *Aeneid* where Anchises is explaining to Aeneas the operation of the underworld, and the cycle of death and rebirth. The "spirit within" is the Stoic world soul that infuses all of the material order and sets all matter in motion (see also at 1:7).

but of its daily paths: That is, setting aside the question of whether the Preacher thought the sun had its own soul or was moved by an external force (God), the thing to note is that in Eccl 1:6 the phrase *whirling in whorls* refers to the daily (twenty-four-hour) cycle of the sun rising and setting. As noted above, Jerome has failed to realize that the subject of this portion of the verse is actually the wind rather than the sun.

oblique and broken...to the east: An explanation for this may be found in Gregory of Nyssa, who shares a common cosmological frame of reference with Jerome: the sun passes over the southern regions

of the earth when it is visible, and then after it sets, passes over the
northern regions on the opposite side of the globe as it makes its
way back to the east (Gr. Nyss. *Hom. I–8 in Eccl.* 1.8). This would be
its course if it traveled along the surface of a plane that bisected the
earth; in fact, the tilt of the earth ensures that the sun remains over
the same latitude as the earth rotates.

lifted high up: In addition to noting that the celestial bodies moved
around the earth in predictable patterns, the Greeks and Romans
also believed that these bodies moved closer and farther away from
the earth. Pliny offers an extremely complicated description of these
motions in *Nat.* 2.13.62–17.81.

evils blaze out upon the earth: Possibly a reference to the Germanic
tribes of the north. When Jerome wrote this work, the disastrous battle
of Hadrianople (AD 378), in which the emperor Valens and two-thirds
of the eastern Roman army had been killed by the Goths, would still
have been fresh in Jerome's mind. He also noted in *Vir. ill.* 135 that
the Goths had been responsible for the destruction of his hometown
of Stridon.

Pliny attributed the fierceness of the northerners to the chill of
the air (Plin. *Nat.* 2.80.189).

all things to himself: An allusion to John 12:32, in which Christ says
that he will draw all people to himself after he has been lifted up.

all in all: 1 Cor 15:28.

1.7

founder of these waters: The Latin word for founder (*conditor*)
appears only once in the Vulgate (Heb 11:10: "For he looked forward
to the city which has foundations, whose builder and founder
[*conditor*] is God"). The equation of Jesus with God's creative activity
grew out of the influence of Stoic philosophy on Christian theology.
Among the Stoics, the λόγος (*logos*: its meanings include "reason" and
"rationality," as well as "word") was the creative and organizing force
immanent in all creation. The term was picked up by the first-century
Jewish philosopher Philo of Alexandria and employed to describe the
instrument used by an immutable and unchanging God to create the
material realm (Ph. *Cher.* 127).

The word λόγος is first applied to Jesus in the Gospel of John:
"In the beginning was the word [λόγος] and the word [λόγος] was with
God and the word [λόγος] was God" (John 1:1). The early Christian
apologists adopted this identification and made Christ (the λόγος) the
creative aspect of God's person (cf. Tert. *Apol.* 21; Pelikan, *Catholic*

Doctrine, 186–89). See also Aug. *Ciu.* 20.30 for the identification of Jesus with the foundation of heaven and earth.

torrents...soon die down: Etymologically, the Latin word *torrentes* ("torrents") is derived from the verb *torreo* ("to dry, parch, burn"). The distinction Jerome draws between a torrent and a river (*flumen*) suggests that he would label a wild, rushing stream that materializes in the desert during a flash flood a *torrens*, while the river that does not dry up during the summer would be a *flumen*. See the note below on the Kidron torrent.

roiled waters: Jerome's Latin term *turbidae aquae*, which we have translated "roiled waters," appears only once in the Vulgate, in Jer 2:18, where the prophet chastises the people of Israel for wanting to return to Egypt in order to drink the roiled waters.

You will give...your pleasure: LXX Ps 35:9 [Ps 36:8].

torrent Kidron: An allusion to John 18:1: "After Jesus had said these things, he went out with his disciples, across the Kidron Valley, where there was a garden." The garden is Gethsemane, where Jesus was arrested. The Kidron Valley runs along the eastern edge of Jerusalem, separating the Temple Mount from the Mount of Olives. The stream (torrent) that flows through the valley is dry for most of the year but is subject to flash flooding during the winter months.

Cherith...dries up: An allusion to 1 Kgs 17:1–7. Elijah had prophesied to Ahab, king of the Israelites, that no rain would fall on the land unless Elijah permitted it. He then hid himself in the wilderness near the Cherith. When the stream dried up, God sent him to Zarephath.

not sated: An allusion to Prov 30:15: "The horse-leech has two daughters, crying, 'Give, give.'" Jerome is referring to the Hebrew text in his citation; in the Septuagint, the horse-leech has three daughters.

1.8

A man will not...troublesome discussions: Jerome has translated this verse based on the Hebrew text, rather than following the Septuagint, which reads: "All words are wearisome; a man will be unable to speak them" (LXX Eccl 1:8). This leads to a slightly different interpretation (see notes below) from that offered by Gregory of Nyssa, who based his comments on the Septuagint.

natural sciences...ethics: Jerome noted at 1:1 that ethics and natural sciences were the first two divisions of knowledge taught by philosophers, and that these areas corresponded to Solomon's first two books, Proverbs and Ecclesiastes.

Speech...height of knowledge: Gregory of Nyssa, commenting on the

Septuagint version of this passage, drew two possible meanings from this verse. First, he recognized that the literal meaning of the text made little sense; why would a person be unable to speak? There is nothing easier than speaking (Gr. Nyss. *Hom. I–8 in Eccl.* 1.11; cf. Gr. Thaum. *Eccl.* 1.8). Since this is the case, this verse must have an allegorical sense. Since it is not difficult to speak, it is essential to consider what sort of words are difficult. Gregory found an answer in 1 Tim 5:17, where Paul discussed the elders who labored in the "word," an obvious reference to the teaching of virtue. In order to become a true elder, a person needed to sweat and labor to overcome a disorderly way of life. This was the hard or wearisome work required as a prerequisite to speaking a word that would instruct the young.

Gregory's second interpretation (*Hom. I–8 in Eccl.* 1.12) comes much closer to what Jerome suggests here. Perhaps the reason a person cannot speak a word is that the human mind is too frail to articulate spiritual realities in words (a point suggested by Paul in 2 Cor 12:4). When the mind turns from the material world presented by the senses and ponders the spiritual order, it perceives things that cannot be translated back into speech.

Jerome's interpretation is based on a very literal rendering of the Hebrew text (see note above), singling out a person's inability to say anything substantive about difficult topics. The reason for this is not that the contemplative is unable to articulate the spiritual realities that the mind sees but rather, because trapped in this world of vanity and illusion, humans are unable even to perceive spiritual things clearly (see further discussion in the Introduction).

Gregory Thaumaturgos offered a similar interpretation with his suggestion that although there were many words, there was little point to be found in this ongoing, foolish talk (Gr. Thaum. *Eccl.* 1.8).

see with a mirror...in an enigma: The first of many allusions to 1 Cor 13:12: "For now we see with a mirror, in an enigma, but then we will see face to face."

prophesy in part: An allusion to 1 Cor 13:9: "For we know in part and we prophesy in part."

all words are troublesome...great labor: Jerome's second version of this verse is much closer to the Septuagint. His emphasis on the difficulty of learning these words has a certain correspondence with Gregory of Nyssa's exegesis (*Hom. I–8 in Eccl.* 1.11; see note above), but whereas Gregory located the difficulty in the effort of mastering oneself, Jerome focused on the task of developing a knowledge of the Bible.

This stands against...expressing wishes: The idea that Christians could be taught directly by the Holy Spirit and thereby avoid the

difficult task of scriptural study and a need to understand the rules
that underpinned proper exegesis was condemned also by Augustine
in *Doct. chr.* Pref. 8. For a discussion of Jerome's portrayal of scriptural
study as an ascetic discipline (like fasting or prayer), see Williams,
Monk and the Book, passim.

1.9

the things he enumerated above ... has not existed before: Augustine
noted that some people considered Eccl 1:9 to support the Platonic
and Stoic doctrine of an endless series of cycles that the universe
passes through. Augustine, possibly following Jerome, asserts that the
Preacher was simply referring to what he had written in earlier verses,
or to the passing of the generations of humans (Aug. *Ciu.* 12.14).
balanced over the waters: The Hebraic view that the earth was founded
upon the waters may be found in Pss 24:2; 136:6; see also Gen 1:6–9.
Nothing has been...said before: Ter. *Eunuch.* Prol. 41. Terence was
commenting on the reuse of stock characters and themes in the play
he was adapting from Greek.
Donatus: Aelius Donatus was one of the most famous grammarians
of late antiquity. He was Jerome's teacher in Rome and wrote an
influential textbook on Latin grammar that was used for centuries. He
also wrote commentaries on the works of Vergil and Terence that were
designed for classroom use. His works had little originality and drew
heavily on the writings of earlier authors (Kelly, *Jerome,* 10–11).
Curse those...before us: Don. *Comm. Ter. Eunuch.* Prol. 41.
seventh day: An allusion to Gen 2:2, which states that after six days
spent in the act of creation, God rested on the seventh.
If everything...under the sun: Or. *Princ.* 1.4.5. Origen was attempting
to solve the question of what God was doing before he began creating.
Either material things are co-eternal with God (uncreated) or there
was a time when he turned to creating them. Origen's solution was to
suggest that neither of these was true, and that all material things were
prefigured or preformed in the Logos, thus having an existence from
all time, even though they did not receive physical form until later.
This, according to Origen, is what the Preacher meant when he wrote
Eccl 1:9–10: all things have existed forever in a prefigured form.

   In a later chapter (Or. *Princ.* 3.5.3), Origen gave a different
answer to the question of what God was doing before he began
creating, by positing an unending sequence of ages, one following
another in an unbroken chain. Thus, as each new age rises to replace
the former and there never is a time when God is not creating. As
Jerome notes, most of the church did not accept Origen's views,

and he was formally condemned a few years after the *Commentary on Ecclesiastes* was completed, at a council of Alexandria (AD 400).

But this view...created before heaven: If all things were in some form of prefigurative existence before the heaven and earth were materially created, then insignificant things would have a preeminence over the greatness of heaven.

1.10

word: Here Jerome is evidently translating directly from the Hebrew, whose word דבר (*dābār*) may mean either "word" or "thing," not from the Septuagint.

Epicurus: Greek philosopher (ca. 341–270 BC). Epicurus founded a philosophical school in Athens, where he advanced a number of doctrines that Christians would later dispute, including that both body and soul were destroyed by death, that gods were dissociated from the human world, that the universe is the product of chance, and that pleasure should be the highest goal of humanity.

same people: Jerome's attribution to Epicurus of a cyclically recurrent history (in either this world or separate worlds with identical histories) is incorrect (our thanks to Professor David Sedley for his help on this point). In a letter written to Avitus (ca. 410) he seems to have realized his mistake. Writing about Origen's views found in *On First Principles,* Jerome asserts that Origen had posited a plurality of worlds, not, as Epicurus had, multiple parallel universes running at the same time, but rather a succession of worlds, with each new one coming into being as the old one came to an end (Hier. *Ep.* 124.5).

The view that Jerome has put forward here is actually the position held by the Stoics, who believed that the universe passed through an unending series of cycles. At the end of each cycle, the universe was consumed in a great conflagration (ἐκπύρωσις [*ekpyrōsis,* "conflagration"]) and began anew, with all events repeating themselves (see Long, *Epicurus to Epictetus,* 256–82; for a Christian perspective on this doctrine, see Or. *Princ.* 2.3.4; Or. *Cels.* 4.67–68; 5.20–21).

Otherwise Judas...recur in the same cycles: This argument against the world and events repeating in endless cycles is taken, with virtually no modification, from Or. *Princ.* 2.3.4.

before the foundation of the world: Eph 1:4.

1.11

face and feet of God: An allusion to Isa 6:2, where the prophet reports his vision of the heavenly court. Origen claimed that his Hebrew teacher had told him that the Seraphim veiled the face and feet of God because the beginning and ending of all things was hidden from the angels, principalities, and powers. Only Jesus and the Holy Spirit knew these things (Or. *Princ.* 4.3.14). Elsewhere (*Princ.* 1.3.4) Origen states that his Hebrew teacher had taught him that the two Seraphim *were* Jesus and the Holy Spirit.

There is considerable ambiguity in the Hebrew text at this point, as Jerome notes in *Is.* 3.4. It is not clear from the Hebrew whether the Seraphim are veiling their own faces and feet or (as he puts it here) the face and feet of God. In his *Commentary on Isaiah,* he finally decides that the text must mean that the Seraphim are veiling God's face and feet, and that this is to be understood allegorically as a reference to things past (which are hidden) and things to come. Like the Seraphim, the apostles also reveal the message of salvation to the believers and hide it from the unfaithful (Hier. *Is.* 3.4).

first and last things are covered: Jerome's exegesis draws out the literal sense of the verse: what has happened in the past is now forgotten, while future events cannot be known.

Gregory of Nyssa interpreted this verse allegorically: the former was humanity's blessed state before the Fall and the appearance of evil. The final state was how we would be after the resurrection, when evil will be consigned to oblivion and our souls returned to their original primordial perfection (Gr. Nyss. *Hom. 1–8 in Eccl.* 1.14).

Septuagint translators...in the end: Jerome has elected to translate the Hebrew words לראשנים (*lārī'šōnîm,* "to the former ones") and לאחרנים (*lā'aḥărōnîm,* "to the later ones") as references to things or events. These two Hebrew masculine words can also designate human beings (Murphy, *Ecclesiastes,* 6 n. 11b). The Septuagint translators made this interpretation possible (although not necessary) by employing the masculine/neuter Greek adjectives τοῖς πρώτοις (*tois prōtois*) and τοῖς ἐσχάτοις (*tois eschatois*). Nevertheless, there is no reason for Jerome to take these as "things," but then in his rendering of the Septuagint version to take them as "people"; in both Hebrew and Greek, they could be either. Nor is there any obvious reason for him to regard—as his comment shows he does—the Septuagint version as taking "first and last" as concerning importance, when he himself has correctly taken the Hebrew as referring them to time. The only real difference between the Greek text itself and Jerome's version of it is that he has put "those going to be last" where the Greek has "those that have become last." The Hebrew uses the same verb form in both "going to be last" and in "going to be at the end"; so either Jerome is silently correcting the Greek, or he has made a slip, or his Greek text was different from ours.

last of all: An allusion to Matt 19:30: "But many who are first will be last, and the last first." This is a very dubious proof-text for Jerome's interpretation, dealing as it does with the reversal of fortunes in the afterlife for those who enjoyed prominence during their lifetime (they, although once first in this world, will be last, or the least, in the kingdom). The point of the Septuagint translation is that people have no memory of the generations that have preceded them.

There is not memory...eternity: See Eccl 2:16.

1.12

his women: An allusion to 1 Kgs 11:1–8, where the writer describes Solomon's seven hundred wives and three hundred concubines. Many of these women were not Israelites, and they led Solomon to turn away from Yahweh and follow the false gods of their nations. The Targum expands this verse greatly, telling how Solomon fell because of his pride, avarice, and marriages to foreign women. The Lord then took away his signet ring and drove him from his throne. Solomon wandered, town to town, crying, "I was king over Israel" (*Tar. Qoh.* 1.12). Because of Solomon's dubious reputation, there was a long-running debate among the Jews as to whether Ecclesiastes belonged in the Hebrew canon (see discussion in Murphy, *Ecclesiastes,* xxiii; Christianson, *Ecclesiastes,* 89–92).

1.13

*anian...*περισπασμόν: The Hebrew word עִנְיָן (ʿinyan), which Jerome transliterated as *anian,* means "task" or "occupation." This word is found only in Ecclesiastes and has a root that means "toil." The Septuagint translators employed the word περισπασμόν (*perispasmon,* "distraction" or "distracting circumstances"). Jerome follows Symmachus's interpretation by translating it as *occupatio* ("business"). Murphy notes that this word generally signifies a disagreeable work, one that here is an evil (*Ecclesiastes,* 11 n. 13d).

Latin interpreter: Jerome refers to one of the Latin (*Vetus Latina*) translations of Ecclesiastes that predated the Vulgate. See the Introduction for a discussion of Jerome's sources.

ἀσχολίαν...occupation: ἀσχολία (*ascholia*) means "occupation," "engagement," or "business," as Jerome suggests.

frequently mentioned...book: The nominal and verbal forms of the word עִנְיָן (ʿinyan) occur ten times in Ecclesiastes (Murphy, *Ecclesiastes,* 11 n. 13d).

Preacher...pursuit of wisdom: Here Gregory of Nyssa and Jerome part ways dramatically in their interpretations. For Gregory, the Preacher is Christ. Consequently, this verse explains the incarnation. Why did

God take on human form? So that he might investigate what had come about in the creation. There was no need for God to investigate the state of heaven, for he already knew that there were no evils there. But the creation was in the grip of a disease, and, like a doctor, God became incarnate in order to investigate its condition firsthand (Gr. Nyss. *Hom. 1–8 in Eccl.* 2.2).

Jerome, reading the text literally, sees in this verse a clue as to where Solomon began to go wrong: he attempted to investigate things that were not permissible for a mortal to know.

infants seized by a demon: Probably to be understood as a reference to convulsions or fits.

Providence: Providence is the view that a god (or gods) ordered the universe and was responsible for exercising divine guidance and care over the events that occur in creation. Lactantius noted that Greco-Roman philosophers had been divided on the question whether providence existed or not. He listed the Epicureans as representatives of the view that there was no providential force guiding the affairs of humanity, and the Stoics as advocates for providence (Lact. *Inst.* 1.2). Lactantius thought that providence was so easily established just by looking at the world around us (the orderly movement of the heavenly bodies, for instance) that there was no need to enter into a lengthy debate about its existence.

unnecessary concern: Lat. *superflua cura.* In Vulg. Eccl 4:4 Jerome used the same words (although reversed in order) to translate the Hebrew phrase רעות רוח (*rĕ'ût rûaḥ*), discussed below at 1:14.

Wanting to know...permissible to know: This interpretation, set in reported speech and attributed to Solomon (although the sentence does not occur in Ecclesiastes), is foundational for Jerome's exegesis of this work. Throughout the rest of the commentary, Jerome will argue that the human desire to understand the reasons and causes of apparently random events is a punishment from God, one that leads the speculative thinker into heresy. Some knowledge belongs to God alone, and those who probe these deliberately hidden mysteries usually fall into heresy (see Hier. *Ep.* 130.16). With this reading Jerome shows that he has no sympathy for the fundamental project that the Preacher has taken on in this work.

cause fairly set out in advance: That is, because Solomon did something first (sought knowledge beyond what was permissible, the "cause"), God responded with a judgment (unnecessary concern or anxiety). Jerome's point is buttressed by the four proof-texts that follow (three from Romans and one from 2 Thessalonians). In each of these texts, God meets sinful behavior (the cause) with punishment.

therefore God...disgraceful passions: Rom 1:26.
Therefore he has surrendered...they should not: Rom 1:28.
Therefore God handed...to filth: Rom 1:24.
For that reason...error to them: 2 Thess 2:11. This verse is drawn from the description of the lawless man who will come in the end-time to lead people astray. Because those who follow him did not love the truth (cause), God sends them a powerful delusion (punishment), making them vulnerable to his lies. The Latin word Jerome uses here, *operationem* (which we have translated "working"), can also be a "religious performance" or "duty."
an evil stretching: Although Jerome has followed Symmachus in translating *anian* as "occupation" in his translation of the verse, here he reverts to the rendering of the unnamed Latin translator and employs the noun/verb pair *distentio...distendo* ("stretching...stretch").
of their own will: Jerome's argument here, supported by his four proof-texts, is that God amplifies humankind's worst inclinations, turning them into punishments. Because the Preacher delved into forbidden knowledge, God increased the desire for this knowledge until it became an all-consuming obsession. In the same way, God inflames the evil desires of those who worship idols, the lust of those who indulge in improper sexual relationships, and the delusion of those who do not love the truth. The craving to know more than we ought is a punishment from God.

Gregory of Nyssa argued that it is wrong to believe that God gave the evils described above to humans, for God can only give good things. God gave the good gift of free will to humans. Humans misused their free will and this led to their experience of the evils of sin.

Gregory went on to state that the Bible often expresses this concept in this way and cites two of the verses Jerome used above (Rom 1:26, 28) as examples of this practice. Nevertheless, it is the capacity to make choices, our free will, that God has given, not (as Jerome reads it) the evils themselves (Gr. Nyss. *Hom. I–8 in Eccl.* 2.3).

Gregory Thaumaturgos also seems to reject the idea that God gives evils to humans. In his paraphrase of the Septuagint text, he removed the noun Θεός (*Theos,* "God") and altered the verb to form an impersonal construction: "it is given to man to work upon the earth" (for discussion, see Jarick, *Thaumaturgos' Paraphrase,* 20).

1.14

presumption of spirit: for this rendering of the Hebrew phrase רעות רוח (*rĕʿût rûaḥ*), see following notes.

routh: The abstract Hebrew noun רעות (*rĕ'ût*) has been derived by interpreters from various roots. One, רעע (*rā'a'*), means "break": hence "breaking, affliction," which is the rendering Jerome later chose for the Vulgate, *adflictio spiritus.* A second Hebrew root, רעה (*rā'â*), means "feed": hence "pasture," as Jerome reports from Aquila, Theodotion, and Symmachus. Another use of the root *rā'â* has the meaning "desire" or "will," which is the meaning of *rĕ'ût* in the Aramaic portion of Ezra, e.g., 5:17; 7:18. Since the Septuagint translated this with the word προαίρεσις (*proairesis,* "purpose," "plan"), Jerome claims that the translators had based this on the Aramaic rather than the Hebrew meaning. The ambiguity of *rĕ'ût* is compounded by that of the second word in this favorite phrase of the Preacher's, namely רוח (*rûah*), as either "wind," breath," or "spirit"; as a result, a phrase that probably meant "chasing the wind" turns into phrases as remote as "affliction of spirit" and "pasture of the soul." For further discussion, see Barton, *Ecclesiastes,* 85–86.

νομήν: *nomēn,* "pasture."

βόσκησιν: *boskēsin,* "pasturing."

Syrian: When Jerome writes "Syrian," he actually means Aramaic. In Hebrew, the word *Aram* means Syria.

προαίρεσιν: *proairesin,* "purpose," "plan."

presumption: The Latin word *praesumptio,* for which we have used the direct English derivative "presumption," is used as a calque of προαίρεσις (*proairesis,* lit. "taking in advance," "taking in preference").

good and evil: An allusion to the title of Cicero's work *On Definitions of Good and Evil.* The second sentence of this work (Cic. *Fin.* 1.1) reads: "Some people (and not just the uneducated ones either) are dissatisfied with the whole subject of philosophy."

routh...will: See note on *routh,* above. The phrase רעות רוח (*rĕ'ût rûah*) is common in Ecclesiastes, with examples occurring in 1:17; 2:11, 17, 26; 4:4, 6, 16; 6:9; 11:5.

Sufficient to the day...trouble: Matt 6:34. The Latin word *malitia* (Gk. κακία [*kakia*]), which is translated here as "trouble," literally means "badness." Like κακία, it is sometimes used in later Latin in the sense of the Greek word κακά (*kaka,* "misfortunes," lit. "bad things"), as well as in the sense of the word "wickedness."

κακουχίαν: *kakouchian,* "distress."

1.15

The twisted man...be adorned: Jerome follows the Septuagint in this verse, translating ἐπικοσμηθῆναι (*epikosmēthēnai,* "to be adorned," "to be decorated") with the Latin infinitive *adornari*. This leads him into an unsustainable argument, namely, that the straight person receives adornment, while the bent one gets correction. While *adornari* is a literal translation of the Greek, it does not capture the underlying idea of a proper arrangement or order bound up in the Greek verb κοσμέω (*kosmeō*, "to order," "to arrange").

The twisted man: Jerome has taken the Hebrew word מעות ([*mĕʿuwwāt*, "distorted") as a masculine noun. In context, however, it must be taken as a neuter, a thing rather than a person (Murphy, *Ecclesiastes*, 12 n. 15a). The Preacher's point is that there is no value in attempting to straighten what cannot be straightened, or counting what cannot be numbered (Jarick, *Thaumaturgos' Paraphrase*, 23).

Gregory of Nyssa takes the Septuagint's rendering (διεστραμμένον [*diestrammenon*, "the one who was/the thing that was distorted"]) as a reference to a thing, human nature, which has been twisted and now no longer can fit with creation (Gr. Nyss. *Hom. I–8 in Eccl.* 2.4).

Twisted is not said...distorted from the straight: One of the explanations offered in the Midrash Rabbah for this verse is that the twisted man was straight at first and then became crooked by following teachers who had abandoned the study of Torah (*Qoh. Rab.* 1.15.2).

introduce certain natures: Jerome here employs the Latin verb *introduco* ("to lead in," "to introduce"). A heretic introduces his own twisted nature into theological discourse, and produces nothing of value.

firstborn of Israel...omitted: The quotation is an allusion to Num 1:1–46, where God ordered Moses to count the number of men available for military service. Only men of age twenty or older were counted; those who were ineligible for military service (women, slaves, and children) were not counted. The diminution that Jerome describes is the lessening of the strength of an army, which must support and defend not only itself, but also the noncombatants.

Gregory of Nyssa noted that a diminution is something that is lacking or left out. This verse refers to the idea that our nature has been twisted and we are no longer numbered among God's one hundred sacred sheep (the rational beings). Consequently, Christ, the Good Shepherd, has been sent to find the one sheep (our nature) that has strayed (an allusion to Luke 15:3–7) and recover it from its wandering in the vanity of the unreal (Gr. Nyss. *Hom. I–8 in Eccl.* 2.4).

The sense may also be: Having suggested his preferred interpretation of this verse (that it was written about heretics) Jerome now offers three further possibilities, eschewing any comment on these additional alternatives.

When everyone has been…in his error: A modified version of Origen's doctrine of apokatastasis, the view that in the fullness of time, all created spirits will return to the perfection in which they were created and be reunited with God (Or. *Princ.* 1.6.3; 3.6.5; Patrides, "Salvation," 467–69). While Origen does not appear to have suggested explicitly the rehabilitation of Satan, this potential is implicit in his views. Jerome here excludes Satan, but later in his life he rejected the system entirely (Hier. *Ep.* 124.3, 11), as did Augustine (Aug. *Ciu.* 21.17).

will of the devil…spirit of malice: This interpretation sits well with Gregory Thaumaturgos's paraphrase of this verse: "Everything down here is full of a strange, foul spirit" (Gr. Thaum. *Eccl.* 1.15; trans. Jarick, *Thaumaturgos' Paraphrase*, 21).

flock of the Lord by the devil: This interpretation evokes Gregory's analogy (see note above) of our nature wandering like a lost sheep. It is possible that both writers are here following Origen.

1.16

wisdom and knowledge: Jerome follows the Hebrew text here, omitting the additional clause found in the Septuagint: "I also gave my heart to know wisdom and knowledge."

Jerusalem: Archaeologists believe that the site of Jerusalem has been occupied since the fourteenth century BC. The city came into Jewish possession around 1000 BC, when David captured Jerusalem and made it the capital of his kingdom (2 Sam 5:1–9). Although Jerome here compares Solomon's wisdom to that of those who ruled Jerusalem before Solomon (the Jebusites), in 2.7 he interprets this passage spiritually as a reference to Christ. Solomon's wisdom is a secular gift of knowledge, and does not compare to the spiritual wisdom given to Abraham, Moses, the prophets, and the apostles (cf. 1.1; 2.9).

Books of Kingdoms: See LXX 3 Kgdms 3:5–9 [1 Kgs 3:5–9].

much wisdom and knowledge: Gregory of Nyssa noted that Solomon actually had an experiential basis for his ultimate condemnation of the things of this world, which gave him an advantage over a person who simply gives good advice without having experienced the things under discussion. He had sampled everything he wrote about and therefore could not be countered with the possibility that things like wealth and great positions might actually be found to be good, if they were possessed (Gr. Nyss. *Hom. I–8 in Eccl.* 2.5).

1.17

The first principle…devoid of foolishness: Hor. *Ep.* 1.1, 41–42.

educated toward wisdom: Jerome here offers a view of why bad things are found in God's good creation: they exist for our education and spiritual perfection. Origen has a very similar idea, suggesting that the material world was created for the training of the souls that had been cast down from their primordial perfection (Or. *Princ.* 3.5.4). See also 7.15.

presumption of spirit...suffice: See 1.14.

This is a phrase: The Hebrew phrase רעות רוח (*rĕ‘ût rûaḥ*); see the discussion at 1.14.

1.18

from one...more is demanded: An allusion to Luke 12:48.

And who is there...sad by me: 2 Cor 2:2.

meditation and study: Jerome does not follow the interpretive line taken here by Dionysius of Alexandria, who reads in this verse a condemnation of the pursuit of worldly knowledge, given by the devil, which is not spiritual and leads to vanity (1 Cor 3:19). Solomon, according to Dionysius, sought this kind of knowledge (Dion. Al. *Fr. Eccl.* 1.18).

Jerome is much closer to Gregory of Nyssa on this point, who argued that the acquisition of knowledge is a difficult, painful struggle (Gr. Nyss. *Hom. 1–8 in Eccl.* 2.6). See also Gregory Thaumaturgos, who wrote: if wisdom follows knowledge, then trouble accompanies wisdom (Gr. Thaum. *Eccl.* 1.18).

CHAPTER 2

2.1

I said in my heart...even this was vanity: The Septuagint translators followed the Hebrew text in a very literal, mechanistic way when they rendered this verse. Jerome's translation follows the Septuagint, preserving both the sense and word order of the Greek text. The verse was substantially altered in his later Vulgate translation. Jerome appears to have realized that the references to the heart signified an interior discourse, rather than the belief that the Preacher was addressing a part of himself (his own heart) and threatening to subject it to pleasure and good. This refined understanding (also present in the following paraphrase of the verse) of the Hebrew is reflected in the Vulgate version: "I said in my heart: 'I will go and abound in delights and enjoy good things.'"

grief and labor...pointless and endless struggle: A discovery noted above at Eccl 1:17–18. Gregory Thaumaturgos's paraphrase offered an interpretive key that Jerome overlooked here: the characterization of the pursuit of wisdom as futility was the conclusion of an earlier experiment, before God had granted the gift of the highest wisdom to Solomon (1 Kgs 3:9–12; 5:12; 10:23). It was not until he received God's wisdom that he was able truly to value the pursuit (cf. Gr. Thaum. *Eccl.* 1.6–2.1; Jarick, *Thaumaturgos' Paraphrase*, 23–28).

Jerome, convinced that flawed humanity cannot possess true spiritual knowledge, was content to read this verse literally (cf. 2.12): the pursuit of answers to questions that only God possessed was a futile endeavor.

pleasure once drained...does not satisfy: A similar view is expressed at Gr. Nyss. *Hom. I–8 in Eccl.* 2.8.

not only physical joy...spiritual joy: As the following verses make clear, the Preacher investigated a wide number of material pleasures in his attempt to see if there was anything real in them worthy of a life's devotion. Jerome here interprets "joy" broadly, moving beyond the Preacher's material pleasures to condemn spiritual joy as well.

goad: The goad (Lat. *stimulus*) was a spike used to encourage animals to move faster. It was also employed as an instrument of torture, and metaphorically could be anything that caused ongoing torment or distress.

goad prodding...will not be conceited: An allusion to 2 Cor 12:7. In this verse Paul reports that he had received a thorn in his flesh to keep him from becoming too full of self-importance after his experience of spiritual visions in the third heaven.

Give me neither riches...poverty: Prov 30:8.

Lest I become full...watches me: Prov 30:9.

devil, too, fell...good things: Origen had suggested that some spirits, suffering from mental deficiencies or out of a desire for material things, had fallen away from God after they were created (Or. *Princ.* 1.3.8–1.4.2).

He must not be swollen...of the devil: 1 Tim 3:6. That text warns about the danger of selecting a new Christian believer to be an ἐπίσκοπος (*episkopos*, "bishop" or "overseer"). This man, elevated before he has matured in the faith, may grow conceited and succumb to pride. Jerome has taken the verse out of context to make a less plausible point about the dangers of spiritual joy.

in which the devil also fell: A clarification, unpacking the phrase "judgment of the devil" to show that it means not "judgment by the devil," as these words might have been taken, but "the same sentence as that to which the devil was condemned"—that is, eternal damnation.

see it with a mirror...truth: An allusion to 1 Cor 13:12. Also found in 1.8; 3.8; 5.1; 7.1; and 7.24, 25.

2.2

I said to laughter...you doing this: Here Jerome follows the Septuagint in his translation, which closely matches the sense and order of the Hebrew text. The verse was significantly altered in the Vulgate, where he incorporated Aquila's translation of the Hebrew word מהולל (*mĕhôlāl*), rendering the verse: "I counted laughter an error." The second half of the verse goes beyond what is found in either the Hebrew or the Septuagint: "I said to joy, 'Why do you mislead [humans] without reason?'" Joy becomes an active principle, bent upon deception for no apparent good reason. Jerome's Vulgate reworking is much darker, more pessimistic than what he offers here.

molal: מהולל (*mĕhôlāl*, "mad").

πλάνησιν: *planēsin*, "error."

θόρυβον: *thorybon*, "uproar of a crowd," "a commotion."

περιφοράν: *periphoran*, "a circuit," "revolution," "going around."

a revolution: Gregory of Nyssa defines περιφοράν (*periphoran*) as a "frenzy" or "madness," and supports his interpretation by citing the unseemly behavior of people who laugh: they lose control of themselves, they breathe convulsively, flare out their cheeks, bare their teeth, gums, and the back of their mouths, and shake their bodies. How could this behavior be anything other than madness (Gr. Nyss. *Hom. I–8 in Eccl.* 2.7)?

wind of doctrine: An allusion to Eph 4:14, Paul's description of the church's teaching ministries. These pedagogical activities are intended to bring the believers to a mature state in which they will be stable and no longer tossed about by every wind of doctrine.

changed to tears: An allusion to Luke 6:25: "Woe to you who laugh now for you shall grieve and weep."

lament past vices: Cf. Dion. Al. *Fr. Eccl.* 2.2: Madness produces laughter, and this laughter does not allow a person to mourn past sins.

2.3

I planned in my heart...persist in foolishness: There is a significant difference between Jerome's translation here (which closely follows the Septuagint) and what is found in the Vulgate: *cogitavi in corde meo abstrahere a vino carnem meam ut animum meum transferrem ad sapientiam devitaremque stultitiam donec viderem quid esset utile filiis hominum...* ("I planned in my heart to drag my flesh away from wine, in order to carry my soul to wisdom and to avoid foolishness, until I saw what was profitable for the sons of men..."). It is difficult to believe that Jerome was responsible for what is found in the Vulgate: not only does it deviate dramatically from what is found in the Hebrew and Septuagint texts, but it makes no sense in the context of either the verse or the chapter (what was the experiment proposed here? Abstinence from wine and the avoidance of folly? And if so, why does the Preacher plant vines for himself [Eccl 2:4] and have wine stewards to serve him [Eccl 2:8])? In fact, this is most probably a pious alteration made by a medieval copyist.

I wanted to live…unconsciousness in pleasure: Both Gregory of Nyssa and Gregory Thaumaturgos took this verse to mean that the Preacher had made a test to see if his heart (Gr. Nyss. *Hom. I–8 in Eccl.* 2.7) or soul (Gr. Thaum. *Eccl.* 2.3) could restrain the lusts and desires of the flesh. Gregory of Nyssa concluded that the Preacher had been successful in this experiment, and, with a mind that remained in control, had sampled material pleasures and found them wanting (Gr. Nyss. *Hom. I–8 in Eccl.* 2.8; 3.3).

Gregory Thaumaturgos, on the other hand, suggested that material pleasures had overwhelmed the Preacher; his thinking was corrupted to such an extent that he began to consider these pleasures a good (Gr. Thaum. *Eccl.* 2.10).

God, the Author…even into sinners: This could be an allusion to Rom 1:18–21, in which Paul asserts that the wicked are without excuse because God has disclosed himself to humankind, and, moreover, his nature is clearly revealed in his creation.

thinking and natural reason…drew me back: Jerome is here looking ahead to the conclusion of the Preacher's experiment, offered in Eccl 2:11, the view that having immersed himself in all manner of pleasures, his reflection on them led him to reject them as vanities.

search for wisdom…their own life: Here Jerome looks ahead to Eccl 2:12, where the Preacher, having abandoned his attempt to find good in material pleasures, resumes his careful examination of wisdom.

exchange pleasure for wisdom…spiritual joyfulness: The books that Jerome mentions here were probably the works of the Cyrenaics or Epicureans. The Cyrenaics, reputedly founded by Aristippus (an associate of Socrates) in the late fourth century BC, were the school of ancient philosophy most closely associated with the pursuit of pleasure. In their system the pursuit of pleasure and the avoidance of pain were humanity's highest good. Epicurus and his followers rejected the Cyrenaic emphasis on pleasure, arguing that freedom from distress (non-perturbation, or ataraxy) was the true pleasure, in contrast to the ongoing drive to experience pleasure that lay at the heart of the Cyrenaic system (Konstan, "Epicureanism," 244–45).

It is unlikely that Jerome would have appreciated the differences between the two schools of thought, and he often slanders adversaries by referring to them as "Epicurus and Aristippus," that is, those more devoted to their own pleasure than to a proper Christian lifestyle (see Hier. *Ep.* 33.5; 50.5). Lactantius was quite possibly his source of information for their views; Lactantius suggested that Epicurus believed the chief good to be pleasure of mind while Aristippus thought the chief good was pleasure of body (Lact. *Inst.* 3.7).

avoided: See 1.17 for the value of harmful things in teaching a person to pursue what should be craved in this life. Dionysius noted that although wine makes the heart merry, a body regulated in a controlled and moderate fashion does the same (Dion. Al. *Fr. Eccl.* 2.2).

2.4

Before I discuss...understood: What follows is Jerome's paraphrase of the contents of Eccl 2:4–14. In this paraphrase he offers a historical reading of the text, but when he treats the verses individually, in the following chapters, he will interpret them allegorically.

Gregory of Nyssa, on the other hand, thought that the deeds described in this passage were to be understood literally, although he was undecided if they had all happened or were a literary artifice. According to Gregory, these verses were a public confession, intended to serve as a salutary example for the church. For a Christian, confession produced modesty and a welcome sense of shame for wrongs done. The Preacher here was confessing acts that no one who aimed at the life of virtue would ever want to participate in. Through this confession, he offered a model for Christians, as well as a condemnation of the pursuit of these forms of pleasure (Gr. Nyss. *Hom. 1–8 in Eccl.* 3.2–3).

As king...good in this age: Jerome's paraphrase focuses on the historical elements found in the following verses. Modern scholars (Murphy, *Ecclesiastes,* 17) believe that the list of pleasures investigated in these verses is drawn from the account of Solomon's life, found in the Hebrew Bible. Although Jerome does not specifically identify the king as Solomon here, he has stated his view that the work was composed by Solomon (see 1.1; 1.17), and there is no reason to think that he did not view these words as a historical description of Solomon's deeds.

Nevertheless...in the world: Jerome goes far beyond what the Preacher actually asserts in this section of his paraphrase. The Preacher does not condemn material pleasures, and in fact he explicitly states that his heart took joy in his work (Eccl 2:10). Nevertheless, the Preacher's verdict on this experiment is that it has been ultimately pointless, a vanity (Eccl 2:11), presumably because he will ultimately have to relinquish the good life he has made for himself when death comes. The scathing condemnation of the experiment belongs to Jerome, not the Preacher.

follower of the virtues: In Greco-Roman philosophical thought, the four cardinal virtues were bravery, moderation, prudence, and justice. To this list Christianity appended the supernatural virtues: love, faith, and hope. A list of fundamental virtues was also enumerated by the apostle Paul in his description of the fruits of the Holy Spirit: love, joy, peace, patience, kindness, goodness, faithfulness, gentleness, and self-control (Gal 5:22–23).

The one...his works great: This verse earned Gregory of Nyssa's condemnation: the Preacher did not say that he made his works great for God, but rather great for himself. The things described in the following verses were done not for God but rather to sate the desires of the Preacher (Gr. Nyss. *Hom. I–8 in Eccl.* 3.4).

Jerome, on the other hand, departs from the literal/historical interpretation offered above, and begins to interpret these verses allegorically, with the Preacher symbolizing either Christ or, as here, the model Christian.

image of the Creator: This elevation, in which a human is restored to image of the Creator (*imaginem conditoris*), has echoes in New Testament verses such as Col 3:5–10, in which the Christian is urged to put to death the old vices and be regenerated in the image of the Creator. See also 2.7 for the *imaginem conditoris* as the end of the Christian life.

houses...live in them: In a letter to the Roman senator Pammachius discussing the monastic buildings that he and his patron Paula were constructing in Bethlehem, Jerome noted that they were building them so that if Joseph and Mary came to visit, the pair would have a place to stay (Hier. *Ep.* 66.14). Here he is speaking of allegorical houses, a probable reference to the place a believer constructs within the self to serve as a dwelling place for God (cf. John 14:23; 2 Cor 6:16).

Gregory of Nyssa discussed (at considerable length) the folly of those who build great mansions and fill them with luxury items that go well beyond a person's need for simple shelter (Gr. Nyss. *Hom. I–8 in Eccl.* 3.4).

donkey: An allusion to Christ's triumphal entry into Jerusalem, seated on the back of a young donkey (Matt 21:2–11; Mark 11:2–10; Luke 19:28–36).

This verse also earned Gregory of Nyssa's censure. What, he asked, was the primary cause of mental agitation and wild behavior? The Preacher had erred, ignoring the beneficial examples contained in the Hebrew Bible. There was the case of Noah, who had planted vineyards, made wine, and then displayed his nakedness in a drunken stupor (Gen 9:20–23); and of Lot, who, while drunk, had committed incest with his daughters (Gen 19:30–38). Wine, suggested Gregory, is a source of such great evils that it is clear that the Preacher is making a confession of sin when he admits that not only did he drink wine, but he also planted vineyards so that he could increase his supply of the pernicious drink (Gr. Nyss. *Hom. I–8 in Eccl.* 3.6).

2.5

mansion of the wealthy man: Jerome's allegory now shifts as the wealthy man (and the Preacher, who is carrying out the experiment) becomes Christ. Christ's mansion is the church. In the church there are greater and lesser vessels, a description of the various stations or ranks of the believers, based on their spiritual maturity.

wood and clay: An allusion to 2 Tim 2:20: "In a great house there are not only vessels of gold and silver, but also of wood and earthenware, and some for noble use, some for ignoble." It is also possible to see here an allusion to Rom 9:19–24, in which Paul characterizes God as a potter who makes one pot for noble use and another for destruction.

vegetables: See Or. *Hom. 1-28 in Num.* 27.1 for the view that the infirm, who were unable to stomach the food eaten by the strong (meat), were pleased with vegetables, for this suited the weakness of their bodies. This physical principle could also, argued Origen, be applied to the spiritual needs of a person (ibid. and also Or. *Or.* 27.5). The infants in the faith, those who were just beginning to acquire an understanding of Christianity, required spiritual milk (cf. 1 Cor 3:2–3); the mature in faith, those who were perfect and could handle advanced spiritual truths, consumed solid food (cf. Heb 5:12–14); and finally, those who were infirm in their faith, able to understand only rudimentary teachings, consumed vegetables (cf. Rom 14:2).

Latin manuscripts: Jerome again points out his dissatisfaction with the translation found in one of his Latin manuscripts of the Hebrew Bible. Eventually this disapproval of these texts led him to produce the Vulgate. See discussion of the Latin texts in the Introduction.

there are different gifts: Lat. *gratiae* (lit. "graces"). Jerome is here
translating Paul's Greek word χαρίσματα (*charismata*) (1 Cor 12:4),
which is also often rendered "gifts" in English Bible translations. This
word is based on the Greek root χάρις (*charis*), a word whose meaning
includes the definition "grace."

Trees are planted...in the church: In this second analogy for the
church, believers are like the different types of trees planted in
orchards and forests. The trees produce fruit, according to their types.
See 2.6 for the trees that do not bear fruit.

different gifts...greater honor: Jerome now links his spiritual allegory to
the analogy that Paul developed in 1 Cor 12:1–30, his characterization
of the church as a human body, with each part (individual person)
having a role that supports the larger body (the church).

tree of life...wisdom: Jerome's analogy evokes Gen 2:9; 3:22, the
description of the two trees (the tree of the knowledge of good and
evil, and the tree of life) that stood in the center of the Garden of
Eden. In the context of his extended analogy, however, the tree of
life, which is wisdom, must be a reference to Christ, who stands at the
center of his church and confers life upon it.

2.6

woodland germinating the wood: Jerome follows the Septuagint
reading: τοῦ ποτίσαι ἀπ' αὐτῶν δρυμὸν βλαστῶντα ξύλα (*tou potisai ap'
autōn drymon blastōnta xyla,* "to water from them a grove growing
timbers"). The Vulgate reading restores the construction in the
Hebrew text: "I built pools of water for myself so that I could water the
forest of growing timber." The Greek word ξύλον (*xylon*) and the Latin
word *lignum* both mean "wood suitable for cutting," that is, firewood
or wood used in building construction; as Jerome points out in his
commentary, the word does not refer to the types of trees that bear
fruit.

Trees of the woodland...streams: Jerome continues the allegorical
reading he began in the interpretation of the previous verse: Christians
are trees that bear different types of fruit; those outside the church are
the trees that do not produce fruit. The former draw their sustenance
(water) from the heavens, while the latter are fed by material things.

At 10.9 Jerome presses this analogy further by asserting that the
trees of the woodland are the heretics.

Egypt...Ethiopia: The two sources of the Nile River, the White and
Blue Nile, originate in Africa. In the ancient world, the land south of
Syene (Aswan) was known as Ethiopia.

Egypt…promised land: Another contrast: the promised land (Israel) is watered from above, while Egypt, which symbolizes enslavement to carnal or material pleasures, is watered from below.

awaits the early and later rain: Jas 5:7. James's verse instructs the reader to wait patiently for the second coming of Christ, much as a farmer waits for the rains (from above) to water his fields.

2.7

homegrown slaves: Jerome's translation of the verse follows both the Hebrew and Septuagint renderings by distinguishing between slaves (male and female) and those slaves born to a household (see discussion in the notes below). In the Vulgate, however, this distinction is lost, as Jerome replaced *vernaculi* ("homegrown slaves") with *multam familiam.* The Latin word *familia* could refer to a large group of slaves, but more commonly it signified all the members of a household (relatives, freedmen, and slaves).

as we said above: See 1.1.

spirit of fear: An allusion to Rom 8:15: "For you did not receive the spirit of slavery to fall back into fear, but you have received the spirit of adoption."

homegrown slaves: Lat. *vernaculos*: a person who was born to an enslaved mother. Under Roman law, this person was also a slave (Iust. *Dig.* 1.5.1; see discussion in Bradley, *Slavery*, 33–35). The Hebrew Bible also distinguished between slaves who were purchased and those who were born in a household (Gen 17:12).

They surpass…slave women: In Roman society the *verna* ("homegrown slave") was usually regarded as having a higher social rank than a slave who had been purchased (Bradley, *Slavery*, 33–35).

given their liberty…by the Lord: Another reference to Roman social practice, the manumission of slaves. Manumission (Lat. *manumissio*, from the verb *manumitto* ["from my hand/authority I send"]) was the process a slave owner could employ (either while living or in his will) that would set a slave free. Under Roman law, manumitted slaves became freedmen (*liberti*).

image of the Creator: See note on this at 2.4. Jerome offers a view of the Christian hierarchy that is lamentably skewed by his own obsessions. Whereas some people might see good works, charity, or loving one's neighbor as the highest expression of Christian faith, Jerome would presumably put those people practicing these commendable acts in with the cows and sheep. For Jerome, it was intensive study of the Scriptures, an intellectual endeavor available to only a small elite, that allowed one to reach the top of the Christian hierarchy and assume the image of the Creator.

above all…in that city: Solomon's father, King David, captured Jerusalem from the Jebusites (cf. 2 Sam 5:1–9).

what Jerusalem is…king in Jerusalem: That is, as Jerome has discussed above, the Preacher is a figure of Christ, who is the head of the church, just as Jerusalem is a figure for the church (see further discussion in the note at 2.9 [however…the church]).

2.8

wine stewards and stewardesses: The Hebrew phrase שדה ושדות (*šiddâ wĕšiddôt,* "many women") is a *hapax legomenon* whose meaning still eludes a complete consensus. It comprises two forms of the same feminine noun, first singular then plural, joined by "and," implying a large number of the same noun; compare the note on 1.2 (magnitude of this vanity). Jerome's distinction of gender between the two words, absent in the Hebrew, is found in the Septuagint and other old versions. Murphy (*Ecclesiastes,* 17 n. 8b) suggests that from its context ("delights of men") this phrase should be taken as a reference to many women, a harem, an interpretation supported by the accounts of Solomon's large number of wives and concubines (1 Kgs 11:3).

The Septuagint translated the Hebrew with the phase οἰνοχόον καὶ οἰνοχόας (*oinochoon kai oinochoas,* "a man to pour wine, and women to pour wine"), and Jerome follows this translation, leading to the lengthy explanation below. By the time he made his Vulgate translation, Jerome was more inclined to follow the view of Aquila (discussed in the commentary), and rendered this phrase: *scyphos et urceos in ministerio ad vina fundenda* ("goblets and pitchers engaged in the service of pouring out the wine").

speech and thought: An idea repeated at 10.19. In Platonic thought, discursive speech, which is involved with the material world, is considered inferior to thought, just as the concerns of the practical man are judged inferior to the lofty thoughts of the philosopher (cf. Pl. *Tht.* 175b–176c). In the Bible, gold was deemed more valuable than silver, and both were better than wood and earthenware (see 2 Tim 2:20), a point Jerome frequently returned to in his letters, when praising sanctified virgins (gold pots) over married women (silver); see Hier. *Ep.* 48.2.

pallor of gold: See LXX Ps 67:14 [Ps 68:13]: "the wings of a dove, covered with silver, its pinions with green gold." In the context of this verse, the dove represents the spoils of war, carried away from a battle. Jerome's spiritual interpretation of the verse has the silver of the dove's wings (speech) concealing a secret wealth, the gold of the body, which is analogous to a person's hidden thoughts.

these are the kings: See the end of 2.7. The Preacher (Christ) is richer in wisdom than all of the secular wise men.

The kings of the earth...one place: Ps 2:2.

white for the harvest: John 4:35.

destroys the wisdom...prudent: Isa 29:14; quoted in 1 Cor 1:19. Jerome's point is that the Christian has access to a higher knowledge than what is possessed by worldly philosophers, an argument developed at 1 Cor 1:18–25.

cantor...materiality: Jerome repeats the contrast between those focused on spiritual things and those focused on material matters, discussed above at 2.6 (trees) and 2.7 (slaves).

ὕλην: ὕλη (*hylē,* lit. "timber") is also a general word for "material" and is used from Aristotle onward for "matter" as opposed to an (immaterial) intelligent or organizing principle.

like matter: Pharaoh's injunction to the midwives to kill the firstborn male children of the Israelites is recorded in Exod 1:16. He had ordered the midwives to kill the male infants because full-grown, male Hebrew slaves had the potential to rebel against their overlords (Exod 1.12). In Jerome's allegorical reading, Pharaoh stands as a figure for Satan, wanting to destroy the spiritual people and allowing only the carnal to live.

produced all daughters: Zelophehad had no sons to inherit his property (Num 26:33), because he had died as a punishment for his own sin (Num 27:3). Zelophehad's daughters petitioned Moses, asking to inherit their father's property. At this time in Hebraic history only sons could inherit property. Moses took the case to God, who agreed with the daughters and decreed that women could inherit a father's property if there were no sons to claim it (Num 27:5–11).

Jerome's literal interpretation of this verse suggests that the production of daughters, rather than an untimely death, was the punishment for Zelophehad's sin. This reading is dubious in view of God's evident favor toward these women.

In his spiritual reading of this text, however, Jerome simply asserts that spiritual people (the saints) are rewarded with spiritual offspring. Zelophehad produced carnal offspring because he was dead in his sins.

placed in danger: Dinah was Jacob's only daughter (Gen 30:21). As a young woman she was raped by Shechem, a prince of the region. This led to a massacre of Shechem's people by Jacob's sons (Genesis 34) and the possibility of retaliation against Jacob.

Delight in the Lord...your heart: LXX Ps 36:4 [Ps 37:4].

You will give them...your pleasure: LXX Ps 35:9 [Ps 36:8].

pourers and pouresses: On the problems of translating this Hebrew phrase, see the note above (wine stewards and stewardesses).

pouresses...does not allow: Jerome is having a bit of fun with his language here. The Latin word for "a man who pours" is *fusor*, a masculine noun. Because Jerome wants to denote both men and women who pour wine, he coins a feminine noun, *fusitrix* ("a woman who pours").

κυλίκιον...κυλίκια: *kylikion/kylikia*, "a small cup/small cups."

in Proverbs...who are passing by: An allusion to Prov 9:2–3, in which Wisdom lays a table for whoever will learn from her.

diluted with ordinary humanity: Jerome's attempt at explaining the nature of the incarnation predates the vigorous ecclesiastical controversy that led to the Council of Chalcedon (451). It goes without saying that none of the parties to that debate would have been satisfied with the explanation that God's divinity was diluted by mixing it with humanity. For an introduction to this debate, see Pelikan, *Catholic Doctrine*, 226–77.

2.9

our Lord: By reading Eccl 2:4ff. as allegorical references to Jesus, Jerome has to solve the apparent problem posed here of a figure who increases in greatness. God/Christ in philosophical thought has always been the same, rather than growing and changing as a human does. The verb used in the Septuagint, μεγαλύνω (*megalynō*, "to make great, powerful"), does imply the idea of change and growth toward something better.

Gregory of Nyssa, interpreting these verses historically, did not face this problem. Solomon had set out to enlarge his works (Eccl 2:4), and the result was that he had been enlarged in worldly terms. The verse simply conveys the result of his quest: much to his detriment, his experience was enlarged by things he should not have undertaken. The wisdom that stood with him was the experiential knowledge garnered from these activities (Gr. Nyss. *Hom. 1–8 in Eccl.* 4.5).

He progressed...favor: Luke 2:52. One solution to the problem of how Christ, who is by definition perfect and unchanging, could be made great was to link Eccl 2:9 to this text, which seems to suggest that Jesus did grow and change during his earthly existence.

wherefore God exalted him: Phil 2:9. A second approach to the problem is to suggest that being made great did not describe a transition from "less great" to "great," but rather represents formal recognition of the greatness (previously undisclosed) that already exists in an individual. Christ is exalted by God, and thus humanity comes to recognize his greatness.

However...the church: At 1.16, Jerome suggests that Solomon had been wiser than all of those before him in Jerusalem. At 2.7, he argued that this phrase could not apply to Solomon on a historical level, because those before him were the Jebusites. Consequently, this must be an allegorical reference to Christ: Jerusalem must symbolize the Jewish people; those before him were the leaders of the Jews; both Jews and their leaders were supplanted by Christ and the church.

face of Moses: An allusion to Exod 34:33, where Moses covers the radiance of his face with a veil. See note at 1.2 (Moses' face).

in full light: An allusion to 2 Cor 3:12–18: Paul wrote that Christ made it possible for humans to look upon God with unveiled faces. Origen argued that a veil, spiritual dullness, lay over humans' hearts and prevented them from understanding the spiritual sense of holy Scripture (Or. *Princ.* 1.1.2).

wisdom remained with him: Dionysius reads this differently: in contrast to all of the transitory pleasures and possessions that the Preacher had accumulated in his experiment, wisdom was the only thing that could be taken into the afterlife. It alone stood with the Preacher (Dion. Al. *Fr. Eccl.* 2.10).

Gregory of Nyssa, on the other hand, suggested that this meant that the Preacher's experience of illicit pleasures had been controlled by wisdom. That is, Solomon's great wisdom had never abandoned him but remained with him and passed judgment on all of the pleasures (Gr. Nyss. *Hom. 1–8 in Eccl.* 4.5).

Gregory Thaumaturgos, pursuing the line that Solomon had departed from a wise course of action, translated the Septuagint's verb ἐστάθη (*estathē*, "was brought to a standstill") as a reference to an action coming to a halt or stagnating. His paraphrase employed the verb ἐλασσῶ (*elassō*, "make less," "diminish") to suggest that the Preacher's wisdom was diminishing (Jarick, *Thaumaturgos' Paraphrase*, 34–35).

standing still with him: This is a second attempt to solve the problem of how Christ could have been made great. The fact that wisdom stood with Christ (i.e., did not grow or change during his earthly sojourn) proves that Christ already possessed perfect wisdom, just as he has complete greatness. Both qualities are always fully present in Christ, and they did not change.

2.10

eyes of the soul...spiritual contemplation: Origen argued that the body parts referred to in the Scriptures not only applied to the visible body but had a spiritual significance as well (Or. *Cant.* Prol. 2.10–11, citing Eccl 2:14). Jerome alludes to that argument here; just as the eyes look upon the visible, material world, the eyes of the soul desire contemplation, the consideration of spiritual realities.

Preacher...in this lifetime: Jerome's "light weight of tribulation" looks back to his quotation of Phil 2:9 in the preceding chapter: because Jesus humbly and obediently accepted death on the cross, he is now raised to the highest place in the kingdom of heaven (Phil 2:6–11).

2.11

worthless...forms of caprice: For Gregory Thaumaturgos, this verse meant that the Preacher had returned to his senses after his long dalliance in pleasure (Gr. Thaum. *Eccl.* 2.11). Wisdom had reasserted itself and the Preacher could assess the world rightly.

abundance: Lat. *abundantia* is the translation Jerome here uses for the Septuagint's περισσεία (*perisseia*, "excess," "abundance"), at the first appearance of the word יתרון (*yitrôn*), a word frequent in Ecclesiastes but used in no other book of the Bible. It basically means "increase," "gain," or "profit." *Abundantia* is used to translate περισσεία again in 2.13 and 3.9, but after that, although the Septuagint continues to use περισσεία, Jerome's regular translation of it is *amplius*, for which we have consistently used the rendering "more." In contexts like Eccl 3:9; 5:15; 6:8; 10:11, "What is there more for a man...?" means "Of what advantage is it for a man...?" Similarly, in the present passage the Hebrew translated *And there is no abundance under the sun* really means something like "And it is no earthly use"—not at all what Jerome interprets it as meaning (for further discussion of יתרון, see Fox, *Ecclesiastes*, xxi).

in the sunlight: LXX Ps 18:5 [Ps 19:4]: *in sole posuit tabernaculum suum* ("he placed his tent in the sun[light]"). Jerome's quotation is identical to the text found in the Gallican Psalter (his first attempt at a new Latin translation of the Psalms), which was based on the Septuagint. The Septuagint and the Gallican Psalter both misunderstand the Hebrew verse, in which God pitches a tent for the sun in the heavens.

In Jerome's later translation of the Psalter, based directly on the Hebrew text, he emends this mistake.

Therefore Christ will not...of the sun: The Preacher's point is that there is no profit to deeds carried out in this life (under the sun), asserted also in Eccl 1:14. Jerome's attempt to allegorize this verse does not seem to work: he notes that Christ had pitched his tent under the sun (presumably an analogy for being within God's radiance) and therefore he cannot abound in a person until that person also comes out into the sunlight (presumably forsaking evil and turning to God). This, however, would imply that abundance could be found only under the sun (in God's presence, united with Christ) which counters the quoted text.

2.12

included everything: See Jerome's synopsis at 2.4.

anagogical sense: That is, he offered mystical interpretations of the verses, relating them to Christ. Jerome here uses the Greek word ἀναγωγή (*anagōgē*), which in patristic and Neoplatonic thought had come to symbolize reading a text in such a way as to lift the reader up to God, drawing out the allusions to hidden meanings about the spiritual world or afterlife.

Septuagint translation: The textual problem comes in the second half of the verse; the clause is ambiguous (and possibly corrupt) in the Hebrew text. There is still considerable debate among modern commentators and translators about how it should be rendered (see Murphy, *Ecclesiastes*, 20 n. 12c, who suggests: "For what can the man do who comes after the king? What they have already done!" as a possible translation). Fox (*Ecclesiastes*, 15) proposes a change in the vowel pointing of the Hebrew text אחרי המלך from *ʾaḥărê hammelek* to *ʾaḥărāy hammōlek*, to give: "Who will succeed me, and who is to rule over what has been built up long ago?"

The Septuagint translators wrote ὅτι τίς ὁ ἄνθρωπος, ὃς ἐπελεύσεται ὀπίσω τῆς βουλῆς τὰ ὅσα ἐποίησεν αὐτήν (*hoti tis ho anthrōpos, hos epeleusetai opisō tēs boulēs ta hosa epoiēsen autēn*, "because who is the man who will follow after the counsel, in everything in which he has made it?").

Gregory of Nyssa, developing his interpretation from the Septuagint text, argued that "counsel" (βουλή [*boulē*]) was a synonym for "Wisdom," a reference to Christ (see discussion in Heine, "Exegesis," 201–5). Consequently, true human wisdom is to turn from transitory delights to follow Wisdom, Christ (Gr. Nyss. *Hom. I–8 in Eccl.* 5.2).

2.13

King and Founder: Jerome has tied his interpretation here to the preceding verse, where he claimed that humans could not know wisdom as clearly as the King and Founder.

light from darkness: Dionysius noted that the Preacher was not making a comparison here. It is not that wisdom is better than foolishness, as Jerome's translation would have it, but that the Preacher had seen that wisdom and foolishness were contraries, opposite states. The two are mutually destructive and cannot be compared; a person chooses to embrace wisdom or folly (Dion. Al. *Fr. Eccl.* 2.13).

Gregory of Nyssa argued that the contrast intended was between something that existed (good/light) and the absence of that real thing (evil/darkness). Neither evil nor darkness has any true essence; they are simply the deprivation of things that do exist, good and light (Gr. Nyss. *Hom. I–8 in Eccl.* 5.2).

2.14

Christ as his head: An allusion to 1 Cor 11:3, in which Paul claims that the head of every man is Christ and the head of a woman is her husband. Both Gregory of Nyssa and Jerome follow Origen (Or. *Dial.* 20) in making this connection (Heine, "Exegesis," 219; Leanza, *L'esegesi di Origene,* 61).

eyes turned to Christ: Dionysius makes it clear that this as a reference to a man's spiritual eyes, the eyes of the mind (Dion. Al. *Fr. Eccl.* 2.14).

Gregory of Nyssa follows a similar line: since all animals have eyes in their heads, this verse must have a spiritual significance. The contrast must be between the head and the rest of the body, symbolizing the division between the soul and the body. When the soul contemplates earthly things, it is in the soles of the feet; when it turns its attention to the spiritual, raising its eyes to the Head (that is, Christ), then it attains pure vision, unaffected by the carnal (Gr. Nyss. *Hom. I–8 in Eccl.* 5.3). This line of interpretation is drawn from Origen (Or. *Cant.* Prol. 2; see discussion at Heine, "Exegesis," 213–18).

2.15, 16

judgment was vain: That is, when the Preacher writes *And I said in my heart that this too was vanity,* the *this too* refers not to the hard work of acquiring wisdom but rather to the judgment that he had just expressed (that there was no advantage to acquiring wisdom).

This verse posed an obvious problem for Jewish and Christian exegetes, who needed to balance the status of Ecclesiastes as inspired

Scripture with the nihilistic sentiment offered by the Preacher. They would believe, as Jerome suggests, that there is a reward for wisdom and the pursuit of virtue, but it comes in the afterlife. To make this theological view fit with the Preacher's statement, early commentators on the text saw in this sentence a condemnation of the previous one.

This was made easier by the translators of the Septuagint, who (as Jerome indicates below) altered the verse by introducing a superfluous διότι ὁ ἄφρων ἐκ περισσεύματος λαλεῖ (*dioti ho aphrōn ek perisseumatos lalei,* "because the fool speaks from excess") at the end of v. 15, which casts doubt on the Preacher's judgment, since at the beginning of the sentence he claimed that he spoke a περισσόν (*perisson,* "excess, superfluous amount") in his heart (another word not present in the Hebrew text).

Consequently, interpreters who followed the Septuagint reading took this to mean that the Preacher was condemning the view offered here, that there was no difference between the wise and foolish (see Gr. Nyss. *Hom. 1–8 in Eccl.* 5.6; Dion. Al. *Fr. Eccl.* 2.15).

Jerome, while remaining faithful to the Hebrew text in his translation, also follows the Septuagint and earlier commentators in reading this as a condemnation of the nihilistic view.

one will go…will go to punishment: In this verse, as in Eccl 3:18–21; 9:1–6, the Preacher questions the value of living wisely, as the same fate (death) waits for both the wise and the fool. The Preacher regards death as an end of human existence, knowing nothing of an afterlife, so death is an unwelcome guest (for discussion, see Murphy, *Ecclesiastes,* lxvii–lxviii).

Jerome and his fellow Christian exegetes worked with the belief that there is life after death, one in which the wicked are sent to hell and the just to heaven. Believing that Ecclesiastes is inspired Scripture, Jerome was forced to find a way to reconcile the Preacher's negative message with Christian hope. Here, Jerome adopts a strategy that was also employed by Gregory Thaumaturgos: asserting that these were views that Solomon had held earlier in life, views that he now renounced (for an account of Gregory's exegetical strategies, see also Jarick, *Thaumaturgos' Paraphrase,* 33–34, 223–24).

Septuagint…Hebrew more clearly: In fact, the Septuagint translators deviate considerably from the Hebrew reading (see note above) in order to make it possible to reconcile the Preacher's nihilistic condemnation of the pursuit of wisdom and virtue with the theological conviction that these qualities would be rewarded in the afterlife.

2.17
grazing of the wind: For this phrase, see notes at 1.14 (*routh*).

the evil one: An allusion to 1 John 5:19: "We know that we are of God and the entire world lies under the evil one."

tabernacle: Cf. 2 Cor 5:1; 2 Pet 1:12–14 for a tent or tabernacle used as a metaphor for the body.

Wretched man...this death: Rom 7:24.

paradise...blessedness of that life: Again, a way must be found to reconcile the Preacher's denunciation of life with Christian theology. Both Gregory Thaumaturgos and Gregory of Nyssa saw here a condemnation of the lifestyle Solomon had chosen for his experiment (described in Eccl 2:3–11). Gregory Thaumaturgos achieves this by interjecting the personal pronoun μου (*mou*, "my") into the verse, changing the blanket condemnation of "life" to a specific condemnation of "my life" (Gr. Thaum. *Eccl.* 2.17; see discussion in Jarick, *Thaumaturgos' Paraphrase*, 44–45). Gregory of Nyssa also followed this line, suggesting that the Preacher had made himself wicked and thus despaired of what he had wrought in his life (Gr. Nyss. *Hom. 1–8 in Eccl.* 5.6).

Jerome avoids this interpretive tack, preferring to read the Preacher more literally: by comparison to what is coming in the afterlife, this life appears horrible, a terrible imprisonment while we wait for release.

holding pen...jail: The idea that human life was a punishment, something to be endured before entering the blessed life, was common in patristic thought. Augustine, for instance, suggested that mortal life is God's wrath upon humans (Aug. *Ciu.* 21.24).

valley of tears: An allusion to LXX Ps 83:7 [Ps 84:6]; Jerome follows the Septuagint rendering (εἰς τὴν κοιλάδα τοῦ κλαυθμῶνος [*eis tēn koilada tou klauthmōnos*, "in the valley of weeping"]) both here and in the two versions of the Psalter he translated for the Vulgate. The Hebrew text (and modern English translations) renders this phrase: "in the Valley of Baca."

sweat of our brow: An allusion to Gen 3:19, in which, after Adam's fall, God sentences humanity to lives of ceaseless toil in order to provide food for themselves. With this reference, Jerome offers a potential explanation for why life under the sun is an evil: the material order was cursed as a consequence of Adam's fall, and humans will not be restored to the fullness of life until they enter the second heaven and earth that will be created after the last judgment (Rev 21:1ff.).

2.18, 19

when we die: An allusion to Luke 12:16–21, the parable of the rich fool who built great barns to store an abundant harvest, and then turned to leisure. But after he had completed his work, God took him away and all that he had prepared passed to someone else.

Rehoboam...like himself: Rehoboam was Solomon's son and successor to his throne. He was a harsh ruler, and when he refused to lighten the service that his subjects owed the crown, ten of the twelve tribes broke away from the kingdom to follow Jeroboam. Rehoboam was left the king of the tribes of Benjamin and Judah, with his throne in Jerusalem. Although Jerome here offers him as an example of a bad son and unworthy heir to Solomon, Augustine noted that responsibility for the division of the kingdom had not rested with Rehoboam but rather was the punishment God inflicted on the Hebrews for Solomon's sins (Aug. *Ciu.* 17.21). Details of Rehoboam's reign may be found in 1 Kings 12 and 2 Chr 10:1—12:16.

think about it more deeply: Jerome now offers an interpretation of this verse that is unattested in earlier (extant) commentaries on Ecclesiastes. Whereas Gregory of Nyssa and Gregory Thaumaturgos saw these two verses as a straightforward continuation of the sentiments expressed in Eccl 2:15–17 (a rejection of the material lifestyle he had embraced earlier in the chapter; cf. Gr. Nyss. *Hom. 1–8 in Eccl.* 5.7; Gr. Thaum. *Eccl.* 2.18–19), Jerome interprets them spiritually as a reference to the misuse of written works by later heretics.

2.20–23

sense here is different...delight of the living: Jerome, expounding the literal sense of the passage, sees that the Preacher has criticized two important elements of inheritance: that an unworthy heir might inherit what has been accumulated, and that there is something fundamentally unfair about a person taking possession of riches he did not earn through his own labor.

labor involved in writing books: Jerome now develops the spiritual sense that he began at 2.18–19, that the labor of the wise man was seeking knowledge and writing books. This exegesis is not without its problems, however: Eccl 2:20 would seem to suggest that the Preacher had disavowed the search for knowledge that would be misused by his heirs.

Gregory Thaumaturgos saw here the end of the experiment with pleasure. The Preacher had renounced accumulating things of the world and returned to the true good, the pursuit of wisdom and virtue (Gr. Nyss. *Hom. 1–8 in Eccl.* 2.20–21).

The man...the stylus: Hor. *S.* I.10.72–3 (with a slight alteration). The stylus, the tool used for writing on a wax tablet, had a point on one end for incising the letters, and a spatula at the opposite end for smoothing over the wax to erase what had been written. Horace's point is that you have to be a perfectionist in order to write well.

And let him give...not labored: Despite the fact that the scholar's work will be left behind to potentially unworthy successors (or at least those who did not put in the hard work to develop the knowledge themselves), Jerome turns this verse into a command for the Christian scholar to persist in this task. In this quotation of the verse he has altered the future verb *dabit* ("he will leave [give]") to the hortatory subjunctive *det* ("let him give"). Now, rather than a prediction of what will happen ("he will leave his own share to a man who has not worked"), there is a command: "Let him leave...." In this way, the work of the Christian scholar is justified, and indeed, commanded.

as I have already said: See 2.18, 19.

2.24–26

except: The Hebrew text at this point reads (אֵין־טוֹב בָּאָדָם שֶׁיֹּאכַל] *ʾēn-ṭōb bāʾādām šeyyōʾkal*], which if translated as it stands would mean, "There is nothing good in a man that he eats...."). As the similar expressions in Eccl 3:12, 22; 8:15 all include a word such as "except," it is assumed that an apparent scribal error has resulted in the "except" dropping out of the Hebrew version (Jarick, *Thaumaturgos' Paraphrase*, 49–50). The Septuagint translators did not notice that this had happened and followed what they found in the text: Οὐκ ἔστιν ἀγαθὸν ἀνθρώπῳ, ὃ φάγεται (*Ouk estin agathon anthrōpōi, ho phagetai*, "There is nothing good for a man that he eats"). Jerome has clearly seen this omission through his study of the Hebrew text and has restored the *nisi* ("except") to the text, even though it offers more problems for his subsequent exegesis.

Gregory of Nyssa, following the Septuagint reading in his exegesis, saw here a debate between the fool and the wise man. The fool believes that only what can be received into one's body (food and drink) is a good. The wise man responds that God has given wisdom and knowledge, food for the higher life (Gr. Nyss. *Hom. I–8 in Eccl.* 5.8).

a gift from God...as the time requires: Jerome's literal paraphrase of the verse understands the Preacher's conclusion: it is not that humans should make the seeking of pleasure and acquisition of material possessions the point of their existence (denied in Eccl 2:11), but rather, in the vanity of existence, eating, drinking, and possessions are God's gifts to humanity and they should be enjoyed when he chooses to grant them (see Murphy, *Ecclesiastes*, 26).

Jerome was not prepared to accept this conclusion and consequently moves on to the spiritual meaning expounded in the subsequent paragraph.

upright man...through cares and sleepless nights: This is not actually what the Preacher wrote: the contrast between the upright and sinners is that God rewards the just with material prosperity in this life, while the unjust devote all of their time and energy to trying to gather these things on their own.

spiritual riches: The task of allegorical exegesis was to bring out the spiritual meaning hidden beneath the literal sense of a text. Often a text would be given an allegorical interpretation when a literal interpretation was thought to be wrong or deemed unworthy (see O'Keefe and Reno, *Sanctified Vision*, 103–7). In the following lines, Jerome moves away from the literal interpretation of the text, because he cannot believe that God would sanction the enjoyment of material possessions, especially those that had been inherited.

body and blood...Lamb: Jerome has allegorized the Preacher's words and decided that the good of eating and drinking must be a prophetic reference to the Eucharist. Dionysius takes the same line, arguing that food and drink do nothing for the benefit of the soul, so clearly this passage must refer to the Eucharist (Dion. Al. *Fr. Eccl.* 2.25).

thrown to the dogs: An allusion to Matt 7:6: "Do not give what is sacred to dogs; do not throw your pearls before swine."

fellow slaves...proper time: An allusion to Matt 24:45: "Who then is the faithful and prudent servant, whom the master has placed over his household to give them their food at the appointed time?"

honey...sufficient: An allusion to Prov 25:16: "If you have found honey, eat only what satisfies you, so that you are not stuffed with it and vomit it."

his own will: Although the *Commentary* predated the Pelagian controversy, this idea that the desire to improve oneself originates in a person's will rather than in God's grace has Pelagian overtones.

Sow...for yourselves: LXX Hos 10:12.

sinner to his own will: A possible allusion to Rom 1:26: "Therefore God gave them up to dishonorable passions."

CHAPTER 3

3.1

universe is self-contradictory...either sky or time: Jerome here offers a platonizing distinction between the material, which is transitory and flawed, and the spiritual, which is perfect. This allows him to uphold the Preacher's ultimate conclusion (that everything under the sun is imperfect and vain) while simultaneously looking beyond this world to the heavenly realm, where there is perfection and purpose.

This line of exegesis was adopted also by Gregory of Nyssa, who, in his homily on this verse, distinguished between the flawed material world and the spiritual. Having demonstrated the futility of existence under the sun in the previous two chapters, the Preacher now turns to offer a practical set of guidelines that will allow a person to seek virtue and a contemplation of the higher reality. Gregory proposed two tests for goodness in the material realm: time and the appropriate moment for doing something. Of the two time, or measure (what course we ought to follow in order to avoid extremes), was the more important. The Preacher's purpose in writing the following verses is to help the seeker of higher things discern the measured path through the material world (Gr. Nyss. *Hom. 1–8 in Eccl.* 6.2).

3.2

From the fear...brought forth: LXX Isa 26:18. Gregory of Nyssa alludes to the same passage in his homily on this verse (which suggests that both authors may have drawn their exegesis from a common source such as Origen), stating that a birth is seasonable when one gives birth to one's own salvation through the soul's labor pains. That is, when we shape our lives by pursuing virtue, we become our own parents and bring ourselves to the light (Gr. Nyss. *Hom. 1–8 in Eccl.* 6.5).

Perfect love...fear: 1 John 4:18.

Nebuchadnezzar: Babylonian king who besieged and captured Jerusalem in 606 BC (cf. Dan 1:1). In 597, he destroyed the temple and carried its treasures and Jewish captives back to Babylon.

Darius: King of Persia (521–485 BC). King Cyrus of Persia had allowed the Jews to return to Jerusalem in 538 and instructed them to begin rebuilding the temple (Ezra 1:2–4). When this project met local resistance from the Samarians, his successor, Darius, confirmed the order and the temple was restored during his reign (Ezra 6.1-14).

Zerubbabel, Ezra, and Nehemiah: Prophets who guided the rebuilding of the temple under Darius.

girdle: Jer 13:1–11. In that passage God uses the figure of a linen waistcloth that has been spoiled by being deposited in the earth to signify Israel's dalliance with pagan gods.

Roman captivity: Jerome is comparing the conquered status of Judea as a province of the Roman Empire, since the first century AD, with the exile of the Jews in Babylonia in the sixth century BC.

hatred...hands on Christ: The idea that the crucifixion of Christ had led to God's anger and the transfer of his covenant promises to the Christians was a commonplace of apologetic literature (see Just. *Dial.* 16; Tert. *Iud.* 13).

Israel shall be saved...nations comes in: An allusion to Rom. 11:25, where Paul writes that the Jewish hearts have been hardened and will remain so until the fullness of the nations comes in.

3.3

It is I...will make alive: Deut 32:39.

time to kill...time to heal: Dionysius suggests that this verse means that those who have committed an unpardonable sin are to be killed, while those with a wound that will respond to treatment are to be healed (Dion. Al. *Fr. Eccl.* 3.3).

Gregory of Nyssa, citing the same verse (Deut 32:39), focused his interpretation on an individual's quest for self-improvement; before one can turn to good things, one needs to kill what is evil within (Gr. Nyss. *Hom. I–8 in Eccl.* 6.7).

In the morning...earth: LXX Ps 100:8 [Ps 101:8].

build and plant: An allusion to Jer 1:10, in which God tells the Jewish people that they have been chosen and placed over the nations.

Once again, Jerome cites the same proof-text from Jeremiah that Gregory of Nyssa employs. Characteristically, Gregory develops this point at much greater length than Jerome, discussing how the buildings of evil within a person must be razed to the ground to make way for the foundations of the good edifices that are to be built in their place (Gr. Nyss. *Hom. I–8 in Eccl.* 6.8).

3.4

time to weep...in the future: Dionysius takes a similar line, suggesting that humans should weep amid their sufferings but laugh at the time of resurrection (Dion. Al. *Fr. Eccl.* 3.4).

Gregory of Nyssa develops this verse by listing a great number of things from this life that are worthy of lamentation. This list ranges from a pitiable childhood through the dementia of old age, culminating in a fiery judgment in the afterlife for those who have made themselves enemies of God. Only a pessimistic attitude toward the "good things" of this world would win a heavenly reward (Gr. Nyss. *Hom. I–8 in Eccl.* 6.9).

Blessed are those...shall laugh: Luke 6:21. Jerome has altered this verse slightly (here and at 3.12–13) by changing the verb in the apodosis from a second person plural form ("you will laugh") to a third person plural ("they will laugh") and emphasizing the "they" by adding the Latin intensive pronoun *ipsi*, for which there is no parallel in the Greek text.

We wailed...did not dance: Luke 7:32. Gregory of Nyssa also cites this verse in his discussion of this passage (Gr. Nyss. *Hom. I–8 in Eccl.* 6.10).

displeased Saul's daughter: An allusion to 2 Sam 6:14–21: when the ark of the covenant was carried into the city of Jerusalem, King David danced before it, dressed in a linen ephod. His wife, Michal, was disgusted by her husband's action, judging it unworthy of a king.

Gregory of Nyssa also cites this example of dancing, but he does not mention Michal. Rather, he suggests that David also played a musical instrument while he danced and made public his devotion to God through the rhythmical motion of his body (Gr. Nyss. *Hom. I–8 in Eccl.* 6.10).

3.5

scholar's ridiculous comment: We have been unable to identify this scholar.

He demolishes...life is inconsistent: Hor. *Ep.* 1.1.100, 99. Here Horace is discussing the inconstancy of the person's mind rather than the building projects of humans; this is another instance of Jerome's parading his secular learning in a way that does not support the point of his argument.

God is able...Abraham: Matt 3:9.

one book: Gregory of Nyssa challenged a similar interpretation, held by those who thought this was a reference to the stoning of Sabbath breakers. He did not believe that such a law, applied literally, could have been worthy of God as human life requires.activity on the Sabbath. On the other hand, this could be read spiritually as a command to take a rest from deeds of evil (Gr. Nyss. *Hom. I–8 in Eccl.* 7.2)

thrown in the law...Gospel: An allusion to John 8:3–11, the story of the woman taken in adultery. The scribes and Pharisees brought a woman to Jesus who had been caught in an act of adultery. Under Mosaic Law the punishment for this crime was stoning. When pressed to pass sentence on the woman, Jesus stated that the punishment should be carried out only by those who were sinless. Convicted of their own unworthiness, the woman's accusers slipped away, whereupon Jesus (the Gospel in Jerome's reading) forgave her.

Do not hold out...time for prayer: 1 Cor 7:5. Jerome's literal and spiritual interpretations of this passage correspond to the exegesis of Origen, found among the fragments of his *Catenas on Ecclesiastes* (Cod. Barber. gr. 388); see discussion in Leanza, *L'esegesi di Origene*, 13–24, 62–63.

Be fruitful...fill the earth: Gen 1:28.

The time...though they had not: 1 Cor 7:29.

Honor her...embrace you: Prov. 4:8.

Further, the human mind...short of sin: Jerome offers a pragmatic reading here, possibly one developed out of his own personal experience: we cannot be constantly focused on God and the pursuit of wisdom. This need to tend to our bodily needs as well as the spiritual can also be found in the early monastic tradition (see Cassian *Coll.* 1.13).

3.6, 7

piecing together...coming of the Lord: A reference to the prophecies of the coming messiah found in the Hebrew Bible and applied to Christ by the authors of the Gospels (e.g., Matt 1:23; 2:6).

conserving Israel...losing and discarding it: Dionysius is a bit more charitable here, suggesting that there was a time for keeping the law and a time for discarding it when the Gospel came (Dion. Al. *Fr. Eccl.* 2.6).

Gregory of Nyssa continued to read these verses in the context of the spiritual life, asserting that it was always time to seek God and to discard evil thoughts that impede our progress (Gr. Nyss. *Hom. I–8 in Eccl.* 7.6).

Pythagoreans: The idea that the Greek philosophers had learned anything good in their philosophy from the Old Testament was a conventional argument among the patristic apologists (see Just. *I Apol.* 44; Or. *Cant.* Prol. 3.4). The claim that Pythagoras had appropriated many of his ideas from the Hebrew Bible can be found at Clem. *Str.* 1.22; 5.5.

without speaking...their education: This practice is ascribed to the Pythagorean school in Clem. *Str.* 5.11. See also the story of Abba Agathon, the Egyptian desert father who held a stone in his mouth for three years until he learned to keep silent (*Apophth. Patr.* Agathon 15).

Gregory of Nyssa interpreted this verse as a reference to the experience of contemplative prayer. The person who contemplates

God will experience things that cannot be expressed in speech, and thus it is pointless to try to put these experiences into words (Gr. Nyss. *Hom. I–8 in Eccl.* 7.8).

instructor's discourse...instead of pupils: The suppression of one's thoughts and ideas, coupled with submission to the understanding and discernment of a spiritual master, was one of the key elements of John Cassian's monastic program (Goodrich, *Cassian*, 45–49).

we are teaching...things we do not know about: Dionysius interprets this verse differently, suggesting that the time to be silent is when your listeners are unworthy of your words (Dion. Al. *Fr. Eccl.* 3.7).

art alone...no instructor: That is, people do not believe that they need to be instructed in Christianity. Cassian makes a similar point about the ascetic life (Cassian *Coll.* 2.11.7).

3.8

stubborn...opposing loyalty: Jerome here envisions a situation where the martyr is forced to choose between his love for his family and love for Christ. He is presumably thinking of a case where the person is offered a chance to make the sacrifices in order to save wife and family. Saving them in this life would be a bad choice, as the person would lose eternal life with Christ, a view shared with Augustine (Aug. *Ciu.* 21.26).

In this time of peace, with the church enjoying the favor of the Roman emperors, it appears peculiar that Jerome and Augustine wrote about martyr trials as if they were an ongoing reality rather than a historical event. This may have been related to a sense that the second coming of Christ, preceded by the tribulations of the Antichrist, was close at hand (cf. Aug. *Ciu.* 21.26; Sulp.-Sev. *Dial.* 2.14). It should also be remembered that the peace of the church was less than one hundred years old and that, as recently as 361, the emperor Julian had attempted to reverse Christianity's position in the empire. The assumption that the persecution of Christians was now firmly in the past may not have been as widely shared as the subsequent centuries would demonstrate.

new moons: The months of the Jewish calendar began with the appearance of the new moon. On this day, a minor holiday (Rosh Chodesh in modern Judaism) was held (see Num 28:11).

time to love...in their place: A conventional apologetic line against the Jews was that the coming of Christ had supplanted the observances of the Mosaic Law (see Just. *Dial.* 45; Tert. *Iud.* 3). Discussion about whether Christians were obliged to adhere to Jewish Law dates back

188 ST. JEROME: *COMMENTARY ON ECCLESIASTES*

to the council held in Jerusalem (Acts 15:1–29), in which the apostles debated whether Gentile converts were obliged to be circumcised and follow Mosaic dietary codes.

mirror...face to face: An allusion to 1 Cor 13:12.

progressing to something better...the object of our love: A similar argument was developed at 1.2.

Gregory of Nyssa used this verse as the basis for a lengthy discussion of true good (the eternal things of God) versus transitory, sensual pleasures (as found in this world). He suggested that this verse implied that we should love the true good and hate evil (Gr. Nyss. *Hom. I–8 in Eccl.* 8.2–3).

time for war: The idea that life is an ongoing war against our sin is a patristic commonplace. See, for instance, Augustine (*Ciu.* 21.15), who asserts that peace comes for the Christian only after death. But better to be enrolled in the army, fighting against one's sins in this life, than to be conquered and a slave to sin.

Gregory of Nyssa takes a similar line, detailing the need to fight against our enemies, the bodily passions, which seek to lure us away from the true good (Gr. Nyss. *Hom. I–8 in Eccl.* 8.4–5).

peace gained: The second element of the name Jerusalem in Hebrew, שלם (*šālēm*, "sound," "whole," "perfect"), is from the same root as the word for peace, שלום (*šālôm*).

Gregory of Nyssa took this as an admonition to seek peace with God by turning away from the temporal passions and enrolling in the army of virtue (Gr. Nyss. *Hom. I–8 in Eccl.* 8.6).

take up arms: An allusion to Eph 6:11, 13, where Paul discusses putting on the whole armor of God.

3.9–11

profit: See note at 2.11 (abundance).

the age: The meaning of the Hebrew word עולם (*ʿôlām*), here translated with the Latin *saeculum* ("age"), is disputed. Murphy (*Ecclesiastes*, 29 n. 11a) suggests that it can mean "duration," "eternity," or "world." Many commentators agree that the RSV's "eternity" is the best translation for the word, but compare NRSV's "a sense of past and future." It might also mean "a desire for a knowledge of the world" (ibid., 34). Fox (*Ecclesiastes*, 23) suggests adapting H. L.Ginsberg's emendation from העולם (*hāʿôlām*, "the world") to העמל (*heʿāmāl*, "the toil") (cf. Eccl 8:17); he posits that *ʿôlām* nowhere else means "eternity."

perverse doctrines...inactivity: This view is expressed by Augustine (although after Jerome had written this work) in Aug. *Gen. Man.* 1.1. Augustine also claimed that the mind is stirred by planned pedagogical error, as in the case of the discrepancies between the Septuagint and the Hebrew text. Since both texts were divinely inspired, variations either represent different prophetic messages offered to separate communities (Aug. *Ciu.* 15.13–14), or they were introduced by the Holy Spirit to exercise reader's minds and drive them to search for a deeper, spiritual meaning (Aug. *Ciu.* 18.44).

content...anxious for tomorrow: Matt 6:34.

It is good...when it is required: The sense of the Hebrew text is that God, who has ordained the times detailed in Eccl 3:1–8, has selected the times for the manifestation of these times in creation, and as an expression of the divine will, these events are good. Jerome's analogy of waking and sleeping does not seem fully to capture this idea.

beginning of the world to its end: Dionysius suggests that God has placed the world as a matter of ignorance in our hearts, and this is to our advantage so that we do not know the limits of our time on earth (Dion. Al. *Fr. Eccl.* 3.11).

3.12, 13

perspective of one...move on to other things: Jerome again puts a Christian spin on the Preacher's message. The Preacher, who does not look beyond this life, resigns himself to enjoying what he has for as many years as he is granted, attributing this enjoyment to God's favor. For Jerome, the existence of an afterlife means that this life is only a preparation for something greater, and the transitory goods of this life are to be held loosely.

Let us eat and drink...we shall die: Isa 22:13.

If we have food...content: 1 Tim 6:8.

anagogical level: For the mystical interpretation of Solomon's discovery that eating and drinking were humanity's greatest good, see note at 2.24–26 (body and blood). For ἀναγωγή (*anagōgē*), see note at 2.12 (anagogical sense).

Gregory of Nyssa also read this verse on a spiritual level, noting that they pointed to a higher truth: food and drinking are to the body what gazing upon God in contemplation is to the soul (Gr. Nyss. *Hom. 1–8 in Eccl.* 8.9).

true food and drink...knowledge of the Scriptures: The Jewish interpretation of "true food and drink" is very similar, with the Midrash Rabbah claiming that it is knowledge of the Torah (*Qoh. Rab.* 3.12.1).

There will be...grief in Israel: LXX Num 23:21.

contradicts this: That is, Balaam's prophecy might suggest that there would be more for God's people than simply having food and drink; there might, in fact, be no hardships of any kind for the people.

hardship and grief: An allusion to 2 Cor 11:22–27, a description of the misfortunes Paul had suffered in the service of Christ.

there will be...Israel: LXX Num 23:21.

blessed are those...who will laugh: Luke 6:21.

and the mouths...filled with joy: LXX Job 8:21.

labor: The Latin word *labor,* translated as "labor" here, is the same word that was translated as "hardship" above in the quotations from Num 23:21 and 2 Cor 11:27.

3.14

them: The pronoun "them" here, not explicit in the Hebrew, refers to humankind.

from his face: Jerome is here translating literally a Hebrew idiom מלפניו (*millĕpānāyw*) that is equivalent to "from him" in English. The Septuagint does the same.

Providence exists: See the discussion of Providence at 1.13 (Providence).

For God's invisible...virtue and divinity: Rom 1:20. In translating this verse, Jerome has misunderstood the Greek phrase ἥ τε ἀΐδιος αὐτοῦ δύναμις καὶ θειότης (*hē te aidios autou dynamis kai theiotēs,* "both his eternal power and divine nature"). Jerome has been misled by the word τε (which can mean "and," but is here meant as "both," leading to the following καί, "and") into thinking that Paul is listing God's eternal power (rather than "virtue") and divinity as attributes separate from his invisible aspects, rather than as being themselves the invisible aspects Paul is talking about.

The face...over the evildoers: LXX Ps 33:17 [Ps 34:16].

3.15

we use...is the same: That is, like every other aspect of the material realm, the sun existed before we were born, and it moves in a cyclical fashion.

καὶ ὁ θεὸς ζητήσει τὸ διωκόμενον: *kai ho theos zētēsei to diōkomenon,* "God will seek that which is pursued." Modern critical editions of the Septuagint have τὸν διωκόμενον (*ton diōkomenon,* "the man pursued"), but Jerome cites it as τὸ διωκόμενον (*to diōkomenon,* "that which is pursued," a neuter noun. The Hebrew does not distinguish masculine from neuter.

persecution by pagans: See note at 3.8 (stubborn...opposing loyalty).

All who desire...suffer persecution: 2 Tim 3:12.

he requires...blood of the slain: an allusion to Gen 9:5.

comes to seek…had been lost: Luke 19:10.
carried the straying…his own shoulders: Luke 15:4–6.

3.16, 17

iniquity: Jerome's *impietas* ("impiety") represents the Hebrew הרשע (*hārešaᶜ* [noun], "[the] wickedness"), while his *iniquitas* ("iniquity") represents הרשע (*hārāšaᶜ* [adjective], "the wicked man"). The consonantal Hebrew text, which is what Jerome would have used, does not distinguish between the two words. The Septuagint uses ὁ ἀσεβής (*ho asebēs*, "an evil man") for both.

volition: The Hebrew text of this verse and Eccl 3:1 both use the same word חפץ (*ḥēpeṣ*). Jerome, however, has rendered this word differently in these two translations. At 3.1 he translated it with the Latin word *rei* ("thing," "deed"); here he used the Latin word *uoluntati* ("volition," "will") for the same term. He also used *uoluntas* for this word at 5.3, where the meaning is "pleasure" (Jerome's "The will is not in the unwise" represents "He has no pleasure in fools"), and at 12.10, where דברי חפץ (*dibrê-ḥēpeṣ*, "words of use") means "useful words" rather than Jerome's "words of will." In each of these three places he has simply followed the Septuagint: LXX Eccl 3:1: ἐν παντὶ πράγματι (*en panti pragmati*, "in everything"); LXX Eccl 5:3: οὐκ ἔστιν θέλημα ἐν ἄφροσιν (*ouk estin thelēma en aphrosin*, "there is not will in unwise people"); LXX Eccl 12:10: λόγους θελήματος (*logous thelēmatos*, "words of will"). Here, however, he has used *uoluntati* where the Septuagint has ἐν παντὶ πράγματι (*en panti pragmati*, "in everything"), as at 3.1.

benches of the judges…bribery: This is a rather conventional statement about the law courts/immorality of the ancient world. The possibility that magistrates could be bribed to gain a favorable decision was a staple of classical writing; see, for instance, Sal. *Cat.* 49.1, for the attempt of Catiline and his fellow conspirators to bribe Cicero into condemning Caesar. For a fuller account of the laws and penalties related to judicial bribery, see Plescia, "Judicial Accountability," 59–61.

volition and their works: Above we noted that Jerome had translated חפץ (*ḥēpeṣ*) with two different words, here and at 3.1. The point of employing the phrase *omni uoluntati* ("for all volition") in this verse becomes clear: Jerome wants to stipulate that humans will be judged on their *res* ("works," "deeds"), that is, what they did, as well as on their *uoluntas* ("will," "desire"), what they wanted to do.

Do not say…in their own time: LXX Sir 39:16.

3.18–21

about the utterance: Jerome, following the Septuagint, has misunderstood a late Hebrew phrase על דברת (*ᶜal-dibrat*), which here and in Eccl 8:2 means "because of" or "concerning" (Murphy, *Ecclesiastes*, 30 n. 18a). Properly translated, the verse should begin: "I spoke in my heart concerning the sons of men," but it looks as if it might mean "on the word."

because God separates...animals to themselves: Jerome is here wrestling with a difficult Hebrew sentence, which modern English translations simplify by omitting redundant words: "I said in my heart with regard to human beings that God is testing them to show them that they are but animals" (NRSV).

Hades: The Hebrew word שאול (*šĕʾôl*, "Sheol") and the Greek word ᾅδης (*Hadēs*) can both be rendered in Latin by the word Jerome uses here, *inferi* (lit. "those below" or "the underworld"). For a discussion of the concept of Hades in Jewish and Christian thought, see Bernstein, *Formation of Hell*, 167–68, 317–18.

In the theology of the church fathers, Hades is the place where the souls of the dead are held before the last judgment (see Ambr. *Bon. mort.* 45–47). Some of the fathers saw Hades as a place of punishment, where the wicked would receive a foretaste of the penalties in store for them after the last judgment, but Augustine advanced the possibility that souls destined to be saved would undergo purificatory punishments in Hades after death, in advance of the last judgment (Aug. *Ciu.* 21.13; 21.16). This speculation evolved into the medieval doctrine of purgatory (see Atwell, "Purgatory," 173–86).

At 9.10, Jerome argues that Christians are not in Hades because they are with Christ (who is not in Hades).

Jacob...Hades: An allusion to Gen 37:34–35. When Jacob believed that his son Joseph had been killed by a wild beast, he tore his clothes, put on sackcloth, and said that he would go down to Sheol (LXX ᾅδου [*hadou*, "Hades"]) to be with his son.

Job...nether regions: See Job 17:13; 21:13; 24:19. Job does not actually state that the just go down to Sheol, although Jerome might have inferred this from Job's desire to go there (Job 17:13).

Abraham...between them: An allusion to Luke 16:19–31. After death, the poor beggar Lazarus joined Abraham in "Abraham's bosom" (v. 22), while the rich man was sent to the portion of Hades where the unjust are tormented. The citation from Luke represents a reconfiguration of the geography of Hades. In earlier Jewish thought, Hades (Sheol) contained all the dead, but by the time of Jesus, divisions had been postulated that separated the just from the wicked. The earliest patristic reference to a place where the just waited for judgment, in sight of their future blessings, known as "Abraham's bosom," is found in a work attributed by some scholars to Hippolytus (*Ex libro adversus*

Graecos; for a discussion of the authorship of this work, see Whealey, "Hippolytus' Lost De Universo," 244–56); for the development of different fates for the dead, see Bernstein, *Formation of Hell,* 154–77.

fiery wheel: An allusion to Dan 7:9. Here the prophet sees the ancient of days whose "throne was fiery flames, its wheels were burning fire."

flaming sword: An allusion to Gen 3:24. When God drove Adam and Eve out of the Garden of Eden, he placed one of the cherubim with a flaming sword at the eastern entrance to prevent their return.

paradise...with the criminal: An allusion to Luke 23:43. When the criminal crucified alongside Jesus begs to be remembered when Christ comes into his kingdom, Jesus replies, "today you will be with me in Paradise."

heavenly realms were closed: Jerome here implies that Christ opened the doors to heaven and now the just go there after death, rather than to Hades. Tertullian disagreed with this position, stating that only the martyrs were allowed to join Christ in paradise before the end of the world and the last judgment (Tert. *An.* 55).

utterance...sunk in silence: As noted above, the Septuagint's mistranslation of the Hebrew term has led Jerome off track, forcing him into this discussion of the difference between mute animals and humans.

made from the ground: In the creation account (Gen 2:7), God shapes Adam from the dust of the earth and then blows life (a soul) into him.

you are dust...you shall return: Gen 3:19.

Who will utter...generation: LXX Isa 53:8.

Lord, who shall ascend...holy hill: LXX Ps 14:1 [Ps 15:1].

And there is a man...knows him: LXX Jer 17:9. The consonantal text ואנש could be read either as *weʾĕnōš* ("and a man"), as the Septuagint and Jerome have taken it, or as *wěʾānūš* ("and sick," "perverse").

Because the Lord...man and beast: LXX Ps 35:7 [Ps 36:6].

I was like...toward you: LXX Ps 72:22 [Ps 73:22].

that men and animals...safely to Jerusalem: Zech 2:4 is a rare reference to men and animals being in Jerusalem as a sign of peace and prosperity (see also Ezek 36:11, a reference to the prosperity of Israel, rather than Jerusalem).

promised land...cattle and herds: An allusion to Deut 6:3; 27:3, verses in which God promises the Israelites a land flowing with milk and honey.

appellation human...being called animal: John Cassian schematized humanity into three classes: the carnal, who are immersed in the fleshy delights of the world; the animal, who are unable to perceive the things of the spirit; and the spiritual, who seek God (Cassian *Coll.* 4.19).

upright man may fall…sinner may rise up: Examples of this catastrophic fall, often near the end of a life that was otherwise unimpeachable, can be found throughout patristic literature. John Cassian, for instance, cited the case of the monk Heron, who had been more rigorous than all of his brothers in his ascetic practices. Despite fifty years of ascetic excellence, his failure to develop discernment had made him vulnerable to the wiles of the devil. He was persuaded to kill himself by leaping into a well, a spiritual as well as a physical fall (Cassian *Coll.* 2.5). See also 11.6–8.

3.22

thief nor bandit…take away: An allusion to Matt 6:20, in which Christ counsels his followers to do good works that will become treasure in heaven, safe from the depredation of thieves or moths.

after death: Once again Jerome puts a Christian spin on the Preacher's conclusion (see also 3.12, 13). The Preacher, pressed by the futility of all of humanity's endeavors, bows to the vanity of a life under the sun and concludes that the best course is to enjoy the work we have been given. Jerome links our present life to future rewards and punishments, thoroughly transforming the Preacher's point.

earlier mistake…ungratefully behind: See discussion at 3.18–21. Jerome again offers an explanation that suggests that this verse should be read as Solomon's recantation after wrong thinking (see also 2.15, 16).

Others have referred…one who does not: See discussion at 2.18, 19.

CHAPTER 4

4.1

false accusations: Lat. *calumnia* (found here, 5.7, and 7.8). In both this work and the Vulgate, Jerome uses *calumnia* as a literal translation of the Septuagint's συκοφαντία (*sykophantia*, "false accusation," "slander"). *Calumnia* is also found at Vulg. Jer 7:6; 21:12; 22:17, but in those passages, the words used in the Septuagint (καταδυναστεύω [*katadynasteuō*, "to overpower," "to oppress"], ἀδικέω [*adikeō*, "to do wrong"], ἀδίκημα [*adikēma*, "a wrong done," "an injury"]) have nothing to do with false accusations. The Hebrew Bible uses words from the same root (עשק [ʿšq]) in all six of these passages. Jerome's translation of this word (which conveys the sense of oppression in general, but not of false accusation in particular) suggests that *calumnia* had widened its meaning, from the classical "false accusation" to a more general "oppression."

Psalm 72: LXX Ps 72 [Ps 73]: the plea of an old man for God's aid in overcoming his enemies.

Jeremiah...book: See Jer 7:6; 21:12; 22:3, 17.

4.2, 3

In that place...voice of the taskmaster: Job 3:17–18.

shipwreck: The shipwreck was a common metaphor in patristic writings, usually employed (following 1 Tim 1:19) as a description of a believer who had turned aside and made a shipwreck of their faith (see Tert. *Idol.* 24; Cypr. *Ep.* 48.1). Clement of Alexandria used the metaphor in a positive manner when he asserted that it was the function of the Instructor (Christ) to steer one through the seas of life and keep one from shipwreck (Clem. *paed.* 1.7). Lactantius equated birth, when a person is cast forth from the womb, naked and defenseless, with a shipwreck (Lact. *Opif.* 3). Jerome's pessimistic description of life as a shipwreck, from which a person escapes into death, appears to be unique in patristic literature.

not yet been born...evils of the world: Jerome's paraphrase captures a sentiment that was surprisingly prevalent in the ancient world. In the Hebrew Bible, it is suggested in Job 3:11–19 and Jer 20:18. This sentiment is repeated in Eccl 6:1–6, where the Preacher asserts that a stillborn infant is better off than a wealthy miser. See further discussion at Jarick, *Thaumaturgos' Paraphrase*, 85.

not yet been born...weighed down with a body: This view was held by Origen and his followers; see note below (dwell in the upper regions).

better not to exist...or to live, unhappily: Gregory Thaumaturgos altered this verse in his paraphrase, writing that the dead were better off than those who lived unjustly or arrogantly (Gr. Thaum. *Eccl.* 4.2). Presumably he believed that people living upright Christian lives were better off than both the unjust living and the dead.

It would have...been born: Matt 26:24.

those who have died...ceased to sin: A Christian reader might wonder why the unjust dead would be better off than the living, as they will have entered (or face) eternal punishment. It is possible that Jerome's comments reflect the same apocalyptic strain found in Gregory Thaumaturgos, who believed that the tribulations of the end-time, described in the book of Revelation, were at hand, and the unjust who were still alive in this period would suffer greatly (see discussion at Jarick, *Thaumaturgos' Paraphrase*, 84).

Elsewhere Jerome was prepared to draw a distinction between the blessed state of the just dead (who were better off than the living) and the worse state of the unjust dead, who were enduring eternal punishment (Hier. *Ep.* 39.3). The former should long for the release of death while the latter should fear it.

John...kingdom of heaven: An allusion to Matt 11:11. Jesus here cited John the Baptist as being great because he fulfilled his prophetic task, preparing the way for Jesus. Jerome's point is that someone in heaven, who has ceased to be troubled by sin, is greater than even John was while he was still present on the battlefield of life.

I am a wretched man...body of this death: Rom 7:24. That is, the person who is least in the kingdom of heaven is no longer able to share Paul's lament.

dwell in the upper regions...choir: The question of when souls were created excited considerable discussion during the patristic period. Origen and some of his followers argued that the soul existed before the body and was assigned a body based on earlier sins or virtues (Or. *Princ.* 1.8.4). A second position, creationism, asserted that God created souls at the moment of birth and placed them into the body. The final option was traducianism, the belief that souls were generated from the souls of the parents (Tert. *An.* 27; Aug. *Litt.* 10.23).

Jerome showed great hesitation in committing himself to one of these three options. In a letter to Marcellinus and Anapsychia (Hier. *Ep.* 126.1), he outlined the three positions and stated that he had already offered his own view in his *Apology against Rufinus* (in fact, he does not commit to a position there either). In the commentary on this verse he seems to support both creationism (above) and Origen's view that souls pre-existed in some form in the upper regions before taking on bodies (although this was apparently rejected above). Later, however, at 12.6–8, he will argue that souls are not created through traducianism (from the souls of their parents) but are individually created by God.

For further discussion of the views of the early church, see Kelly, *Early Christian Doctrines*, 344–46.

4.4

envious man is tormented...exposed to snares: Jerome's point is that working hard to acquire material, transient things is a two-edged sword: it stirs up envy in those who lack what another person owns, and for the owner there is the danger of becoming filled with pride and boastfulness.

Jarick (*Thaumaturgos' Paraphrase*, 86–87) suggests that the Septuagint translators had softened the force of this sentiment by employing the Greek word ζῆλος (*zēlos*), which in classical Greek could mean "zealous imitation" or "zeal," a positive quality. This interpretation is found also in the Targum, where the translators suggested that a person could be encouraged to pursue the good more zealously (*Tar. Qoh.* 4.4). As Jarick (ibid., 87) noted, Gregory Thaumaturgos excluded this potentially positive interpretation by substituting the negative word φθόνος (*phthonos*, "envy," "jealousy," "ill will") for ζῆλος in his paraphrase. Jerome's word, *aemulatio*, covers both the positive and the negative senses of the two Greek words, although his paraphrase leaves little doubt that it is the negative vice of jealousy or envy that he has in mind.

4.5

lazy in Proverbs…poverty comes like a fast runner: Prov 24:34. This resembles Jerome's later Vulgate translation, which rendered the Hebrew phrase ובא מתהלך ריש (*ûbā' mithallēk rêšekā,* "and there comes one walking, your poverty") as *veniet quasi cursor egestas tua* ("your poverty will come like a runner"). Rather like "highwayman," the Hebrew word מתהלך (*mithallēk,* "one walking about," or "a vagrant") is here taken to mean "a robber."

eats his flesh: The consumption of one's own flesh is said to be one of God's punishments (see Isa 49:26).

he who works…envy in this world: See 4.4.

possible alternative explanation…jealousy and spite: This interpretation follows Gregory Thaumaturgos' paraphrase very closely. Gregory expanded the short Septuagint verse to read: "The person who takes it [envy] in and, as it were, clutches it to his breast, takes part in nothing other than the eating of his own soul and the cutting and consuming of it, along with his own body. He regards the success of others as an inconsolable pain" (Gr. Thaum. *Eccl.* 4.5, trans. Jarick, *Thaumaturgos' Paraphrase,* 88).

The word…Haggai: Hag 1:1. Although the Latin word *manus* can mean "work" or "workmanship," Jerome's citation, literally translated from the Septuagint or the Hebrew, clearly seems to signify that the instrumental use of the word is intended in this example: the word of the Lord came to the Hebrews *through* (or *by means of*) the hand of Haggai.

He trains…battle: LXX Ps 143:1 [Ps 144:1].

And so the fool…extend them: A confusing interpretation at best.

Jerome's point seems to be that because "hands" can signify the "works" through which God manifests himself, the clasping of hands would signify not performing the works that reveal God. The person focused on the flesh does not extend his hands to God, preferring to live according to the poverty of the flesh.

4.6

great riches of sinners: It was a rather conventional view among patristic writers that a person or family could not acquire wealth without having cheated someone in the past. Jerome himself expressed this view in *Ep.* 120.1; see also Eucher. *Contempt.* (*PL* 50:716). For a survey of patristic views on wealth, see McGuckin, "Vine and the Elm Tree," 1–14.
A small amount...produce with iniquity: Prov 16:8.
singular number...bad sense: Jerome may be thinking of passages such as Jas. 1:7–8, where a man who is double-minded (*duplex animo*) is branded as unreliable. Nevertheless, positive examples of *duplex* (double) in the Bible could be adduced; see, for instance, 2 Kgs 2:9, where Elisha asks for a double (*duplex*) measure of Elijah's spirit.

4.7, 8

matter of duty: In other words, working to acquire wealth might be permissible if you were working to secure the future of your descendants. Jerome, however, imagines a situation in which the person working does not have an heir to support.
preceding interpretation: Lat. *superiorem interpretationem*; the interpretation Jerome has just offered, pointing out the futility of piling up wealth while not knowing who will inherit it.
disdainful readers: Lat. *fastidiosis lectoribus*. For Jerome's concern about his literary legacy, see note at 2.20–23 (and let him give).
sons of God...adoption: See Rom 8:14–23.

4.9–12

certain heir: See Jerome's discussion above, 4.7–8.
above: See, e.g., 1.1, and particularly in the preceding section (4.7–8).
man's will is left free: Humans have the free will to choose whether or not to have Christ stand with them against the devil.
sometimes be broken: Probably to be understood as a reference to the person who turns away from God (see Jerome's discussion in the last paragraph of 3.18–21).
After the bread...into him: John 13:27.

example from Elisha: An allusion to 2 Kgs 4:32–36: here the Prophet Elisha brought the Shunammite woman's son back to life by lying on top of him.

4.13–16

Bar Akiba: One of the most famous rabbis of the first century. Born around the year AD 50, he was a well-known sage who became a key contributor to the Mishnah. He supported the claim that Bar Kokhba was the long-expected Jewish messiah, and he participated in the Second Jewish Revolt against Rome. He was captured by Hadrian's Roman forces and executed ca. 132.

left-hand path...right: The text here literally reads: "after the philosophers' letter Y." Evidently a fork in the road was called a Y junction, and this junction was employed as a metaphor for the choices a person made in life. See also the citation of Lactantius on this point at 10.3 (*The Institutes*).

In Prodikos's *Choice of Herakles* (Xen. *Mem.* 2.1.21–34) the word ὁδός (*hodos*, "way") is repeatedly used of the choice confronting the young Herakles between the "way of virtue" and the "way of vice," although they are not identified with the left and right.

The idea of making the correct choices in life is a commonplace among patristic authors, and the belief that angels lead men along two different paths as they enter Hades (left going to torments, while the right-hand path leads to rewards) may be found in Hipp. *Graec.* 1. The distinction between the right and left is present also in Christ's description of the judgment of the nations, the separation of the sheep and goats at the last judgment (Matt 25:31–46).

Better is the inner man...in the earlier one: Bar Akiba has allegorized this verse, seeing in it a description of the two ways: the way of the flesh (the first man) and the way of the spirit (the second man). After a person reaches puberty, the age of accountability and reason, he or she is faced with a decision to spend his or her life satisfying the base desires and lusts of the flesh, or to turn to loftier pursuits, the practice of philosophy.

Qoh. Rab. 4.13.1 claims that the poor wise child is the Good Inclination, which comes to a person at puberty and teaches the right way; the old, foolish king is the Bad Inclination, which teaches the way of evil and is called a king because most people serve it.

two men: Allusions to either Eph 4:24 or Col 3:9–10, texts that direct the believer to put off the old nature and adopt a new nature that comes from God.

Man, man: LXX Lev 17:13. The Hebrew phrase איש איש (*ʾîš ʾîš*) is literally "man, man." This is a normal Hebrew idiom that means "anyone," but Jerome is using it as if it supports Bar Akiba's theory of two men in the one human being, an interpretation entirely incompatible with the Hebrew.

Gregory, bishop of Pontus: A reference to Gregory Thaumaturgos. See Introduction for a discussion of Jerome's sources.

But I prefer...opposing spirit: Gr. Thaum. *Eccl.* 4.13–16.

interpreter of Laodicea: Apollinarius of Laodicea (ca. 310–390). Bishop of Laodicea, Apollinarius was a contemporary and supporter of Athanasius of Alexandria during the fourth-century Arian controversy. His christological views, however, came under censure as he neared the end of his life, and he was condemned at the Council of Constantinople (381) and forbidden to preach. In *Concerning Illustrious Men*, Jerome's catalogue of patristic writers, he lists Apollinarius as one of the defenders of Nicene theology (Hier. *Vir. ill.* 86; 120) and has nothing negative to say about him in his own entry (Hier. *Vir. ill.* 104).

The Preacher...dies, another: Apollinarius of Laodicea's commentary on Ecclesiastes is no longer extant.

Origen's view: Origen discussed this passage in *Dial.* 24 (see Leanza, *L'esegesi di Origene,* 42), but he did not offer the interpretation of the verse that Jerome produces here. Origen was considering whether the soul separates from the body at death, or whether it remains in the tomb with the corpse. He argued that the soul goes to be with Christ (citing Phil 1:23 and Luke 2:29). Consequently, Origen claimed that Eccl 4:14 was written about the just person, who, departing from the prison of the body, goes forth to be a king.

Victorinus: Victorinus, bishop of Poetovio in Pannonia (modern-day Ptuj in Slovenia). Little is known about his life, although Jerome claims that he was martyred during Diocletian's persecution of the church (303–311). Jerome lists him at *Vir. ill.* 74, noting that he was an exegete who had written commentaries on several biblical books (including Ecclesiastes), but that his style was inferior.

It is a great thing...boy: Isa 49:6. Jerome here follows the Septuagint translation (Μέγα σοί ἐστιν τοῦ κληθῆναι σε παῖδά μου [*Mega soi estin tou klēthēnai se paida mou,* "It is a great thing for you to be called my child"]). The Hebrew is slightly different: "It is too light a thing that you should be my servant" (NRSV). The Latin word *puer* can mean both "boy" and "servant." Jerome here adopts the interpretation that enables him to employ the quotation from Isaiah in his argument.

he became poor...rich: 2 Cor 8:9.

he increased...God and man: Luke 2:52.

kingship of one who is old: There is a temptation to see the foolish old king as the Jewish King Herod, who ruled when Jesus was born (Matt 2:1; Luke 1:5). However, context and the next several lines show that Satan is the foolish old king that Jerome has in mind.

If my kingship...of this world: John 18:36.

kingdoms of the world...glory: An allusion to Matt 4:8–10; Mark 1:12–13; Luke 4:1–13, when Satan tested Christ, after Jesus had spent forty days fasting in the desert.

So that he might humble...his feet: LXX Lam 3:34.

a distant region: An allusion to Matt 2:13–15: Joseph and Mary took Jesus to Egypt after King Herod gave orders to kill all the male infants.

I am the life: John 14:6.

two groups...are signified: Jerome refers to the translation of this verse: *all who were before them. And indeed the most recent will not rejoice in him.*

who lived before...Jews and apostles: The beginning of this sentence makes it appear that Jerome is going to suggest that an unidentified group of Jews, who lived before the coming of Christ, will be saved. The end of the sentence, however, restricts salvation to those who became disciples and apostles during Christ's lifetime, leaving the fate of those Jews who had not known Christ unresolved.

4.17

Moses alone...to approach: An allusion to Exod 20:18–21: when God descended to Mount Sinai to give the law to the Jewish people, the elders of the tribe were too frightened to approach the mountain and begged Moses to act as an intermediary between God and the people.

obedience and good works: A similar sentiment is expressed in Aug. *Ciu.* 21.27, where Augustine argues that it is not the act of offering alms that makes recompense for sin, but rather the turning away from sin that makes alms efficacious.

Obedience over sacrifice: 1 Sam 15:22.

I desire mercy, not sacrifice: Hos 6:6.

CHAPTER 5

5.1, 2

promises lightly...powers: Jesus warned his disciples against making vows that they might be unable to keep in Matt 5:33–37. The question whether a vow should always be kept was treated by John Cassian in *Coll.* 18; he argued that some vows could be safely set aside if breaking them would yield a better result than keeping them.

multiplication of speeches: At 10.13, 14 Jerome asserts that a fool considers himself wise if he multiplies his speeches, that is, talks at greater length than is required.

Just as someone...into foolishness: Our speculations about God are, like dreams, a fruitless fantasy. On the unreality and untrustworthiness of dreams, see 5.6.

mirror...enigma: An allusion to 1 Cor 13:12.

from much talking...escape sin: Prov 10:19.

5.3, 4

volition...the unwise: For this phrase, see note at 3.16, 17 (volition).

it is better to make no promises: An idea also found in the Mosaic Law in Deut 23:22.

In any case...come to you now: 1 Cor 16:12. This verse details Apollos's reluctance to visit the church at Corinth. Jerome has changed the verb from *veniret* ("he should come") to *venirem* ("I should come") to make it apply to Paul. Paul had encouraged Apollos to go, but οὐκ ἦν θέλημα ἵνα νῦν ἔλθῃ (*ouk ēn thelēma hina nyn elthē*, "it was not [his] will that he should go now"). Context would lead a reader to believe that Apollos's will was keeping him from journeying to Corinth, but the ambiguity of the Greek leaves the possibility open that a greater will (of God) was stopping Apollos.

worshiped idols: Idolatry was forbidden in the Ten Commandments (Exod 20:3–5; Deut 5:7–9). The reminder that the Jews had not kept their promise to refrain from idol worship was a commonplace in patristic polemics against the Jews (see Just. *Dial.* 19, 22; Tert. *Iud.* 1).

Whatever God commands...do it all: Exod 24:3. This was the promise that the Israelites made after Moses presented the law he had received from God.

beating and stoning...Son himself: An allusion to Matt 21:33–41, Jesus' parable of the vineyard.

The servant...a severe beating: A paraphrase of Luke 12:47.

5.5

sight of an angel: The Septuagint translators had rendered this phrase πρὸ προσώπου τοῦ θεοῦ (*pro prosōpou tou Theou*, "before the face of God"). The Hebrew text, instead of "God," employs the word המלאך (*hammalʾāk*, "the messenger" or "the angel"). Jerome's translation clearly favors the Hebrew interpretation put forward by his teacher (see below), although modern commentators suggest that this verse is a reference to the rituals described in Num 15:22–29 for sins of inadvertence. In this case, the *mal'āk* would actually be the temple priest (Murphy, *Ecclesiastes*, 50–51).

angel present...close by: See also at 10.20. After the exile, angels came to play an increasingly important role in Jewish thought. They mediated between God and humanity (see Zech. 1:8–19) and also served as guardians over cities and individual humans (LXX Ps 33:8 [Ps 34:7]). The most explicit statement about guardian angels may be found in Christ's teaching on the subject (Matt 18:10). Jerome clearly believed in guardian angels: "How great the worth of souls, that each one should have been assigned to the care of a guardian angel from the point of birth" (Hier. Matt 18.10).

You are not to give...so as to sin: Although Jerome's Hebrew teacher glosses over the "flesh" in his interpretation, his view is more plausible here, seeing Eccl 5:5 as a continuation of the point made in Eccl 5:4. It is better not to make a vow than to make a vow and fail to carry it out. The mouth leads the flesh (the person; see Murphy, *Ecclesiastes*, 46 n. 5a) into sin when it makes this careless vow.

our view...sense is different: That is, the Christian interpretation differs from the Hebrew exegesis of this passage.

the flesh: Jerome indicates that his Hebrew teacher's understanding of the passage was defective because he did not take proper account of the term *the flesh*. Jerome here takes too much account of it and attempts to tie it into Paul's discussion of the flesh and the will found in Romans.

For I do not do...do not want: Rom 7:15.

Hebrew *segaga*...sin is his fault: Jerome has translated the Hebrew word שגגה (*šĕgāgâ*, "inadvertent error") with the Latin *ignorantia* ("ignorance"). As he notes, Aquila had rendered the word with the Greek ἀκούσιον (*akousion,* "not on purpose"). Jerome faults Aquila's translation because it would seem to suggest that God is somehow culpable in inadvertent sin (see 5.6).

5.6
above: See 5:1–5.

Someone who believes...silly vanities: The Hebrew position does not mesh neatly with the importance Jerome had recently placed on his most famous dream: the account of his condemnation in the heavenly court for being a "Ciceronian" rather than a "Christian." Jerome related this dream to Eustochium (Hier. *Ep.* 22.30) in 384, about three years before the *Commentary on Ecclesiastes* was written. According to

Jerome, the dream had disturbed him so deeply that he had promised never to read pagan literature again. He maintained this vow for at least a decade (Kelly, *Jerome*, 43), but eventually returned to his reading of classical literature. Years later, when Rufinus challenged him for breaking his promise, Jerome stated that a person was not to be bound by a promise made in a dream (Hier. *Ruf.* 1.31), a sentiment that accords well with the interpretation he offers here.

give your mouth...flesh sin: See 5.5.

5.7, 8

Christ's garment...crucifiers: An allusion to John 19:23–24: at the foot of the cross the soldiers divided Jesus' clothing, but his tunic was seamless, so they chose to cast lots to see who would receive the garment.

Savior commanded...to the apostles: Luke 8:27–35; Matt 8:28–34; Mark 5:1–20. The Gerasene demoniac wore no clothes while he haunted the tombs. After Jesus expelled the demons that had possessed him, the Gospel accounts report that the people of the nearby town found the man, fully clothed, speaking with Jesus. Hence Jerome's inference, that Christ had ordered his apostles to provide clothing for the healed man.

Above...and the rest: See 5.5.

It was against those...he had said this: The Epicureans were known for their view that the gods took no interest in human affairs, nor did they guide the world to a predetermined end. See note at 1.9–10 (Epicurus).

blessed in the Gospel: Matt 5:3; Luke 6:20. Jerome alludes to the Beatitudes, in which Jesus states that the poor are blessed because they will see the kingdom of God.

grain to be separated...put into the fire: An allusion to the parable of the weeds (Matt 13:24–30): a man plants grain in his field, but during the night, an enemy sows weeds in the same field. When this is discovered, the man's servants want to root up the weeds immediately, but the owner of the field opts to allow the two types of plants to grow together, waiting until the harvest to separate them.

parable...weeds and the grain: See Matt 13:24–30, the parable of the weeds.

5.9, 10

ἀργύριον: *argyrion*, "silver," "money."

pecunious: From Lat. *pecuniosus* ("wealthy," "having an ample supply of money"). This is an adjective formed from *pecunia* ("money").

peculia: Plural of the Lat. *peculium,* whose main meaning is "money for use by one (e.g., a slave) not its legal owner." The surviving passage of Cic. *Rep.* 2.16 that refers to the derivation of the Latin word *pecuniosus* from words that mean "livestock" does not mention *peculium* at all; but other authors who give this derivation do mention *peculium* (e.g., Var. *L.* 5.95 [5.19 in some editions]; Col. *Rust.* 6 Pref. 4). Probably Jerome's memory of the Cicero passage is blurred; he seems wrong in asserting that *peculium* ever meant "livestock."

pecora: The Latin word for "cattle."

Cicero tells us...other meaning: Cic. *Rep.* 2:16.

The miser...needy: Hor. *Ep.* 1.2.56.

Greed is not...by shortage: Sal. *Cat.* 11:3.

5.11

to one working: The Septuagint translators and Gr. Thaum. *Eccl.* 5.11 translated the Hebrew word העובד (*hāʿôbēd,* "the one working") with the Greek word δοῦλος (*doulos,* "slave," "servant"). Jerome restores the sense of the Hebrew text with his *operanti* ("to one who is working").

Woe to you...consolation: Luke 6:24.

5.12–16

his own wealth himself: See 5.9, 10.

accumulated to his heir: A point made at 4.7, 8.

litigation: It was a patristic commonplace that wealth could not be acquired without cheating or stealing from someone else (see note at 4.6 [great riches]). In antiquity, as now, litigation was one possible means of acquiring wealth.

I will destroy...I will thwart: 1 Cor 1:19. Paul cites this text while developing his argument that the wisdom of the cross is superior to the wisdom of the wise, an apposite quotation for the view Jerome expresses here.

But the Jerusalem...mother of us all: Gal 4:26.

They are worn out...with a search: LXX Ps 63:7 [Ps 64:6]. The Septuagint, which Jerome is following here, differs very markedly from the Hebrew text. It renders the Hebrew phrase in Ps 64:7, תמנו חפש מחפש (*tamnû ḥēpeś mĕḥuppāś,* literally "we [*or they*] have accomplished a devised device"), with ἐξέλιπον ἐρευνῶντες ἐξερευνήσει (*exelipon ereunōntes exereunēsei,* "they gave up searching with a search").

are carried...wind of doctrine: Eph 4:14.

storing up wrath...day of wrath: Rom 2:5.

5.17–19

By comparison: That is, by comparison with the rich miser (see 5.12–16 and 6.1–6) who does not use his wealth. For Jerome's view that this verse is not approving the enjoyment of food and drink but only stating that these are a better thing than parsimony and miserliness, see 7.3.

God distracts him...by thought: Jerome develops the literal sense of this verse: God allows certain wealthy people to enjoy their possessions in this life. This is a gift from him, and their enjoyment and delight in what they have distracts them from the harsh realities and apparent unfairness of life.

spiritual food...given by God: An allusion to 1 Cor 10:3–4. Here Paul offered an allegorical reading of the Israelite's sojourn in the wilderness. The Israelites ate manna, a supernatural bread, in the wilderness (Exod 16:4–35) and drank from a supernatural rock when Moses struck it with his staff (Exod 17:6). According to Paul, the spiritual food and drink was Christ. Jerome's point, then, is that God leads people into happiness by allowing them to participate in the Eucharist (eating and drinking). This is not the first time he has preferred a spiritual interpretation to the Preacher's more earthly command to enjoy eating and drinking (see 2.24–26; 7.3).

περισπασμός: *perispasmos,* "wheeling around," "distraction." The Septuagint text (LXX Eccl 5:19) reads: ὁ θεὸς περισπᾷ αὐτόν (*ho theos perispa auton*), which could be rendered as "God distracts him." See note on *anian...*περισπασμόν at 1.13.

CHAPTER 6

6.1–6

rich miser...others are to devour: A theme already explored in Eccl 2:18–23; 5:12–16.

one hundred children...one thousand years: A long life and many descendants were traditional indicators of God's blessing (see Gen 25:8; 35:9–12; Murphy, *Ecclesiastes,* 53–54).

as Adam did: According to Gen 5:5, Adam lived 930 years.

The kingdom of God...producing its fruits: Matt 21:43. This verse comes from the conclusion of the parable of the vineyard, in which Jesus appears to criticize the guardians of Judaism, the chief priests and Pharisees. Jerome's interpretation of this verse, that it refers to the Jews losing God's favor, is a commonplace in patristic writings (see Aug. *Psal.* 63.14).

Our father is Abraham: John 8:33, 39. Jesus' Jewish listeners asserted that they had no need to become his disciples because they were already children of Abraham. Jesus rejected this claim, stating that if the Jewish leaders were children of Abraham, then they would do what Abraham had done, and understand his words.

body is cast away unburied: In ancient cultures it was very important that a body receive a proper burial. This view emerges, for instance, in Vergil, where the souls of the unburied are seen crowded onto one bank of the river Styx, unable to cross (Ver. *Aen.* 6. 327–28), or in fallen Mezentius's plea that his body be buried rather than surrendered to the hatred of his enemies (Ver. *Aen.* 10.904–6). A proper burial was important also in Jewish thought. Jezebel's body was left in the street where it fell and was consumed by the dogs before it could be buried (2 Kgs 9:33–37); Isaiah predicted that the body of the king of Babylon would be cast out, away from its sepulcher (Isa 14:19); and the body of Jehoiakim was to be given the burial of an ass: dragged outside the gates of Jerusalem and left to rot (Jer 22:18–19).

Augustine played down the importance of burial when he asserted that there was nothing anybody could do to hurt a body after it had died; unburied Christians were not separated from heaven (Aug. *Ciu.* 1.12).

passing...cattle: Sal. *Cat.* 1.1. Sallust argued that a man must distinguish himself somehow in life if he is to rise above the beasts of the field who exist simply to fill their bellies. A man could set himself apart on the battlefield or in politics, or could gain eternal fame by writing history.

Jerome also believed that the cultivation of a reputation that will endure after death is important (see 7.2).

6.7, 8

seems to bestow pleasure...in the throat: Jerome stands in a long line of ascetic thinkers who denigrated luxurious foods. See Hier. *Ep.* 22.8–9 for his view that anything more than water and coarse fare were unsuitable for the monk.

poor man goes...wealth: The meaning of Eccl 6:8b is unclear, even to modern biblical commentators (Murphy, *Ecclesiastes,* 54). A literal rendering of the verse would read: "What to the poor knowing to go in front of/over/against/facing life/living people?" The LXX glossed this difficult passage as ὁ πένης οἶδε πορευθῆναι κατέναντι τῆς ζωῆς (*ho penēs oide poreuthēnai katenanti tēs zōēs,* "the poor man knows how to walk over against life"). Jerome picked up the Greek adverb κατέναντι (*katenanti,* "over against, opposite") and translated it with the Latin adverb *contra.* To make sense of his spiritual exegesis (the poor churchman cannot go against Christ, who is life), it seems clear that he intended *vadat contra* ("he goes against [life]") to mean something more like "he encounters life." Gregory Thaumaturgos solved the problem by radically recasting the verse as: "justice of life mostly leads a person to poverty" (Gr. Thaum. *Eccl.* 6.8, trans. Jarick, *Thaumaturgos' Paraphrase*, 146).

blessed…Gospel: Matt 5:3; Luke 6:20. Another reference to the Beatitudes in the Gospels. Here, the verse is a natural support for his argument (the churchman is poor in material things, but wealthy because his desire for learning will lead him to the kingdom of God).

constricted, narrow…leads to life: An allusion to Matt 7:14: "For the gate is narrow and the road is constricted which leads to life, and there are few who discover it."

6.9

reasoning…eye of the soul: The faculty of reason as the inner eye or eye of the soul was a philosophical commonplace (see Pl. *Rep.* 518c; Arist. *EN* 1144a29-31).

Those who walk…their own heart: An allusion to Ezek 11:20-21. The prophet relates God's plan to give his people a new heart to replace their stony heart. With this new heart, they will keep his commands and be his people. But God will reject those whose hearts pursue detestable things.

grazing of the wind: See note at 1.14 (*routh*).

ruha: Heb.: רוח (*rûaḥ*). The same is true of Latin, where *anima* can mean either "spirit" or "wind."

6.10

called by his name: An allusion to Isa 9:6: "and his name will be called 'Wonderful Counselor,' 'Mighty God,' 'Father of eternity,' 'Prince of Peace.'"

known to the prophets…being a man: The Hebrew prophets had foretold the coming of a man, the messiah, who would establish God's kingdom in the world and redeem his people (see, e.g., Micah 5:2; Zech 9:9-10). Patristic authors, naturally, applied these prophecies to Jesus.

The Father…greater than I: John 14:28. Jerome asserts the humanity of Christ, and thus his subordination to God.

he was made…this way or that: See Job 40:1—42:6 on Job's inability to respond to God; also Rom 9:19-21, where Paul asserts that the clay pot has no right to question the potter's will for the pot.

CHAPTER 7

7.1

Because there are...under the sun: Modern English translations place these two verses at the end of chapter 6 of Ecclesiastes. The Vulgate, on the other hand (which the CCSL follows), places the second verse at the beginning of chapter 7, resulting in a numbering system that does not match English translations. Since Jerome discusses Eccl 6:11 in this section, we have transferred this verse to chapter 7.

unaware of his own condition: That is, unable intellectually to grasp spiritual truths. Augustine attributed this to the Fall; before Adam sinned in the Garden, he was able to understand these higher realities. After the Fall, he no longer could grasp spiritual truths such as the justice of God condemning certain people to hell (Aug. *Ciu.* 21.12). This spiritual understanding will be restored, however, in heaven, where the saved will see God face to face, as the angels, who did not fall, currently do (Aug. *Ciu.* 22.29).

in a mirror...in representation: An allusion to 1 Cor 13:12.

in much speech...escape sin: Prov 10:19; see also Eccl 5:2.

7.2

lasting reputation: The converse of this sentiment, condemnation of the person who does not make a reputation that endures, may be found at 6.1–6.

birth fetters...death releases it again: This is an ancient Greek idea that can be found as early as Plato (see Pl. *Grg.* 493a; Pl. *Cra.* 400c). The binding of pre-existent souls to material bodies is described in Pl. *Ti.* 43a. These texts have been analyzed by C. J. de Vogel ("Soma-Sema Formula, 79–95), who concluded that, while Plato did not see the body as being a punishment for the soul, it is possible to read later Christian authors as interpreting the struggle between body and soul in this way. Origen, for instance, attributed this binding to a body as a soul's punishment for its failure to persist in the good (Or. *Princ.* 1.8).

7.3

in which...every man: Like the Hebrew and the LXX, Jerome's translation leaves it unclear that the clause *in which is the end of every man* has *a house of mourning* as its antecedent. His comment, however, does resolve this difficulty.

above: See Eccl 3:13; 5:18.

avarice and excessive thrift...for the moment: See 6.1–6 for Jerome's condemnation of the parsimony that prevents a miser from enjoying the things he has accumulated, which ultimately results in these goods being left to a stranger.

7.4

We should be angry...angry with others: Was it appropriate for Christians to be angry? Different answers were advanced by various patristic authors. Lactantius argued that anger was appropriate only when it existed within God-given limits. A parent was permitted to employ anger to discipline children, but anger was not to be directed at those equal in age for fear of stirring up dissension (Lact. *Inst.* 6.19). Gregory of Nyssa suggested that anger was only to be used like a watchdog: to attack the sins creeping into a person's mind (Gr. Nyss. *Virg.* 18.3). Augustine affirmed Jerome's position when he suggested that anger directed toward a sinner was a passion that no reasonable person could condemn (Aug. *Ciu.* 9.5). John Cassian disagreed, stating that a monk must strive to expel anger from his soul; if an erring brother required correction, this should be done without growing angry (Cassian *Inst.* 5.1).
Woe to those...shall mourn: Luke 6:25.

7.5

Blessed...shall be comforted: Matt 5:4.
days of his life: See 1 Samuel 15:34.
sorts of sins: See 2 Cor 12:21.
is praised...his consolation: For "is praised," all the manuscripts have "is mourned," which makes no satisfactory sense in this context. With our textual emendation (see Appendix, n. 37), this sentence combines two scriptural references: Matt 6:2 (the hypocrites in the synagogues who boast about their almsgiving in order to be praised by the people) and Luke 6:24–25 (the rich who have their consolation in this life, but not hereafter). Undoubtedly angry over his recent exile from Rome (see also 3.6, 7; 7.6, 9; 10.19), Jerome seems here to be attacking successful preachers whose sole aim, he writes, is to impress the crowds.

7.6, 7

thorns under a pot...of a fool: The Hebrew word for "thorns," סירים (*sîrîm*) is formed as the plural of the word for "pot" (סיר [*sîr*]); thus the text contains an assonance amounting almost to a pun.

Wounds...from an enemy: Prov 27:6.

cares of this world...thorns: An allusion to the parable of the sower, in which Jesus equates the cares of the world with thorns that choke the growth of the sown grain (Mark 4:18–19; Matt 13:22; Luke 8:14).

one is tied in bonds: This free translation suggests that Symmachus ignored the meaning "pot" (see above) and took the phrase to mean "like thorns under a thorn"—that is, like a tangled thicket which traps someone.

7.8

Reprove a wise man...love you: Prov 9:8.

false accusation: See note on this at 4.1.

εὐτονίας αὐτοῦ...mattānâ: Symmachus has correctly rendered the reading מתנה (mattānâ, "gift," here "bribe"), which is now found in Hebrew Bibles (Eccl 7:7). The translation "courage" or "vigor" seems to go back to an ancient variant מתנים (motnayîm, "loins" or "strength").

Bribes...wise men's eyes: Deut 16:19.

7.9

epilogues...exordium: Jerome here draws a parallel from the practice of oratory. In classical rhetoric, an *exordium* was the introductory section of a speech in which the orator aroused the interest of his listeners, revealed the purpose of his discourse, and sought to conciliate those who might be hostile to his cause. The *epilogus* concluded the speech and was devoted to emotional appeals to the audience.

that which...has come: 1 Cor 13:10.

high in spirit: Jerome here uses the Latin word *spiritus,* which is derived from the same stem as English "respire"; its original meaning is "breath," but it was also commonly used in the sense in which it has come into English, "spirit." Jerome uses the word to translate רוח (rûah), which does have both those meanings but is also used at times in the Bible to mean "anger." However, neither "spiritus" in Latin nor πνεῦμα (pneuma), the Greek word used here in the Septuagint, is found elsewhere with the meaning "anger"; so either Jerome has worked directly from the Hebrew here and found the meaning "anger" better suited to this context than the commoner one of "spirit," or perhaps he found the Greek word θυμός (thymos), which can mean "anger" as well as "spirit," in Aquila, Symmachus, or Theodotion. See also notes at 6.9 (ruha) and 10.4 (excessive self-importance).

Anger is better...laughter: A reference back to 7.4.

poor in spirit: Matt 5:3.

7.10
said above: See Eccl 7:9.

7.11
Blessed are…have believed: John 20:29.
You were running…the truth: Gal 5:7.
Having begun…ending with the flesh: Gal 3:3.

7.12, 13
Wisdom is good…one who has it: This verse, as found in the Masoretic manuscripts, is difficult to interpret (Kugel, "Qohelet and Money," 43–44). "Shade," for a desert people, is a metaphor for protection. Therefore, Qohelet is stating that wisdom offers the same kind of protection to a person as wealth, a point Jerome discusses below.
we become heirs…with Christ: Rom 8:17.
sun of justice: Mal 4:2. See 1.5 and 1.6 for Jerome's identification of Christ as the sun of justice.
Those understanding…stars of heaven: Dan 12:3. Jerome has altered the force of this verse slightly to support a point that it does not make. In Dan 12:3 the repetition is simply an example of Hebraic parallelism: "Those who are wise shall shine like the brightness of heaven, those who turn many to justice will be like the stars forever." The verse is not drawing a contrast but rather restating a proposition. Jerome, however, interposes the adversative conjunction *vero* ("but," "however") between the two clauses in order to make the verse support his exegesis.
talents and minas: These measures, originally representing weights (sixty minas to a talent), are used in Greek as sums of money. Matthew's version of the parable (Matt 25:14–28) uses "talents"—hence the English transferred meaning of that word—and Luke 19:12–25 uses "minas."
the sun shall not…by night: LXX Ps 120:6 [Ps 121:6]. The explanation for Jerome's citation may be found in the preceding verse (LXX Ps 120:5 [Ps 121:5]): "The Lord watches over you—the Lord is your shade at your right hand."
shadow: The Latin word *umbra* is used as both "shade" and "shadow."
breath: Here *spiritus* has its original meaning of "breath" (contrast note on 7.9 [high in spirit] above).
And the breath…among the nations: Lam 4:20.
until the day…flee away: Cant 2:17; 4:6.

7.14

twisted: From the Latin verb *perverto* (lit. "turn wrong"). Jerome uses parts of this verb for "perverse" in the Psalm quotation later in his commentary on this verse, and for "contrary" in the Leviticus quotation; here we have translated it as "twisted." See also 1.15, and the relevant notes there.

contemplation of the elements...what has happened: The citation of Romans at the end of this chapter suggests that he has Rom 1:20 in mind here, the view that God's creation testifies to his nature and qualities, a revelation that is sufficient for human understanding.

Who made a man...Lord God: Exod 4:11.

With the pure...will be perverse: LXX Ps 17:27 [Ps 18:26].

If they walk...in my fury: Lev 26:27–28.

Pharaoh's heart: See Exod 7:3. Jerome draws the example of the sun liquefying wax and hardening mud directly from Origen's discussion of the hardening of the Pharaoh in Or. *Princ.* 3.11.

signs in Egypt: An allusion to Exod 7:1–12:30.

storing up wrath...day of wrath: Rom 2:5.

7.15

in order to speak: The Hebrew phrase עַל־דִּבְרַת (ʿal-dibrat, "on account that," "in order to" [Eccl 7:14]) was misunderstood by the Septuagint translators, who wrote περὶ λαλιᾶς (*peri lalias*, "on account of talking") and Jerome, who translated it *ad loquendum*. See also the note at 3.18 (about the utterance). This mistake is emended in the Vulgate.

The world itself...bad and good: An allusion to Ov. *Met.* 1:19–20, in which the poet discusses the primordial, warring state of the elements before the god gave them a semblance of order. The distinction between opposites and contraries is made at Arist. *Metaph.* 1018a12–b6.

free will in choosing...complain of his own condition: See note at 1.17 (educated toward wisdom); God has allowed good and evil things in creation so that humans will have the chance to choose for themselves.

7.16

He who finds...will find it: Matt 10:39.

Maccabees: Jerome refers to the Judean revolt of 168–167 BC, led by Judah, the son of Mattathias, an event chronicled in the intertestamental books 1–4 Maccabees. The Judean freedom fighters rebelled when the Hellenistic king Antiochus Epiphanes attempted to impose Greek cultic practices on the Jews. The rebellion was successful and led to the creation of an independent Jewish state that endured until 63 BC. The Jewish festival of Hanukkah commemorates Judah's victory over the Hellenistic king.

ate pork...sacrificed to idols: Antiochus Epiphanes sent letters throughout his kingdom in an attempt to establish religious conformity (1 Macc 1:44–49). One of his commands was that pigs should be slaughtered on the altars. Many of the Jews refused to eat pork and were killed (1 Macc 1:62–63).

A parallel situation arose under the Roman emperor Decius (AD 249–251), when all Roman citizens were commanded to offer a sacrifice to the traditional Roman gods. Those who complied with this edict were given a certificate (a *libellus*) that proved that they had made the sacrifice. Since worship of other gods was forbidden to Christians, many refused to make the sacrifice. These believers were arrested, tried, and executed; other Christians complied with the edict, made the sacrifice, and were allowed to go free (see Rives, "Decree of Decius," 135–54).

not coming down...sinners for their wrongdoing: But see 7.18 for Jerome's claim that sometimes the wicked are punished in this life to serve as examples that will rehabilitate others.

inappropriate fire: An allusion to Lev 10:1–2. In this story, Nadab and Abihu, the sons of Aaron, mixed fire with incense in their censers. The writer of Leviticus noted that this was unauthorized fire, and the two men were consumed when fire came out from the presence of God, in the Holy of Holies.

The unauthorized fire is fire that does not come from the outer altar of the Holy of Holies (Lev 16:12).

Manasseh...lived a long time: Manasseh was the son of King Hezekiah. During his reign (687–642 BC), Judea was a vassal state of the Assyrian Empire. At one point the Assyrian king had Manasseh hauled before him in chains (2 Chr 33:11), evidently suspecting him of planning to revolt against his Assyrian overlords (Bright, *History,* 311). Eventually Manasseh was released and allowed to return to Judea. 2 Chr 33:12–20 seems to suggest that Manasseh had been reformed and returned to the worship of Yahweh, while the account of his rule found in 2 Kgs 21:1–18 maintains that he led the people astray and ruled wickedly. In Hier. *Ep.* 77.4, written ca. 399, Jerome offers King Manasseh as an example of a person who repents and changes his life.

Jerome repeats this claim about the sons of Aaron and Manasseh at 8.14.

7.17

Judge not...not judged: Luke 6:37.

no one is without sin...only a day: The idea that even newborn infants are tainted by original sin, and thereby guilty in the Lord's eyes, was most famously argued by Augustine (Aug. *Enchir.* 52), who suggested that babies who died before baptism would be sent to Hades, but would only suffer the lightest punishments there (Aug. *Peccat. merit.* 1.21; Aug. *Nat. et grat.* 9.8).

A heavy weight…to the Lord: Prov 20:23. Jerome is here translating the Septuagint version of the Proverbs text: δισσὸν στάθμιον (*disson stathmion,* "a double weight"); the Hebrew ואבן אבן (*'eben wā'eben*] literally means "stone and stone," that is, "a weight and a weight."

In philosophy…as a vice: This idea can be traced back to Aristotle, who, in the *Nicomachean Ethics,* argued that the master of any art avoided both excess and defect, seeking the intermediate path between extremes (Arist. *EN* 1106b36–1107a27). The same idea appears in Christian writers such as Gregory of Nyssa (*Virg.* 8) and, later, John Cassian (*Coll.* 2.16).

Why does he…his will: Rom 9:19.

Who are you…back to God: Rom 9:20.

recipient no good: A possible allusion to 1 Cor 2:14, in which Paul suggests that an unspiritual person cannot receive the gifts of God because they seem foolish to the unenlightened mind. Jerome's point is that even if God did choose to reveal hidden knowledge, it is so far beyond human comprehension that it would make no sense anyway.

Agag…put to death: An allusion to 1 Sam 15:9. The Targum reshapes this verse as a command to avoid being overly soft-hearted by failing in the duty of putting a condemned person to death (*Tar. Qoh.* 7:16). *Qoh. Rab.* 7.16 is similar to Jerome's exegesis, using Saul's failure to slaughter all of the living things in the city of Amalek (1 Sam 15:9) as an example of being too just.

fellow slave off: An allusion to Matt 18:23–34.

7.18

I do not desire…turn back and live: Ezek 33:11. The Hebrew, Septuagint, and Jerome's own Vulgate texts all concur in using a word meaning "wicked man." Either Jerome's memory slipped at this point, or "dying" is a copyist's error.

celandine…dittany: These two examples, and indeed the entire argument, are taken directly from Tertullian (*Paen.* 12). Tertullian's zoological examples were probably drawn from Pliny the Elder. The claim that stags who have been wounded by archers use dittany to expel the arrows from their wounds is found in Plin. *Nat.* 8.41.97. Likewise, the suggestion that swallows use celandine as a balm for their chick's sore eyes may be found in Plin. *Nat.* 8.41.98.

Korah, Dathan...earthquake: See Num 16:1–35. Korah, Dathan, and Abiram led a rebellion against Moses, and the Lord punished them by having the earth open and swallow them (Num 16:31–33).

7.19
household of faith: See Gal 6:10.
anyone who asks: See, for example, Jesus' command to give freely to someone who asks for something (Matt 5:42).
rains...just and the unjust: An allusion to Matt 5:45; God sends his blessings (rain) on both the just and the unjust.
to do good...discrimination: An allusion to the story of Cornelius the centurion, found in Acts 10, especially v. 28; when Peter realized that God had given Cornelius (a Gentile) a vision, he realized that God did not discriminate between Jew and Gentile.
A God-fearing person...crushed by adversity: A Stoic sentiment. The sage sought to avoid elation or despondency over things beyond his control.

7.20, 21
angels...decad: Arist. *Metaph.* 986a8 refers to Pythagoras as holding that ten, the decad, is the perfect number. The decad is the sum of the first four numbers (the tetrad: 1+2+3+4).
Wisdom...Jesus Christ: Jerome follows a long tradition of linking Jesus with the personified quality of Wisdom. Prov 8:1–36 speaks of Wisdom as one of the firstborn of God's works, an intelligent force that taught people how to live just lives. The early Christian apologists equated Wisdom with Christ (see Just. *Dial.* 61; Ign. *Smyrn.* 2; for New Testament references, see 1 Cor 1:30; Col 2:3). It should be noted that other patristic authors, such as Irenaeus, identified Jesus as the Word and the Holy Spirit as Wisdom (see Iren. *Haer.* 4.20.3).
We healed Babylon...his country: Jer 51:9.
touch of his hem: An allusion to Luke 8:43–48, the story of the woman who was healed after she touched the hem of Christ's garment.
To any that has...added to him: Matt 13:12.

7.22, 23
fleck...beam in one's own: An allusion to Matt 7:3.

7.24, 25
Books of Kingdoms also testify: See 1 Kgs 3:5–15; 4:29–34 (LXX 3 Kgdms 3:5–15; NETS 5:9-14, older versions 4:29–34).
revealed face to face: An allusion to 1 Cor 13:12.

7.26, 27

Symmachus translated it…to investigate: In his Vulgate translation, Jerome was closer to Symmachus's version.

had said above: See 7.25.

Woman: In isolation, the Hebrew phrase האשה אשר־היא (*hāʾiššâ ʾăšer-hîʾ*) and the Greek τὴν γυναῖκα ἥτις (*tēn gynaika hētis*) both have a literal meaning of "the woman who." The most natural interpretation would see this as a reference to a single woman who entraps men. In context, however, it is clear that the Preacher is condemning women as a class, a view that Jerome endorses with his comments.

they are all…like a furnace: Hos 7:4. The pronouns "they" and "their" are masculine in Latin, as in the Hebrew text. In the context of the verse in Hosea, "they" are the Israelites, fickle in their relationship with God.

assurim: אסורים (*ʾăsûrîm*, "bonds").

ensnared by women: See 1 Kgs 11:1–8, which describes how Solomon was turned away from worshiping Yahweh by his foreign wives.

in Zechariah…lead weight: An allusion to Zech 5:7–8. These verses describe a vision of the prophet in which he saw a basket. The angel who was with Zechariah said that the basket contained the iniquity of the Israelites. When the lead cover was raised, Zechariah saw a woman sitting in the basket. In the Hebrew text it is clear that the lid of the basket was made of lead; it is possible that Jerome has misunderstood the Septuagint version (which has no word implying that the lead mentioned was a cover) as meaning that she was sitting on a lump of lead inside the vessel.

stolen loaves…stolen water: An allusion to Prov 9:17, where the reward of pursuing Folly is stolen loaves and water.

7.28–30

one to one: The word for "one" here, in both the Hebrew and the LXX, is in the feminine gender. Jerome takes this as support for his argument of the preceding chapter that women are a trap and snare for men.

thoughts: The translation "thoughts" (*cogitationes*) treats the Hebrew word here, חשבנות (*ḥiššĕbōnôt*), as the plural of חשבן (*ḥešbôn*, transliterated as *esebon* by Jerome), the word translated as "reason" in vv. 26–27; but dictionaries list it as a distinct word meaning "contrivances." In consonantal Hebrew texts such a distinction is invisible.

λογισμός…thought: All the definitions suggested would apply to both the Greek word λογισμός (*logismos*) and the Hebrew word חשבון (*ḥešbôn*).

from youth up: An allusion to Gen 8:21.

woman...more prone to fall: The tendency to pin the blame for Adam's fall on Eve (one possible way to read Gen 3:6) has a long pedigree in patristic thought (see Iren. *Haer.* 3.22; Fort. *Carm.* On Easter; Aug. *Bon. coniug.* 30; Ambr. *Off.* 1.2.7).

Ever fickle...woman: Ver. *Aen.* 4:569–70.

Ever learning...of the truth: 2 Tim 3:7. A reference to the weak-willed women who are swayed by the wicked men who insinuate themselves into the women's homes.

Where we normally use...feminine gender: Jerome here offers an explanation of the differences between Hebrew and Latin grammar. In Latin, when using the pronouns *hic* ("this") and *iste* ("that") to refer to things (rather than people), Latin usually employs the neuter forms. Hebrew, on the other hand, uses the feminine gender of these pronouns to express the same idea.

One thing...seek after: LXX Ps 26:4 [Ps 27:4].

one in the neuter: That is, expressing the same meaning as the Latin neuter form *unum* ("one thing").

CHAPTER 8

8.1

Who is as...word: CCSL, following the verse divisions of the Vulgate, numbers this verse as Eccl 7:30. Since Jerome discusses this verse here, we have chosen to combine this verse with Eccl 8:1, following the verse numbering employed by the LXX, the Masoretic Text, and modern English translations.

The Hebrew word דבר (*dābār*) can mean both "word" and "thing." See also notes at 8.2 (evil word) and 8.5 (evil thing). Since the Hebrew text that Jerome used lacked the vowel pointing of the later Masoretic Text, it was also possible to read this word as *deber* ("death") or *dibbēr* ("he spoke"). At Hier. *Ier.* 9:28, Jerome discusses this point, countering the erroneous readings of Origen, Symmachus, Aquila, and the Septuagint. This is one instance where Jerome's ability to understand Hebrew is manifestly apparent (for discussion, see Brown, "Jerome and the Vulgate," 357).

Above he had taught...volition: See 7.28–30.

no one was as wise as he himself: But see 1.16 where Jerome asserts that Solomon was not as wise as Abraham or Moses, but only was wiser than the Jebusites.

problems: See 1 Kgs 3:16-28.

beyond all men…in his appearance: The only biblical reference that might conceivably be taken to imply that Solomon's wisdom was visible from his outward appearance is 1 Kgs 10:4 [2 Chr 9:3]: "And the queen of Sheba saw Solomon's wisdom." The context makes such an inference most unlikely, especially as the Hebrew verb for "see," ראה (rāʾâ), is often used for other kinds of perception, for example, in Eccl 1:16.

The wisdom…hated for his appearance: Despite the fact that Jerome followed the Hebrew text in his translation of the verse above, here he is commenting on the LXX version.

However, we all…glory of the Lord: 2 Cor 3:18.

The light of your countenance…marked upon us: LXX Ps 4:7 [Ps 4:6].

Marcion and Valentinus … Demiurge: Marcion of Pontus (d. ca. 160) and the Gnostic Valentinus (ca. 100–160) were infamous heretics who both believed that the material world had been created by a flawed divinity, the Demiurge. For both men, the Demiurge was to be identified with the evil or warped Yahweh, the God of the Hebrew Bible. The idea of the Demiurge, a being intermediate between the material world and an immutable God, goes back to Plato, who, in the *Timaeus*, discussed the operation of the Demiurge (see Pl. *Ti.* 41a7 ff.).

8.2–4

I guard the mouth … God's oath: The Hebrew text is ambiguous here. Most modern commentators have seen the second clause as offering a reason for obeying the king's command: because the person has sworn an oath before God to do so. Gregory Thaumaturgos probably offered a more accurate understanding when he read this as two separate commands: pay attention to the words of the king *and* avoid swearing an oath in God's name (Gr. Thaum. *Eccl.* 8.2). This would be consistent with the advice given at *Eccl.* 5:4–5, where Qohelet recommends that his readers avoid making vows (see Jarick, *Thaumaturgos' Paraphrase*, 196–97).

evil word: For this term, see note on דבר (dābār) at 8.1 (Who is as… word).

like the Apostle: See Titus 3:1.

Lord, the king…your strength: LXX Ps 20:1 [Ps 21:1].

God, give your judgment…king's son: LXX Ps 71:1 [Ps 72:1].

Father does not judge…to the Son: See John 5:22.

It is good to conceal…of the king: Tob 12:7.

Let his delight…of the Lord: An allusion to Ps 1:2.

oath of God: According to Augustine, the oath of God was the oath God took when he stopped Abraham from sacrificing Isaac. In this story, God swears by himself that he will bless Abraham and make his descendants as numerous as the stars in the sky and the sand on the seashore (Gen 22:16–17). This oath supplanted God's earlier covenants with Abraham, because before this God had promised to bless Abraham but had never sworn to do so (Aug. *Ciu.* 16.32). The significance of this oath for Christian history is also discussed in Heb 6:13–20.

And like Moses...see his back: See Exod 33:18–23.

8.5

Who although...him to be sin: 2 Cor 5:21.

evil thing: A valid translation; on the Hebrew word דבר (*dābār*), see note at 8.1 (Who is as...word).

8.6, 7

The mind of man...future destiny: Ver. *Aen.* 10.501. Jerome refers to the scene in which Turnus slays Pallas and then takes the fallen hero's belt. He exults in his prize, unaware of what Fate holds in store for him.

resh and *daleth*...corner: The Hebrew letter ר (*reš*) is very similar in appearance to the letter ד (*dalet*). As Jerome notes, the difference is so small that it would be possible to mistake one for the other.

***daath*...*raath*:** The Arabic version, as well as the Greek versions mentioned, has a translation implying the reading דעת (*daʿat*, "knowledge"), but Jerome is right to prefer רעת (*rāʿat*, the construct state of רעה [*rāʿâ*], "evil"). This is another example of the advantage that his knowledge of Hebrew gave him over previous translators (compare note on 8.1 [Who is as...word]).

evil: Above, Jerome used *afflictio* ("affliction") for רעת (*rāʿat*), which basically means "badness" or "something with a bad quality" (i.e., misfortune or wickedness). Here he uses the more literal rendering *malitia* ("badness," "evil," "ill will").

we have now...Hebrew: Of the two translations Jerome has given of v. 7, the one that is "word for word from the Hebrew" is the translation in the heading text; that, then, is the one he means by "now." We may infer that the translation he has just offered, in the last part of the commentary on the verse, comes from an Old Latin version, and so would be more familiar to his readers.

8.8

shut our mouths...fleeing life: Possibly an allusion to Hom. *Il.* 9.408–9, in which Achilles states that there is no way to win a man's life back once it has passed the guard of his teeth. For a short discussion of the ancient belief that the soul of a dying person departed through the mouth, see Duncan, "Weasel in Religion," 48.

cannot accept any conditions...spiritual action: Lit. "cannot accept laws of breathing." The verb *spirare* ("to breathe") is used as the natural action of *spiritus* ("spirit," but lit. "breath").

The spirit...in whorls: Eccl 1:6.

peace of God...all understanding: Phil 4:7.

The shoots you send out...fruit of apples: Cant 4:13. The Hebrew noun used here is משלחת (*mišlaḥat,* "a sending," so here "release," "leave of absence"). From the same stem שלח (*šlḥ*) comes the *hapax legomenon* שלחיך (*šĕlāḥayik*) in Cant 4:13, customarily translated "shoots." Because the Septuagint used the same word ἀποστολή (*apostolē,* "a sending away") in both places, Jerome makes this forced and unwarranted link between them.

8.9–11

For the sinner...iniquities is blessed: LXX Ps 9:24 [Ps 10:3].

We can use this testimony...better things: Jerome now initiates a critique of the bishopric. In earlier letters he had noted that not all bishops were worthy shepherds of the flock (Hier. *Ep.* 16.9), and while he generally holds the office in esteem (Hier. *Ep.* 52.6–7), he knows, probably from firsthand experience in Rome, that not all men undertook the episcopate from the worthiest of motivations: "To be a bishop is much; to deserve to be a bishop is more" (Hier. *Ep.* 69.4).

8.12

from his face: The Hebrew expression מלפניו (*millĕpānāyw,* "from his face") means "of him." See note on this at 3.14.

however the wicked man will...face of God: The second part of this translation from Symmachus is actually the next verse, Eccl 8:13.

It is obvious...maath: Jerome is drawing attention to the fact that there are three conflicting renderings: that of the Septuagint (also, probably the Old Latin) version; that of Symmachus and the other two Greek versions; and his own. The Hebrew phrase is עשה רע מאת (*ʿōśeh rāʿ mĕʾat,* "he does evil a hundred times"). The Septuagint translators must have read the third word (with the same consonants, but pronounced differently) as *mē'ēt* ("from then"); and the other three as *mēt* ("he died").

Here Jerome's knowledge of Hebrew enables him to present the first correct translation that his readers will have seen. He knows that its unfamiliarity will disturb them, so he defends its use in detail, in accordance with the policy he had stipulated in the last sentence of the Preface to this work.

For the sinners...from the belly: LXX Ps 57:4 [Ps 58:3].

little sinners tell a lie...seem to make sense: Jerome again seems to be alluding to Origen's doctrine of the pre-existence of souls. Souls take on bodies the farther they fall away from God (see Or. *Princ.* 1.8 and note at 7.2 [birth fetters...death releases it again]).

8.13
If only they...disturb you: Gal 5:12.
Alexander, the coppersmith...to his works: 2 Tim 4:14.
For the face...evil things: LXX Ps 33:17 [Ps 34:16].
Few and evil...my days: Gen 47:9.
My days...hay of the field: LXX Ps 101:12 [Ps 102:11].
For man...illusion: LXX Ps 38:7 [Ps 39:6].

8.14
rich man in purple...poor man, Lazarus: See Luke 16:19–31.
72nd Psalm: Psalm 73 in the Hebrew and English Bibles.
sons of Aaron...Manasseh: A point that Jerome has already made at 7.16. See the relevant notes there. Neither the Targum nor the Midrash mentions the interpretation that Jerome ascribes to the Hebrews. The Targum suggests that the just are punished in this life for their minor sins so they may enjoy a complete blessing (free of punishment) in the next life. The wicked, on the other hand, are allowed to enjoy rewards for the minor good they do in this life; they will only receive punishment in the next (*Tar. Qoh.* 8.14).

8.15
amply above: See 3.12, 13; 5.17–19; and 7.3.
blessed in the Gospel: An allusion to Matt 5:5–6.
the *food* and the *drink* spiritually: See 2.24–26 where Jerome states that the Eucharist is the food and drink that people are to enjoy.
next sentence: Eccl 8:16.

8.16, 17

tormented by his own investigation: At 1.18 Jerome suggested that a wise person found it a torment that these secrets were cloaked in mystery and inaccessible.

causes for all things...grasped by human beings: Jerome closes this chapter with a profound statement of faith: the fact that humans cannot understand why things happen as they do in this flawed world does not mean that God does not know why things happen.

CHAPTER 9

9.1

because: Heb.: אשר (*ʾăšer*, "which," "that," "because," etc.). In the Latin of this period the word *quia*, translated here as "because," may also mean "that," as we translated it just above in Jerome's own version of this verse. We have given what seems the likeliest meaning in each place, but either translation is possible in both.

in the face of them: Jerome translates the Hebrew לפניהם (*lipnêhem*) literally as "in the face of them" to mean "in front of them," and so "in the future," despite having rendered Symmachus's Greek by a Latin expression literally meaning "in their presence," and so (metaphorically, as in our translation) "in their view," or "in their opinion." The Hebrew expression could mean any of these.

9.2

indifferent...secular philosophers: Jerome refers here to the doctrine of the Stoics, who believed that only virtue and vice had moral content; all other things were morally neutral or indifferent (Lat. *media* or *indifferentia*; see, e.g., Sen. *Ep.* 117.9). His familiarity with this doctrine is evident here and at Hier. *Is.* 4.11.6–9, where he attributes it to the Stoics. For discussion, see Colish, *Stoic Tradition,* 76, 117.

contrite heart...to God: LXX Ps 50:19 [Ps 51:17].

9.3, 4a

Because who is there...the living: Here Jerome, following Symmachus, has missed the connection between the two halves of v. 4, dividing them by the following lines of commentary and altering the sense. The Septuagint offers a better translation by keeping the entire verse together.

9.4b–6

he had said earlier: See Eccl 9:4a.

living sinner...just man's virtues: Jerome, as a Christian exegete, believed in life after death and a last judgment that would determine where each person would spend that life. Consequently, he interprets this verse to mean that, while a sinner lives, there is still the possibility of repentance and deeds that will render that person greater than a dead, just man for whom no more acts (either wicked or just) are possible. This interpretation is far removed from the position advanced by the Preacher, which is that, because there is no life after death, even a miserable person, clinging to life, is better off than someone who is dead, whose memory is growing dim among the living.

I have been given...from the heart: LXX Ps 30:13 [Ps 31:12].

I am not of this world: John 8:23.

sun of justice: Mal 4:2.

lion Moses: See *Qoh. Rab.* 9.4. The Roman emperor Hadrian asked a rabbi if he was not better than Moses, because a living dog is better than a dead lion. The rabbi challenged Hadrian to forbid his people from lighting a fire for three days. Hadrian did so, but looking out over the city in the evening he saw that the order had been disobeyed. The rabbi then noted that although Hadrian's order had been flauted, no Jew would disobey the command of the dead lion (Moses) and light a fire on the Sabbath.

Your faith has saved you: Mark 5:34.

Behold the people...rampant lion: LXX Num 23:24.

Do I not hate...over your enemies: LXX Ps 138:21 [Ps 139:21].

Phineas: Phineas is held up as an example of zeal in 1 Macc 2:54 LXX.

knees shake: Mattathias was consumed with zeal during the Maccabean revolt when he saw a Jew coming to sacrifice an unclean thing on the altar (1 Macc 2:24–26 LXX).

My portion is the Lord: LXX Ps 72:26 [Ps 73:26].

9.7, 8

like fish...upon them: See below, Eccl 9:12.

earlier section...hearts of the living: See Eccl 2:16.

No strife...air above: Ver. *Aen.* 11.104.

prosopopoeia: This Greek word, literally "character-making," is a figure of speech in which the speaker speaks in an assumed character. Jerome's point is that the Preacher does not really believe what he is saying, but is simply offering an alternative point of view. Gregory Thaumaturgos handled this passage by claiming that the Preacher was taking on the role of Deception in uttering these words (Gr. Thaum. *Eccl.* 9.7).

as there is nothing: Jerome makes his character begin with a much-quoted line from Sen. *Tro.* 398.

Epicurus: For Epicurus, see note at 1.9, 10 (Epicurus).

Aristippus: A Greek philosopher (ca. 435–356 BC), a contemporary of Socrates, from the North African colony of Cyrene. Believed to have been the founder of the Cyrenaics, he taught that pleasure, especially sensual pleasure, should be seized whenever offered. Humanity's highest end was the experience of pleasure, even if this pursuit of pleasure went against social conventions.

Cyrenaics: The Cyrenaic school of philosophy was founded either by Aristippus (see preceding note) or his grandson. Like Aristippus, members of the school believed that pleasure was the supreme good, and that the impressions formed by the senses were the only way to apprehend reality.

If God does not rule...watch in vain: LXX Ps 126:1 [Ps 127:1].

At a time...reckoning on it: A possible allusion to Matt 24:42; Luke 12:40.

Whether you are eating...name of God: 1 Cor 10:31.

Drink wine sensibly: A possible allusion to 1 Tim 5:23.

true bread: John 6:32–35. Once again Jerome interprets these problematic verses spiritually, referring the bread and wine advocated by the Preacher back to Christ and the Eucharist (see also 2.24–26; 3.12, 13; 5.17–19).

vines of Sorek: This is a reference to LXX Isa 5:2: ἄμπελον σωρηχ (*ampelon sōrēch*, "vine of Sorek"). At Hier. *Is.* 2.5.2, Jerome noted that there had been some confusion in the way the Hebrew word שׂרק (*śōrēq*) had been translated in the Greek versions. Only Symmachus had translated it "choice." Jerome continues: "The Hebrews say that Sorek is the best type of vine because it produces plentiful and long-lasting fruit."

You desired wisdom...provide it for you: LXX Sir 1:26.

Also, lest you should say...utterly contemptuous: Isa 48:7, 8.

Anyone who thirsts...drink: John 7:37.

Come, eat my loaves...my wine: Prov 9:5.

sinful people...mourning: This is a reference to the custom, mentioned in Latin authors, whereby a Roman who was being prosecuted on a nominally capital charge would put on shabby, dark clothes, as if he were dressed for mourning.

put on light: Possibly an allusion to Rom 13:12: "put on the armor of light."

Let him wear...garment: Interestingly, Jerome seems here to be translating directly from the Hebrew of Ps 109:18, reading the consonants

וילבש (*wylbš*) as *wĕyilbaš*, "and let him wear" (thus making the sentence into a curse), rather than *wayyilbaš*, "and he wore," as in LXX Ps 108:18 (ἐδύσατο [*edysato*]) and in modern translations.

bowels of compassion...patience: Col 3:12. Jerome's Latin version (*viscera misericordiae*) is a literal translation of the Greek phrase σπλάγχνα οἰκτιρμοῦ (*splanchna oiktirmou*, "intestines of pity"). In the Hebrew Bible, the word for intestines is used to signify the seat of affections and emotions, just as we use "heart."

When you have been stripped...renewed: Col 3:9–10.

Therefore God, your God...your fellows: LXX Ps 44:8 [Ps 45:7].

With this oil...be made glad: An allusion to LXX Ps 103:15 [Ps 104:15].

fasting man's head...be anointed: An allusion to Matt. 6:17: "When you fast, put oil on your head and wash your face."

There is no liniment...nor bandages: Isa 1:6.

The oil of the sinner...my head: LXX Ps 140:5 [Ps 141:5].

9.9

Love her...shall encircle you: Prov 4:8.

Apostle also...something to say: See, for instance, Gal 1:4.

9.10

Work while it is day...able to work: John 9:4.

Samuel, truly, was in Hades: An allusion to 1 Sam 28:7–19, in which the distraught King Saul has a witch summon Samuel from the dead.

law of Hades: See discussion of patristic views on Hades offered in the notes at 3.18–21 (Hades).

It is better...be with Christ: Phil 1:23.

9.11

because wickedness...lead weight: Zech 5:7; see the notes on 7.26–27 for a discussion of this passage.

They are loaded...heavy load: LXX Ps 37:5 [Ps 38:4].

I have finished...kept the faith: 2 Tim 4:7.

When the battle...takes place: An allusion to Eph 6:12 , a discussion of the spiritual enemies that stand against a Christian.

Sanctify war: Jer 6:4. Jerome is not following the Septuagint reading, which has παρασκευάσασθε ἐπ' αὐτὴν εἰς πόλεμον (*paraskeuasasthe ep' autēn eis polemon*, "Prepare yourselves for war against her"), but is translating literally a Hebrew word קדשו (*qaddĕšû*) used here with the meaning of "inaugurate (war) with proper ritual."

bread of heaven: John 6:33–35.

Come, eat my loaves: Prov 9:5.
To become rich…good works: 1 Tim 6:18.
You have become rich…knowledge: 1 Cor 1:5.
The ransom…his real wealth: Prov 13:8.
I have labored…grace that is in me: 1 Cor 15:10.
His grace in me…without effect: 1 Cor 15:10.
At the end…everyone is to ensue: An allusion to Mark 13:33.
anagogical sense: See note on this at 2.12.
Because it is not…God's mercy: Rom 9:16.

9.12
We have said…above: See 9.11.
The kingdom…cast in the sea: Matt 13:47.
heretics have a net…for destruction: The Psalter often uses the image of the just being ensnared by the nets of the wicked; see, for example, Pss 10:9; 35:7–8; 57:6; 140:5; 141:10.
wickedness is multiplied…grown cold: Matt 24:12.
signs and portents…led astray: Matt 24:24.
sons of *Adam*: The Hebrew word אדם (*ʾādām*) simply means "man."

9.13–15
smaller world…philosophers too: The idea of a person as a smaller version of the world was stated explicitly by Democritus of Abdera (fl. ca. 420 BC), *frag.* 34. In Pl. *Rep.* 434d2–435b2, a similar analogy is made between a person and a city.
who became poor: An allusion to 2 Cor 8:9, in which Paul states that Christ became poor for us, so that we might become rich.
Wisdom itself: A possible allusion to 1 Cor 1:30, in which Paul notes that God made Christ to be our wisdom, justice, sanctification, and redemption.
seen the lion: For the devil described as a lion, see 1 Pet 5:8.

9.16
No one remembers…fit to listen: Jerome here simply offers a paraphrase of the Preacher's verse. The "I" denotes the Preacher, but the reference to the preceding interpretations clearly points to the views Jerome has assembled.

9.17
Whenever you see anyone…of the audience: Jerome registered his disapproval of popular preaching and teaching at 7.5 and will take up this thread again at 10.19.

9.18

and he who commits...much goodness: Jerome is right about the ambiguity in the Hebrew text here, an ambiguity not present in the Septuagint.

he who has one...them all: This is a tenet of Stoic philosophy. It is interesting that on this occasion Jerome does not seek to parade his classical learning by attributing it to Cicero, who in *Off.* 2:35 shows that his previous argument for this tenet is one not likely to win acceptance with ordinary people.

all the vices: An allusion to Jas 2:10.

CHAPTER 10

10.1

flies of death: A Hebrew idiom meaning *dead flies.*
comment above: See Eccl 9:18.
innocence of doves: An allusion to Matt 10:16, in which Christ counsels his disciples to be as cunning as serpents and innocent as doves.
The flies which...Egyptian river: See Isa 7:18, where the flies that come from Egypt symbolize the Egyptian army that the Lord sent to invade Judea.
Beelzebub: Originally Beelzebub was a Philistine god, associated especially with the city of Ekron (see 2 Kgs 1:2, 6). The Hebrew word בעל זבוב (*baʿal zĕbûb*, "lord of the flies") is a play on Baalzebul ("lord of the world"), one of the names of Baal. In time, Beelzebub was identified with Satan, the prince of demons, and the name is used in the New Testament (see Matt 12:24). For further discussion of the term, see Maclaurin, "Beelzeboul," 156–60.

10.2, 3

left hand...right hand is doing: See Matt 6:3.
present the left cheek...other cheek: Matt 5:39: "turn the other cheek also" (στρέψον αὐτῷ καὶ τὴν ἄλλην, *strepson autōi kai tēn allēn*). In Jerome's commentary on Matthew, he notes, "We are not commanded to offer our left cheek for striking, but our other cheek. That is, our other right cheek. The just person does not have a left cheek" (Hier. *Matt.* 1 [5:39–40]).

According to John Cassian, the other right cheek stood for the cheek of the inner man. When the outer man had been physically abused, the inner man was to be offered up to the tormenter as well (Cassian *Coll.* 16.22).

just man does not…only the right in him: Jerome is probably recalling the exegesis of Origen, who had noted that the holy did not have a left in them, as the left is associated with evil (see, e.g., Or. *Hom. Jud.* 3.15, where, discussing Ehud, he notes that Ehud was not described as having a left hand, but only another hand). Cassian picked up this idea as well, stating that the holy ones never had the Lord present on their left because holy people have nothing of the left within them, only the right (Cassian *Coll.* 12.5).

sheep will stand…goats on the left: An allusion to Matt 25:33, the separation of the sheep and goats at the last judgment.

The Lord knows…are to the left: LXX Prov 4:27.

The right-hand road…to impious Tartarus: Ver. *Aen.* 6.540–44.

Our Firmianus: Lucius Caelius Firmianus Lactantius (ca. 240–320). Lactantius was a North African teacher of rhetoric who served under the Emperor Diocletian in Nicomedia and later was the tutor for Crispus, the eldest son of the Emperor Constantine. He wrote several apologetic works, including *The Divine Institutes* and *On the Death of the Persecutors.*

The Institutes…virtues and vices: Lact. *Inst.* 6.3.6. Here Lactantius compares the philosophers' conception of the two roads (virtue and vice) with what is held by Christians. The philosophers believed that every young man reached a Y in his life, forcing him to choose between virtue and vice. The young man who chose virtue would seek out a human teacher who would stand on his right and teach him to follow the path of virtue. Proof of the path that he had chosen would be reflected in the honors or punishments accrued over the rest of his life.

The Christians believed that the selection of a path had eternal consequences. Two invisible powers (God and Satan) served as permanent guides to all humans (not just young boys). By following the teaching of one or the other, the person would ultimately be led to heaven or hell (see also Jerome's discussion at 4.13–16).

Do not deviate…to the left: Prov 4:27.

middle path…direction of vice: See note at 7.17 (in philosophy…as a vice).

10.4

Apostle also mentions: See Eph 2:2; 6:12.

give it any further room…thought by action: In this statement, Jerome is fully in accord with the teaching of the early Egyptian monks, who believed that it was impossible to stop thoughts from coming into the mind, but a Christian could refuse to dwell on the evil thought and, even more important, could avoid taking the action that would convert the potentiality of the thought into an actual sin (see Cassian *Coll.* 7.8).

If they do not...greatest fault: LXX Ps 18:14 [Ps 19:13].

marphe...**fit the sense:** It is not entirely clear what Jerome means here. It is possible that he thought Symmachus was connecting this verse with its opposite, the flies who taint the purity of the perfume, in Eccl 10:1. The Hebrew word מרפא (*marpēʾ*) means "healing" or "calmness."

excessive self-importance: Jerome's Hebrew teacher takes the Hebrew word רוח (*rûaḥ*, "spirit") (see note at 7.9 [high in spirit]) as meaning something like "feeling." Jerome thus reports his Hebrew as suggesting an interpretation that is something like: "If a sense of power comes over you."

10.5–7

ὡς ἀκούσιον: *hōs akousion*, "as something unintentional."

blind are led...into the pit: An allusion to Luke 6:39.

fast ponies: An allusion to Hor. *Epod.* 4.14.

If the spirit...relinquish your place: Eccl 10:4.

And your riding...salvation: Hab 3:8. The passage in Habakkuk describes the prophet's vision of the Lord coming to save his people. Here, Jerome followed the Septuagint in his Latin translation of the verse, using *equitatio* ("riding") for the Greek word ἱππασία (*hippasia*, "riding," "chariot driving"). In his later Vulgate translation of this passage, Jerome employed the Latin word *quadriga* ("four-horse chariot"), which better reflects the Hebrew text. For Jerome's discussion of horses in the Scriptures, see Hier. *Abac.* 3.8.

10.8

He who sets up...caught in it: Jerome's memory has slipped here: his quotation is from the Wisdom of Ben Sirach (Sir 27:26), not the Wisdom of Solomon.

He has opened...he has made: LXX Ps 7:16 [Ps 7:15].

If he descends into Hades...it will bite him: Amos 9:3, misquoting "into Hades" for "into the depths of the sea."

10.9

In Zechariah...rolled on the earth: Zech 9:16. Jerome is again using the Septuagint text, which mistranslates the Hebrew phrase כי אבני־נזר מתנוססות על־אדמתו (*kî ʾabnê-nēzer mitnōsĕsôt ʿal-ʾadmātô*, "as stones of consecration sparkling [or swaying] on his land") as διότι λίθοι ἅγιοι κυλίονται ἐπὶ γῆς αὐτοῦ (*dioti lithoi hagioi kyliontai epi gēs autou*, "because holy stones will roll over his land"). He retained this translation in the Vulgate.

from these living stones...Book of Revelation: Rev 21:18–21.

apostle also talks...built of them: 1 Pet 2:5, quoted also at 1.1, where see note (living stones).

takes away a stone...dirt and ash: A reference to Lev 14:40–45, a passage that gives directions for the purification of the house of a leper.

being compelled...church of Christ: Jerome has extracted a spiritual meaning from the Levitical code and applied it to a Christian priest's duty to excise those who are spiritual lepers from the body of the church.

Weep with those weeping...those mourning: Rom 12:15.

Who is weakened...do not burn: 2 Cor 11:29.

woodland is without useful fruit: See 2.6 for Jerome's discussion of symbolic meaning of the different types of wood.

prohibited for a grove...temple of God: This is explicitly prohibited in Deut 16:21, because sacred groves were associated with the worship of Baal (see Judg 6:25, 28).

If his ax is blunted...spoiled its edge: Eccl 10:10.

he will be strengthened in his strength: Jerome has taken both the Hebrew and the Septuagint text of these words as passive, although they are both unambiguously active, meaning literally: "And he will strengthen strength(s)." Since he gives a further passive translation ("reinforced") of the same word at 10.10, both in the text and at the end of his commentary on the verse, it must be a mistake of his own, and not that of a copyist. This is a surprising slip: his knowledge of Greek is perfectly sound, even if his Hebrew is much less assured. It seems unlikely that either his Septuagint or his Hebrew text had a passive version.

10.11

not more: For the Hebrew expression behind this phrase, see note on 2.11 (abundance).

tongue: Here Jerome is using the double sense of the Latin word *lingua* ("tongue," "language") in a manner that is difficult to reproduce in translation.

human tongue...those close to one: See Prov 15:2, 4; 18:21.

confess his wound...able to help him: See Cassian *Coll.* 2.11–13 for an extended discussion of the fundamental principle that a novice needs to disclose thoughts to an elder in order to conquer vices and develop discretion.

10.12
listening ear: Possibly an allusion to Prov 20:12.

10.13, 14
multiplication of talking...sin: An allusion to Prov 10:19.

10.15
O Lord...likeness in your city: LXX Ps 72:20 [Ps 73:20]. The Hebrew root בזה (*bzh*) is correctly translated by the Septuagint here as "despise." Apparently Jerome, working from the Hebrew, has confused it with the root בזר, "scatter."
The rush of the river...city of God: LXX Ps 45:5 [Ps 46:4].
The city placed...cannot be hidden: Matt 5:14.
I am the firm city...attacked: LXX Isa 27:3.
They have lost their way...to his abode: LXX Ps 106:4 [Ps 107:4].

10.16, 17
In Isaiah...which flows silently: See Isa. 8:6.
diverted the old pool: See Isa 22:11.
currents of Damascus: This is an allusion to the story of Namaan the leper, who, when told to wash himself in the Jordan River in order to cure his disease, bridled and asserted that certainly Abana and Pharphar, rivers of Damascus, were just as good as Israel's holy river (see 2 Kgs 5:12).
And I will make...their masters: LXX Isa 3:4.
the ancient of days: Dan 7:9.
white as snow...like white wool: See Rev 1:14.
Jeremiah too...reckoned as wisdom: Jer 1:6.
Absalom rebels...against a parent: See 2 Samuel 15–18.
Let us eat...we will die: Isa 22:13.
sin was not the master...they were truly free: Jerome is making an allusion to Gal 4:1–31, in which Paul argues that Christians have been set free from the law and are no longer slaves like the descendants of Hagar.
no shoot, no bud...burst forth into flower: Jerome's point seems to be that Mary did not go through the normal cycle of conception and

procreation. Metaphorically speaking, she did not show the signs that normally precede a plant's display of fruit (putting out shoots and buds), but leapt over these intermediate steps to produce the fruit (Jesus).

I am the flower...lily of the valleys: LXX Cant. 2:1.

Behold those who serve...will hunger: Isa 65:13.

Behold those who serve...be ashamed: Isa 65:14.

10.18

storms from above...rain clouds: Jerome's interpretation of this verse reflects the parable of the foolish and wise builders (Matt 7:24–27; Luke 6:47–49).

10.19

roof collapses: See 10.18.

Titus is admonished to do: See Titus 1:9.

neglect the grace...laying on of hands: 1 Tim 4:14.

Blessed are those...they who will laugh: Luke 6:21.

silver...speech: See also the note at 2.8 (pallor of gold).

For the utterances...purified seven times: LXX Ps 11:7 [Ps 12:6].

bridegroom with them...mourn and to fast: See Matt 9:15.

Isaac received his name...laughter: See, for example, Gen 21:6, where the Hebrew word for "will laugh," יצחק (*yiṣăḥāq*), has the same consonants, and practically the same sound, as the name Isaac (*yiṣḥāq*].

every holy man...teacher of the church: See Matt 28:19–20.

five talents...and the one: See Matt 25:15.

ten minas: See Luke 19:13.

10.20

the walls themselves...hide what they hear: An ancient version of the maxim: the walls have ears.

love the Lord...neighbor as yourself: Matt 22:37–39.

angels...the ministering spirits: See Heb 1:14.

We circled the earth...inhabited and silent: LXX Zech 1:11.

Like birds...thoughts to heaven: Origen expressed a similar view about the role of angels. He suggested that they searched the thoughts of humans and then bore this information up to heaven, where it was offered to God (Or. *Hom. Lev.* 9.8.5).

CHAPTER 11

11.1

encouragement to almsgiving: Many modern commentators suggest that the Preacher was actually recommending that people invest in maritime trading ventures (Jarick, *Thaumaturgos' Paraphrase*, 277; Longman, *Ecclesiastes,* 255–56). This view is strengthened by Eccl 11:2, which recommends diversification of investments and points to the dangers of land-bound commerce. Ancient commentators, however, including the Targum, Gregory Thaumaturgos, and Jerome all regarded this as an encouragement to almsgiving.
Rivers of living water...his vitals: John 7:38.
Blessed is the man...ox and ass tread: LXX Isa 32:20.

11.2

flights of seven and eight...to the temple: See Ezek 40:26, 31.
one hundred and eighteenth: Numbered Psalm 119 in English translations of the Bible.
fifteen step Psalms: LXX Ps 119 [Ps 120] and the next fourteen Psalms have the superscript "A Song of Ascents."
ogdoad: The Latin word *ogdoas* basically means "the number eight." Why Jerome uses this here, rather than the more common *octo,* is unclear, unless he is simply trying to strike a more mystical tone.
Marcion: One of Marcion's more controversial positions was his rejection of the Old Testament and Judaism. Marcion believed that Yahweh was the flawed, evil god who had created the world. Jesus, on the other hand, had been sent by a good God to redeem humankind and free humans from Yahweh's grasp. See note at 8.1 (Marcion and Valentinus) for additional biographical information on Marcion.
Mani: A Persian mystic (ca. 216–276) who mixed elements of Christianity, Zoroastrianism, and Gnosticism to form a new religion, Manichaeism, a dualistic faith that emphasized the ongoing battle between light and darkness. Like Marcion, Mani rejected the Old Testament.
Sabbath and the circumcision: In Judaism, the Sabbath is celebrated every seventh day, and infants are circumcised on the eighth day after birth.

11.3

Your truth...up to the clouds: LXX Ps 35:6 [Ps 36:5].
I will command...shed rain on it: Isa 5:6.

May my discourse...awaited like rain: Deut 32:2.

Let the earth...words of my mouth: Deut 32:1.

God will come from Teman: Hab 3:3. At *Nom. Hebr.* (*PL* 785), Jerome defines "Teman" as *auster* ("south," "south wind") or *Africus* ("wind from Africa," "southwest wind").

other translators...from the south: In *Abac.* 3.3, Jerome noted that Theodotion had substituted *auster* ("south wind," "the South") for "Teman" in his translation of this verse.

Get up, north...come, south wind: Cant 4:16.

I will say to the north wind...Do not hinder: Isa 43:6. The Hebrew word used here, דרום (*dārôm*), means, unambiguously, "south." Jerome's translation uses the Latin word *africus*, meaning "the south-west wind"; it exactly renders the Septuagint's λίψ (*lips*, "the wind from Libya"). This has misled him into taking it, in the next sentence, as the opposite of "east." It is hard to see how he can then have thought that the pairing, in this sentence, of north and south-west winds as opposites of south and east repectively, "has this same meaning" as his opposition in the previous sentence between north and south. In his Vulgate version of this sentence in Isaiah, Jerome uses not *africus* but *auster*, the word he has used throughout this passage to mean "south."

11.4

in season...out of season: 2 Tim 4:2.

As that rain...wisdom and praise impiety: Prov 28:3, 4.

11.5

breath: Or "wind," or "spirit." See note on the translation of the Hebrew word רוח (*rûaḥ*) at 7.9 (high in spirit).

winds and clouds...mentioned above: See 11.4.

It is not a matter...God's mercy: Rom 9:16.

11.6–8

on the day...free him from death: The belief that a person could live a long, virtuous life but then lose salvation through a sinful lapse in old age was common in patristic thought. John Cassian illustrated this point in a series of stories about certain desert monks who, after long years of strict asceticism, had been misled by demons and gone astray near the end of their lives. For Cassian, the ever-present danger of losing one's salvation, right up to the moment of death, could only be met through the cultivation of discretion, the virtue that served as a shield against the wiles of the demonic forces (see Cassian *Coll.* 2.3–8).

sun of justice: Mal 4:2.

I will give you...late rain: Deut 11:14. Both here and in the Vulgate, Jerome renders in only two terms "seasonal rain and late rain" what both Hebrew and Septuagint, in our texts, express in three: "rain in season, the early and the late."

evangelists and the apostles...there is to hear: See Or. *Princ.* 4.3.1–4 for the argument that the Bible should not be read for the literal sense alone.

sun of justice: Mal 4:2.

CHAPTER 12

12.1

Be glad, young man...folly are vanity: Modern translations place this material as vv. 9 and 10 of chapter 11. Since Jerome discusses these verses with Eccl 12:1, we have chosen to place them here.

will: For this use of "will," see notes at 3.16, 17 (volition and their works).

as many opinions...there are people: An allusion to Ter. *Ph.* 454, which had become proverbial.

surrounding ocean: The Greek philosopher Pythagoras (ca. 575–490 BC) and his followers had determined that the earth was a sphere, but the ancient view of the world as flat with a great river (*oceanus*) flowing around it dated back to the Homeric epics and the works of Hesiod (for discussion, see Wright, *Early History,* 99–100).

Babylonian and Roman captivity: Judea was conquered by the Babylonian king Nebuchadnezzar, and the prominent citizens were exiled to Babylon (ca. 597–586 BC; see 2 Kgs 24:14–16; 25:11).

In 64 BC, Judea came under Roman control when Pompey the Great captured the city of Jerusalem after a three-month siege. Under the emperor Augustus the kingdom was ruled by dependent kings (the Herods), but in AD 6, Augustus deposed King Archelaus and made Judea a Roman province, governed by a procurator. Judea remained a Roman province during Jerome's lifetime.

the whole passage from...God, who gave it: Eccl 12:2–7.

Nebuchadnezzar: Nabu-kudurri-ushur, as the name is spelled in cuneiform inscriptions, was the king of Babylon who captured Jerusalem after a siege in 597 BC and again, in 586, after a revolt by the puppet king he had installed there (see note above).

Titus son of Vespasian: Both Vespasian, Roman emperor AD 69–79, and his son Titus, who eventually succeeded him (79–81), commanded Roman forces sent to suppress the First Jewish Revolt (66–70). Besieged by Titus, Jerusalem fell and the temple was looted and destroyed.

summoned by the prophets...their prophecies are fulfilled: A variety of prophecies were recorded in the Old Testament about the coming of the Babylonians and the downfall of Judea (e.g., Jer 25:8–11; Hab 1:6). Patristic writers found a prophecy of the Roman invasion also in Nebuchadnezzar's dream (Dan 2:31–35), in which the king saw a great statue made of four materials: a gold head, silver chest and arms, bronze belly and thighs, and feet made of both iron and clay. According to Hippolytus, the golden head was Babylonia; the silver chest, Persia; the iron legs, Rome; and the feet of mixed materials, the ten democracies that were to arise in the end times (Hipp *Schol. Dan.* 2.31; Hipp *Dan.* 2.1).

Jeremiah's words: See Jer 1:15.

death of Sennacherib: Sennacherib was the king of Assyria (704–681 BC). In 701 he attacked Judea in order to suppress a rebellion led by King Hezekiah and supported by Egypt. According to the Old Testament, when Sennacherib besieged Jerusalem, the Lord struck down 185,000 Assyrian soldiers and the defeated Sennacherib withdrew (2 Kgs 19:35–36; 2 Chr 32:20–22). An Assyrian account of the battle is found on Sennacherib's Prism, a cuneiform tablet containing annals of the king. It states that Sennacherib withdrew from Judea only after King Hezekiah paid a tribute of thirty talents of gold and eight hundred talents of silver. 2 Kings 19:37 is the only ancient source for Sennacherib's death; it reports that he was killed by his sons while worshiping his god, Nisroch.

Jeremiah saw...of his prophecy: See Jer 1:11.

away into his tent: Based on Jerome's exegesis of this passage at 12.5, "tent" is a metaphor for the man's tomb.

return to Babylon...loins of Abraham: The patriarch Abraham came from northwest Mesopotamia, Ur in Babylonia (see Gen 11:28; 24:4–10).

He had said: See Eccl 11:6–8.

Epicureanism: The philosophical system founded by Epicurus (on whom see note at 1.9, 10). The essence of Epicurus's ethical teaching is that the guiding principle of our actions should be pleasure; the fact that he defined pleasure as avoidance of painful sensations was ignored by opponents, who regarded his teaching as being a scandalous encouragement to immoral self-indulgence.

12.2

There will be tribulation...will be moved: Matt 24:21–29.

original branches have been broken...sound olive tree: See Rom 11:17–21. This is an allusion to Paul's claim that the Gentiles had been incorporated into God's salvific purpose, like a wild olive branch grafted in among the cultivated branches.

Among whom you shine...principle of life: Phil 2:15–16. Here Jerome translates λόγον ζωῆς (*logon zōēs*, "word of life") by *rationem vitae* ("principle of life"); in the Vulgate he has *verbum vitae* ("word of life"). For the view that stars were living creatures with souls, see Or. *Princ.* 1.7.3; 1.7.5 and the note at 1.6 (living thing...portion of its own).

Star differs...in glory: 1 Cor 15:41.

watered the hearts...their own rain: See 2.6 for Jerome's contrast between heavenly rain, which nourishes believers, and groundwater, which does not.

12.3

the Gospel parable: Phrases from two versions of the parable, Matt 12:25–29 and Luke 11:17–23, are here combined.

there are those...to the human body: This is certainly the case of the Jewish scholars who made the Aramaic translation of Ecclesiastes, the *Targum Qoheleth*. Although written at least two hundred years after Jerome's death, the Targum interprets this passage in relation to the weakening of the human body as it nears death (see following notes for specific examples).

what follows: See Eccl 12:5–8.

love of many grows cold: See Matt 24:12.

bread of heaven: See John 6:32.

I shall put you...see my back: Exod. 33:22.

caves: Here Jerome is probably thinking of Plato's famous allegory of the cave (Pl. *Rep.* 7.514a1–520d8).

two women grinding...the other left: See Matt 24:41.

They suppose that...become worn or fall out: A view found in the Targum: "the teeth of your mouth will become useless so that they are unable to chew food" (*Tar. Qoh.* 12.3, trans. Knobel, *Targum of Qohelet*, 52).

They think *those looking*...vision is impaired: *Tar. Qoh.* 12.3: "your eyes which look out of the opening of your head will become dim" (trans. Knobel, *Targum of Qohelet*, 52).

12.4

silly girls in the Gospel: See Matt 25:1–12 for Jesus' parable of the foolish bridesmaids.

the way leading to life...wide and spacious: See Matt 7:13–14.

love of many grows cold: See Matt 24:12.

call of the archangel: See 1 Thess 4:16.

I trust in the Lord...to the mountain: LXX Ps 10:1 [Ps 11:1].

I was awake...sparrow on the roof: LXX Ps 101:8 [Ps 102:7].

Even the sparrow...a house: LXX Ps 83:4 [Ps 84:3].

doors closed...old man's impaired gait: Jerome continues to offer the Jewish exegesis of this passage. See *Tar. Qoh.* 12.4: "And your foot will be impeded from going out on the street" (trans. Knobel, *Targum Qohelet*, 52).

refer to his jaws...chew the food: *Tar. Qoh.* 12.3: "the teeth of your mouth will become useless so that they are unable to chew food" (trans. Knobel, *Targum Qohelet*, 52).

his breathing...only just be heard: *Tar. Qoh.* 12.4: "your lips shall tremble so that they cannot utter songs" (trans. Knobel, *Targum Qohelet*, 54).

he wakes up...middle of the night: *Tar. Qoh.* 12.4: "you will awaken from your sleep by the sound of a bird as if it were the sound of thieves" (trans. Knobel, *Targum Qohelet*, 52–54).

going deaf: There is nothing in this unusual use of the Hebrew root שחח (*šḥḥ*), which basically means "be low" or "sink down," to justify Jerome's preference for "deafness" here, as opposed to "dumbness." In the original context, the singers are plainly meant to be singing no longer, so that "dumb" is plainly the required meaning. He seems to be twisting the meaning to fit his preferred interpretation of the phrase as referring to deafness in old people, presumably in the expectation that none of his readers will know enough Hebrew to challenge his interpretation.

Barzillai says to David...across the Jordan: See 2 Sam 19:32–36.

12.5

But: Although the commonest Hebrew word for "and" (ו [*wĕ*]) is also used where we would put "but," the word used here is not that one, but גם (*gam*), a word that can only mean "also." For this the Septuagint has καί γε (*kai ge*, "and moreover"). As Jerome used *et* ("and") in his summary of the entire passage at 12.1, it seems that he is here merely varying the wording in a way he regards as unimportant.

The almond blossom...buttocks shrinks: This Jewish exegesis is reflected in the Targum: "the top of your spinal column will protrude because of deterioration like an almond tree" (*Tar. Qoh.* 12.5, trans. Knobel, *Targum Qohelet*, 54).

opening of Jeremiah: See Jer 1:11–12.

*soced...*nut and wakefulness: The Hebrew word שקד (*šāqēd*) means "almond tree"; a change of vowel pointing yields *šōqēd*, "(I am) watching."

double sense of *aagab...*weighed down with gout: This exegesis is odd and seems linguistically unlikely, given the very slight resemblance between the Hebrew words החגב (*heḥāgāb*, "the locust") and העקב (*heʿāqēb*, "the heel"). Nevertheless, the rabbis made the same connection at *Qoh. Rab.* 12.5.

*abiona...*caper berry: האביונה (*hāʾăbîyônâ*, "the caper berry.")

old men's libido...sexual organs waste away: *Tar. Qoh.* 12.5: "you will be prevented from having sexual intercourse" (trans. Knobel, *Targum Qohelet*, 54). At *Qoh. Rab.* 12.5, the rabbis interpreted this verse as a reference to the failure, in old age, of the sexual desire that brings peace between a man and his wife.

Laodicean: Apollinarius of Laodicea; for biography, see Introduction and note at 4.13–16 (interpreter of Laodicea).

12.6–8

hyperbaton: Lat. *hyperbaton*. A hyperbaton is a rhetorical figure of speech in which words that are normally used together are separated in order to add emphasis to them.

bright life: The Jewish exegetes took *the silver cord* as a reference to the spinal cord (*Tar. Qoh.* 12.6; *Qoh. Rab.* 12.6).

breath: The word used here is not *spiritus*, which can mean either "breath" or "life" (see note at 7.9 [high in spirit]), but *spiramen*, which means only "breath."

This makes...instead of by God: Jerome here criticizes the Traducian view of the creation of souls, which elsewhere he seems to accept (see notes at 4.2, 3 [dwell in the upper regions...choir]).

opening of his book: Eccl 1:2.

12.9, 10

will: For a discussion of this word, see the note at 3.16, 17 (volition).

proclaims the wisdom...the whole human race: See 1 Kgs 3:12.

Lord spoke to the public...to them in private: See, for instance, the parable of the sower (Matt 13:10, 11).

I shall see the heavens...your fingers: LXX Ps 8:4 [Ps 8:3].

12.11

Moses...God was angry at first: Exod 4:14.

had not undertaken voluntarily: See Exod 3:11—4:17 for Moses' reluctance to serve as God's chosen leader of the Hebrews.

This passage counters those…of the old law: See the notes on Marcion and Mani at 11.2.

as we said earlier: See 10.11.

one Shepherd: Jerome is clearly taking "the one Shepherd" as a reference to the Good Shepherd (Christ), as is made clear in the next sentence when the voice of the Shepherd speaks to Paul on the road.

It is hard…against the goad: Acts 26:14 (and in some texts of Acts 9:5).

12.12

for the Lord…on the earth: Rom 9:28. Both here and in the Vulgate, Jerome takes λόγος (*logos*) as "word" and applies it to the Bible, although the context in Romans makes it clear that "account" or "reckoning" is the likelier meaning.

His word is close…in our heart: Rom 10:8, quoting Deut 30:14.

the commandment of the Lord…converting souls: LXX Ps 18:8 [Ps 19:8].

sealed book in Isaiah's discourse: See Isa 29:11.

all Scripture is divine: 2 Tim 3:16.

Ezekiel's and John's…one section: Jerome's Latin word here is *capitulum,* literally "heading." The Hebrew word מגלה (*mĕgillâ*) used in this Ezekiel passage, and in the Psalm quoted in the next sentence, literally means "scroll"; it is derived from a root meaning "roll." One might expect Jerome to use here the correspondingly derived Latin word *volumen;* but as he has used that word just above in the sense of "a whole volume," he needed to find a word unambiguous in the sense of "part" of a book, in order to establish his argument that the Scriptures as a whole constitute one book.

Although *capitulum* is the origin of the English "chapter," it was not yet synonymous with our division of books of the Bible into chapters, so "section" seems the best translation available.

of a book: See Ezek 3:1–3 and Rev 10:9–10.

In a section…written of me: LXX Ps 39:8 [Ps 40:7].

who was in the beginning with God: John 1:2.

From much talking…escape sin: Prov 10:19. This verse is also cited in Jerome's discussions at 5.1, 2 7.1, and 10.13, 14.

I have labored more…which is with me: 1 Cor 15:10.

I have labored, clamoring: LXX Ps 68:4 [Ps 69:3].

12.13, 14

other writings…no longer on record: 1 Kgs 4:32 states that Solomon wrote 3,000 proverbs and 1,005 songs.

The Hebrews say...should also be deleted: A possible reference to the dispute between the rabbinical schools of Hillel and Shammai about whether Ecclesiastes (which was said to make the hands unclean) was canonical or not (see discussion at Murphy, *Ecclesiastes,* xxiii).

Fear is servile...casts out fear: 1 John 4:18.

Those who fear...have no lack: LXX Ps 33:10 [Ps 34:9].

Woe, then, to those...good evil: Isa 5:20.

APPENDIX: TEXTUAL NOTES

The printed editions that have contributed most toward the establishment of a serviceable Latin text of this work are those of Johannis Martianay (Paris, 1699), Domenico Vallarsi (2nd ed.; Venice, 1767, repr., J.-P. Migne in *Patrologiae cursus completus: Series Latina* (221 vols.; Paris: J.-P. Migne, 1844–64), vol. 22 (2nd ed., 1883); and M. Adriaens in vol. 72 of *Corpus Christianorum Series Latina* (Turnhout: Berpols, 1959). Adriaens' edition was a great advance on its predecessors in three ways: it contains a detailed critical apparatus; it was the first to make use of the exceptionally ancient Würzburg manuscript, written within a century of Jerome's own work; and it corrected many of the misprints that had survived into Migne's second edition.

Several other earlier misprints, however, were reproduced by Adriaens unchanged, and a good many new ones appeared; also, in our opinion, his choice between variants did not always give the best reading. We have therefore studied the text afresh and can claim to have made a significant contribution of our own.

For the benefit of those who wish to study the Latin text on which this translation is based, a list follows of all the places where we have preferred a reading different from that printed in Adriaens' CCSL edition.

This excludes almost all of our very numerous differences in punctuation; as early manuscripts had no punctuation at all, that is a matter on which a translator is free to use whatever system of punctuation gives a modern reader the best help in following the sense. Where scans of the Würzburg manuscript were helpful in supplying or confirming a changed reading, the words "(with oldest MS)" appear; where there seemed no doubt of what Jerome wrote, it is not mentioned. The numbers in square brackets refer to chapter and line of the CCSL edition

1. **In [1:17]:** Reading *In* for CCSL's *Id.*
2. **superior [1:85]:** Reading *excellentem* for CCSL's *exellentem.*
3. **smoky vapor [1:99]:** Reading *uaporem fumi* for CCSL's *uaporem sumi.*
4. **εἰσπνεῖ [1:137]:** Reading εἰσπνεῖ for CCSL's εἰσπνεῖ.
5. **same [1:260]:** Reading *isdem* for CCSL's *hisdem.*
6. **were omitted [1:355]:** Reading *praetermissi* for CCSL's *pratermissi.*
7. **that [1:357]:** Reading *ut* for CCSL's *ud.*
8. **find [2:81]:** Reading *reperire* for CCSL's *repperire.*
9. **world [2:80]:** Reading *mundo* for CCSL's *munda.*
10. **numerous [2:133]:** Reading *multa* for CCSL's *multi.*
11. **understood [2:205]:** Reading *intellegitur* for CCSL's *intellegit.*
12. **we will enjoy [2:299]:** Reading *fruebimur* for CCSL's *fruebamur.*
13. **think about [2:313]:** Reading *contemplanti* for CCSL's *comtemplanti.*
14. **He [3:40]:** Reading *Ei occidendi* (with oldest MS) for CCSL's *Et occidendi.*
15. **kills [3:42]:** Reading *occidit* (with oldest MS) for CCSL's *occidi.*
16. **unbelievers [3:115]:** Reading *incredulos* for CCSL's *incredules.*
17. **not to talk [3:119]:** Reading *ʾnon> loqui* for CCSL's *tacere.*
18. **schools [3:123]:** Reading *scholarum* for CCSL's *saeculorum.*
19. **day [3:165]:** Reading *diei* for CCSL's *dici.*
20. **let us spend [3:193]:** Reading *consumamus* for CCSL's *consummamus.*
21. **jointly created [3:215]:** Reading *concreata* for CCSL's *concreta.*
22. **human being [3:287]:** Reading *hominem* for CCSL's *homidem.*
23. **it would be safe…difficulty [3:335]:** Conjectural filling in of words, perhaps ending with …*sit,* missing from MSS after *sit.*
24. **discover [4:10]:** Reading *reperire* for CCSL's *repperire.*
25. **they fall, one [4:116]:** Reading *si ceciderint, unus eriget participem suum* for CCSL's *si ceciderit unus, eriget participem suum.*
26. **alone [4:128]:** Reading *solus* (with oldest MS) for CCSL's *solis.*
27. **will lift [4:141]:** Reading *eriget* (with oldest MS) for CCSL's *erigit.*
28. **when he falls [4:142]:** Reading *cum conruerit* (with oldest MS) for CCSL's *conruerit.*
29. **broken [4:152]:** Reading *rumpetur* (with oldest MS) for CCSL's *rumpitur.*
30. **branching of the roads [4:192]:** Reading *post Y litteram* for CCSL's *hi post litteram.*
31. **the two [4:195]:** Reading *Hos duos* for CCSL's *Hoc duos.*
32. **said [5:23]:** Reading *dixerimus* for CCSL's *duxerimus.*
33. **or [5:72]:** Reading *nec* (with oldest MS) for CCSL's *ne.*
34. **death [7:25]:** Reading *mors* for CCSL's *mores.*
35. **We should be angry [7:43]:** Reading *irascamur* for CCSL's *israscamur.*

36. **where [7:55]:** Reading *ubi* for CCSL's *uni.*
37. **is praised [7:56]:** Reading *plauditur* for CCSL's *plangitur.*
38. **unacceptably [7:112]:** Reading *condecet* (with oldest MS) for CCSL's *concedet.*
39. **the same [7:271]:** Reading *eundem* for CCSL's *eumdem.*
40. **had compassion [7:274]:** Reading *miseritus* for CCSL's *misertus.*
41. **deep [7:325]:** Reading *profundo* for CCSL's *profundi.*
42. **and can weigh up [7:334]:** Conjectural filling in of words, perhaps starting *potest et…*, missing from MSS after *et.*
43. **all things [7:375]:** Reading *uniuersa* for CCSL's *uiniuersa.*
44. **her [7:388]:** Reading *eius* (with oldest MS) for CCSL's *eis.*
45. **gradually [7:402]:** Reading *sensim* for CCSL's *sensu.*
46. **one true human being [7:436]:** Reading *inueni unum uerum* for CCSL's *inueni uerum.*
47. **the wise man [8:19]:** Reading *uirum* (with oldest MS) for CCSL's *uerum.*
48. **powers [8:39]:** Reading *potestatibus* for CCSL's *postestatibus.*
49. **has enjoined [8:74]:** Reading *Praecipit* for CCSL's *Praecepit.*
50. **what [8:75]:** Reading *quid* for CCSL's *quin.*
51. ***daath* [8:92]:** Reading *daath* for CCSL's *dath.*
52. **suffering [9:30]:** Reading *angustiarum* for CCSL's *augustiarum.*
53. **they understand [9:80]:** Reading *intellegant* (with oldest MS) for CCSL's *intellegunt.*
54. **someone…however ignorant [9:89]:** Reading *indoctum eum* for CCSL's *indoctum et eum.*
55. **in God's sight [9:175]:** Reading *coram* for CCSL's *couam.*
56. **clean [9:189]:** Reading *mundum* for CCSL's *mudum.*
57. **anointed [9:203]:** Reading *unguendum* for CCSL's *ungendum.*
58. **so will it be [9:298]:** Reading *sic <erit> cum* for CCSL's *sic cum.*
59. **scent [10:6]:** Reading *odorem* for CCSL's *oderem.*
60. **should be combined [10:9]:** Reading *mixta quae* (with the oldest MS) for CCSL's *mixtaque.*
61. **recalling the fork in the road [10:38]:** Reading *Y litterae meminit* for CCSL's *litterae meminit.*
62. **temple [10:151]:** Reading *templo* for CCSL's *semplo.*
63. **He will begin [10:162]:** Deleting the second *incipiet* and repunctuating as: *sapientia. Incipiet, inquit, fortitudinem habere* for CCSL's *sapientia incipiet, inquit: fortitudinem incipiet habere.*
64. **dulled and confused [10:168]:** Reading *obtusum et turbatum* for CCSL's *obtusum: et turbatus.*
65. **training [10:172]:** Reading *disciplinis* (with oldest MS) for CCSL's *discipulis.*

66. **you will discover [10:273]:** Reading *reperies* for CCSL's *repperies*.
67. **gray hair [10:274]:** Reading *canities* for CCSL's *cani eius.*
68. **height [10:308]:** Reading *altitudo* for CCSL's *altutido.*
69. **dumb [10:321]:** Reading *muti* for CCSL's *multi.*
70. **in Zachariah [10:370]:** Reading *spiritus, in Zacharia* for CCSL's *spiritus; et in Zacharia.*
71. **will be put [11.69]:** Reading *ponetur* (with oldest MS) for CCSL's *ponitur.*
72. **fleshy areas [11:100]:** Reading *carnibus* for CCSL's *canibus.*
73. **holy [12:58]:** Reading *sancto* for CCSL's *sancta.*
74. **wickedness [12:84]:** Reading *malitiam* for CCSL's *militiam.*
75. **will grow dumb [12:161]:** Reading *obmutescent* for CCSL's *obmustescent.*
76. **will go [12:210]:** Reading *praecedet* for CCSL's *praecedat.*
77. **people [12:220]:** Reading *populum* (with MSS) for CCSL's *verbum.*
78. **so-and-so [12:221]:** Reading *ut faciam illud vel illud.* for CCSL's *ut faciam illud. Vel illud.*
79. **are moved [12:256]:** Reading *mouebuntur* for CCSL's *nouebuntur.*
80. **shepherd [12:310]:** Reading *pastore* for CCSL's *postore.*
81. **consultation [12:318]:** Reading *consilio* (with MSS) for CCSL's *concilio.*
82. **consultation [12:323]:** Reading *consilium* (with MSS) for CCSL's *concilium.*
83. **consensus [12:331]:** Reading *consilio* (with MSS) for CCSL's *concilio.*
84. **Hebrews [12:384]:** Reading *Hebraei* for CCSL's *Habraei.*
85. **despised [12:402]:** Reading *contempto* for CCSL's *contemptu.*

BIBLIOGRAPHY

Primary Source Abbreviations

Ambr. *Bon. mort.*	Ambrosius, *De bono mortis*
Ambr. *Off.*	Ambrosius, *De officiis ministrorum*
Apophth. Patr.	*Apophthegmata patrum*
Arist. *EN*	Aristoteles, *Ethica Nicomachea*
Arist. *Metaph.*	Aristoteles, *Metaphysica*
Aug. *Bon. coniug.*	Augustinus, *De bono coniugali*
Aug. *Ciu.*	Augustinus, *De ciuitate Dei*
Aug. *Doct. chr.*	Augustinus, *De doctrina christiana*
Aug. *Enchir.*	Augustinus, *Enchiridion de fide, spe et caritate*
Aug. *Ep.*	Augustinus, *Epistulae*
Aug. *Gen. Man.*	Augustinus, *De Genesi contra Manichaeos*
Aug. *Litt.*	Augustinus, *De Genesi ad litteram*
Aug. *Nat. et grat.*	Augustinus, *De natura et gratia*
Aug. *Peccat. merit.*	Augustinus, *De peccatorum meritis*
Aug. *Psal.*	Augustinus, *Enarratio in psalmos*
Aug. *Symb.*	Augustinus, *De symbolo ad catechumenos*
Bas. *Hex.*	Basilius Caesariensis Cappadociae, *Homiliae in hexaemeron*
Cassian *Coll.*	Cassianus, *Collationes*
Cassian *Inst.*	Cassianus, *De institutis coenobiorum et de octo principalium uitiorum remediis libri*
Cic. *Fin.*	M. Tullius Cicero, *de Finibus Bonorum et Malorum.*
Cic. *Off.*	M. Tullius Cicero, *de Officiis*
Cic. *Rep.*	M. Tullius Cicero, *de Republica*
Clem. *paed.*	Clemens Alexandrinus, *Paedagogus*
Clem. *Str.*	Clemens Alexandrinus, *Stromateis*
Col. *Rust.*	L. Iunius Moderatus Columella, *de Re Rustica*
Cypr. *Ep.*	Cyprianus, *Epistulae*
Dion. Al. *Fr. Eccl.*	Alexandrinus, *Fragmenta in Ecclesiasten*
Don. *Comm. Ter. Eunuch.*	Aelius Donatus, *Commentarium in Terentii Eunuchum*
Eucher. *Contempt.*	Eucherius, *De contemptu mundi*
Eus. *Hist. Eccl.*	Eusebius Caesariensis, *Historia ecclesiastica*

Evagr. Pont.	
Schol. Ecc.	Evagrius Ponticus, *Scholion in Ecclesiasten*
Fort. *Carm.*	Fortunatus, *Carmina*
Gr. Nyss. *Hom. I–8 in Eccl.*	Gregorius Nyssenus, *Homiliae in Eccl.*
Gr. Nyss. *V. Macr.*	Gregorius Nyssenus, *De vita Macrinae*
Gr. Nyss. *Virg.*	Gregorius Nyssenus, *De virginitate*
Gr. Thaum. *Eccl.*	Gregorius Thaumaturgus Neocaesarensis, *Metaphrasis in Ecclesiasten*
Hier. *Abac.*	Hieronymus, *Commentariorum in Abacuc libri II*
Hier. *Chron.*	Hieronymus, *Chronicon Eusebii a Graeco Latine redditum et continuatum*
Hier. *Ep.*	Hieronymus, *Epistulae*
Hier. *Ier.*	Hieronymus, *Commentariorum in Ieremiam libri VI*
Hier. *In. Psal.*	Hieronymus, *Commentarioli in psalmos*
Hier. *Is.*	Hieronymus, *Commentariorum in Isaiam libri XVIII*
Hier. *Matt.*	Hieronymus, *Commentariorum in Matthaeum libri IV*
Hier. *Nom. Hebr.*	Hieronymus, *De nominibus Hebraicis*
Hier. *Ruf.*	Hieronymus, *Aduersus Rufinum libri III, seu Apologia aduersus libros Rufini*
Hier. *Vir. ill.*	Hieronymus, *De uiris illustribus liber*
Hier. *Zach.*	Hieronymus, *Commentariorum in Zachariam libri III*
Hipp. *Dan.*	Hippolytus Romanus, *Commentarium in Daniel*
Hipp. *Graec.*	Hippolytus Romanus, *Ex libro adversus Graecos*
Hipp. *Schol. Dan.*	Hippolytus Romanus, *Scholia in Daniel*
Hom. *Il.*	Homerus, *Ilias*
Hor. *Ep.*	Q. Horatius Flaccus, *Epistulae*
Hor. *Epod.*	Q. Horatius Flaccus, *Epodi*
Hor. *S.*	Q. Horatius Flaccus, *Sermones*
Ign. *Smyrn.*	Ignatius Antiochenus, *Epistula ad Smyrnaeos*
Iren. *Haer.*	Irenaeus Lugdunensis, *Adversus haereses*
Iust. *Dig.*	Iustinianus, *Digesta*
Juln. Imp. *Galil.*	Julianus Imperator, *Adversus Galilaeos*
Just. *Dial.*	Justinus Martyr, *Dialogus cum Tryphone Judaeo*
Just. *I Apol.*	Justinus Martyr, *I Apologia*
Lact. *Inst.*	Lactantius, *Diuinarum institutionum libri VII*
Lact. *Opif.*	Lactantius, *De opificio Dei*
Or. *Cant.*	Origenes, *Commentarius in Canticum*
Or. *Cels.*	Origenes, *Contra Celsum*
Or. *Dial.*	Origenes, *Dialogus cum Heraclide*
Or. *Hom. 1–28 in Num.*	Origenes, *Homiliae 1–28 in Numeris*
Or. *Hom. Jud.*	Origenes, *Homiliae in Judices*
Or. *Hom. Lev.*	Origenes, *Homiliae in Leviticum*
Or. *Or.*	Origenes, *De oratione*

Or. *Princ.*	Origenes, *De principiis*
Ov. *Met.*	P. Ouidius Naso, *Metamorphoses*
Ph. *Cher.*	Philo Judaeus, *De cherubim*
Pl. *Cra.*	Plato, *Cratylus*
Pl. *Grg.*	Plato, *Gorgias*
Pl. *Rep.*	Plato, *Respublica*
Pl. *Tht.*	Plato, *Theaetetus*
Pl. *Ti.*	Plato, *Timaeus*
Plin. *Nat.*	Plinius Secundus, *Naturalis Historia*
Qoh. Rab.	*Midrash Rabbah Ecclesiastes*
Ruf. *Apol.*	Rufinus, *Apologia aduersus Hieronymum*
Sal. *Cat.*	C. Sallustius Crispus, *Catilina*
Sen. *Ep.*	L. Annaeus Seneca, *Epistulae*
Sen. *Tro.*	L. Annaeus Seneca, *Troades*
Sulp.-Sev. *Dial.*	Sulpicus Severus, *Dialogi*
Tac. *Ag.*	Cornelius Tacitus, *Agricola*
Tar. Qoh.	*Targum Qoheleth*
Ter. *Eunuch.*	P. Terentius Afer, *Eunuchus*
Ter. *Ph.*	P. Terentius Afer, *Phormio*
Tert. *An.*	Tertullianus, *De anima*
Tert. *Apol.*	Tertullianus, *Apologeticus*
Tert. *Idol.*	Tertullianus, *De idololatria*
Tert. *Iud.*	Tertullianus, *Aduersus Iudeos*
Tert. *Paen.*	Tertullianus, *De paenitentia*
Var. *L.*	M. Terentius Varro, *de Lingua Latina*
Ver. *Aen.*	P. Vergilius Maro, *Aeneis*
Ver. *G.*	P. Vergilius Maro, *Georgica*
Xen. *Mem.*	Xenophon, *Memorabilia*

Secondary Bibliography

Atwell, Robert "From Augustine to Gregory the Great: An Evaluation of the Emergence of the Doctrine of Purgatory." *Journal of Ecclesiastical History* 38 (1987): 173–86.

Barton, George A. *A Critical and Exegetical Commentary on the Book of Ecclesiastes.* International Critical Commentary. Edinburgh: T&T Clark, 1908.

Bernstein, Alan E. *The Formation of Hell: Death and Retribution in the Ancient and Early Christian Worlds.* Ithaca, NY: Cornell University Press, 1993.

Bradley, Keith R. *Slavery and Society at Rome.* Key Themes in Ancient History. Cambridge: Cambridge University Press, 1994.

Bright, John. *A History of Israel.* 3rd ed. Philadelphia: Westminster Press, 1981.

Brown, Dennis. "Jerome and the Vulgate." In *A History of Biblical Interpretation,* edited by Alan Hauser and Duane Watson, 355–79. Grand Rapids: Eerdmans, 2003.

Christianson, Eric S. *Ecclesiastes through the Centuries*. Blackwell Bible Commentaries. Oxford: Blackwell, 2007.

Cloke, Gillian. *This Female Man of God: Women and Spiritual Power in the Patristic Age, AD 350–450*. London and New York: Routledge, 1995.

Colish, Marcia L. *The Stoic Tradition from Antiquity to the Early Middle Ages*, vol. 2, *Stoicism in Christian Latin Thought through the Sixth Century*. Studies in the History of Christian Thought 35. Leiden: Brill, 1985.

Duncan, Thomas. "The Weasel in Religion, Myth, and Superstition." *Washington University Studies. Humanistic Series* 12 (1924): 33–56.

Fernández Marcos, Natalio. *The Septuagint in Context: An Introduction to the Greek Versions of the Bible*. Leiden and Boston: Brill, 2000.

Fox, Michael V. *Ecclesiastes: The Traditional Hebrew Text with the New JPS Translation*. JPS Torah Commentary. Philadelphia: Jewish Publication Society, 2004.

Glazier-McDonald, Beth. *Malachi: The Divine Messenger*. Society of Biblical Literature Dissertation Series 98. Atlanta: Scholars Press, 1987.

Goodrich, Richard. *Contextualizing Cassian: Aristocrats, Asceticism, and Reformation in Fifth-Century Gaul*. Oxford Early Christian Studies. Oxford: Oxford University Press, 2007.

Hall, Stuart George. *Gregory of Nyssa: Homilies on Ecclesiastes. An English Version with Supporting Studies. Proceedings of the Seventh International Colloquium on Gregory of Nyssa (St. Andrews, 5–10 September 1990)*. Berlin and New York: W. de Gruyter, 1993.

Heine, Ronald. "Exegesis and Theology in Gregory of Nyssa's Fifth Homily on Ecclesiastes." In *Gregory of Nyssa: Homilies on Ecclesiastes. An English Version with Supporting Studies. Proceedings of the Seventh International Colloquium on Gregory of Nyssa (St. Andrews, 5–10 September 1990)*, edited by Stuart George Hall, 197–222. Berlin and New York: W. de Gruyter, 1993.

Jarick, John. *Gregory Thaumaturgos' Paraphrase of Ecclesiastes*. Septuagint and Cognate Studies 29. Atlanta: Scholars Press, 1990.

Kamesar, Adam. *Jerome, Greek Scholarship, and the Hebrew Bible: A Study of the Quaestiones hebraicae in Genesim*. Oxford Classical Monographs. Oxford: Clarendon Press, 1993.

Kannengiesser, Charles. *Handbook of Patristic Exegesis: The Bible in Ancient Christianity*. Bible in Ancient Christianity 1. Leiden and Boston: Brill, 2004.

Kelly, J. N.D. *Early Christian Doctrines*. London: A. & C. Black, 1968.

———. *Jerome: His Life, Writings, and Controversies*. London: Duckworth, 1975.

King, J. Christopher. *Origen on the Song of Songs as the Spirit of Scripture: The Bridegroom's Perfect Marriage-Song*. Oxford Theological Monographs.. Oxford: Oxford University Press, 2005.

Knobel, Peter. *The Targum of Qohelet: Translated with a Critical Introduction, Apparatus, and Notes*. Collegeville, MN: Liturgical Press, 1991.

Konstan, David. "Epicureanism." In *The Blackwell Guide to Ancient Philosophy*, edited by Christopher Shields, 237–52. Oxford: Blackwell, 2003.

Kugel, James. "Qohelet and Money." *Catholic Biblical Quarterly* 51 (1989): 32–49.

Lane Fox, Robin. *Pagans and Christians*. London: Viking, 1986.

Leanza, Sandro. *L'esegesi di Origene al Libro dell'Ecclesiaste*. Reggio Calabria: Parallelo 38, 1975.

Long, A. A. *From Epicurus to Epictetus: Studies in Hellenistic and Roman Philosophy*. Oxford: Oxford University Press, 2006.

Longman, Tremper, III. *The Book of Ecclesiastes*. New International Commentary on the Old Testament. Grand Rapids: Eerdmans, 1998.

Maclaurin, E. C. B. "Beelzeboul." *Novum Testamentum* 20 (1978): 156–60.

McGuckin, John. "The Vine and the Elm Tree: The Patristic Interpretation of Jesus' Teachings on Wealth." *Studies in Church History* 24 (1987): 1–14.

Meredith, Anthony. "Homily I." In *Gregory of Nyssa: Homilies on Ecclesiastes. An English Version with Supporting Studies. Proceedings of the Seventh International Colloquium on Gregory of Nyssa (St. Andrews, 5–10 September 1990)*, edited by Stuart George Hall, 145–58. Berlin and New York: W. de Gruyter, 1993.

Metzger, Bruce M. "Theories of the Translation Process." *Bibliotheca Sacra* 150 (1993): 140–50.

Murphy, Roland E. *Ecclesiastes*. Word Biblical Commentary 23A. Nashville: Thomas Nelson, 1992.

O'Keefe, John J., and R. R. Reno. *Sanctified Vision: An Introduction to the Early Christian Interpretation of the Bible*. Baltimore and London: John Hopkins University Press, 2005.

Patrides, Constantinos A. "The Salvation of Satan." *Journal of the History of Ideas* 28 (1967): 467–78.

Pelikan, Jaroslav. *The Emergence of Catholic Doctrine (100–600)*. Chicago: University of Chicago Press, 1971.

Petersen, David L. *Zechariah 9–14 and Malachi*. Old Testament Library. Louisville: Westminster John Knox, 1995.

Plescia, Joseph. "Judicial Accountability and Immunity in Roman Law." *American Journal of Legal History* 45 (2001): 51–70.

Pope, Marvin H. *Song of Songs: A New Translation with Introduction and Commentary*. Anchor Bible 7C. Garden City, NY: Doubleday, 1977.

Rebenich, Stefan. *Hieronymus und sein Kreis: Prosopographische und sozialgeschichtliche Untersuchungen. Historia*. Einzelschriften 72. Stuttgart: Franz Steiner, 1992.

———. *Jerome*. Early Christian Fathers. London: Routledge, 2002.

———. "Jerome: The Vir Trilinguis and the Hebraica Veritas." *Vigiliae Christianae* 47 (1993): 50–77.

Rives, James. "The Decree of Decius and the Religion of Empire." *Journal of Roman Studies* 89 (1999): 135–54.

Scott, Alan B. *Origen and the Life of the Stars: A History of a New Idea*. Oxford Early Christian Studies. Oxford: Clarendon, 1991.

Vessey, Mark. "Jerome's Origen: The Making of a Christian Literary Persona." *Studia Patristica* 28 (1993): 135–45.

Vogel, C. de. "The Soma-Sema Formula: Its Function in Plato and Plotinus Compared to Christian Writers." In *Neoplatonism and Early Christian Thought: Essays in Honour of A.H. Armstrong,* edited by H. J. Blumenthal and R. A. Markus, 79–95. London: Variorum Publications, 1981.

Whealey, A. "Hippolytus' Lost De Universo and De Resurrectione: Some New Hypotheses." *Vigiliae Christianae* 50 (1996): 244–56.

Whybray, R. N. *Proverbs.* London: Marshall Pickering, 1994.

Williams, Megan Hale. *The Monk and the Book: Jerome and the Making of Christian Scholarship.* Chicago: University of Chicago Press, 2006.

Wright, J. Edward. *The Early History of Heaven.* Oxford: Oxford University Press, 2000.

INDEX

Aaron, 88
sons of, 24, 87, 98, 214, 222
Abraham, 43, 63, 78, 117, 125,
140, 161, 192–93, 207,
237
almsgiving, 64, 119, 234
anagogical exegesis, 51, 60, 85,
106, 176, 186
angels
as deliverers of thoughts to
God, 73–74, 119, 233
as guardians, 124, 203
as interpreters of visions, 217
as rulers over the world, 75,
89, 127, 202–3
Seraphim, 41, 154–55
anger
censured, 83–84, 119, 126
of God, 54, 74, 184
salutary against sin, 82, 210
apokatastasis, 20, 161
Apollinarius of Laodicea
biography of, 21
interpretation of Ecclesiastes,
200, 240
Aquila
biography, 14
in the Hexapla, 10, 13–14,
147
Jerome's use of, 33, 164, 171,
203, 211, 218
translation of, cited, 37, 41,

42, 45, 49, 74, 80, 83, 91,
97, 111, 127
translation of, commended,
113
Aristippus, 103, 165–66, 225
Aristotle, 115, 172, 215
Augustine of Hippo, 3
defense of the Septuagint, 13,
188–89
on Hades, 192
on Jerome's biblical translations, 11, 29
on martyrdom, 187
on original sin, 215
on providence, 5

Bar Akiba, 70
Barania
influence on Jerome, 23
interpretations of, cited, 43,
59, 70, 73, 83, 102, 108,
111, 112, 203, 230
Rufinus' contempt for, 23, 31
Bethlehem, 4, 16, 28–30, 33,
135–36
bishops
condemned, 96, 97, 117–18,
221
Blesilla
death of, 4, 5
as stimulus for commentary,
33